D1603023

MAKING A MODERN POLITICAL ORDER

RECENT TITLES FROM THE HELEN KELLOGG INSTITUTE SERIES ON
DEMOCRACY AND DEVELOPMENT

Paolo G. Carozza and Aníbal Pérez-Liñan, series editors

The University of Notre Dame Press gratefully thanks the Helen Kellogg Institute for International Studies for its support in the publication of titles in this series.

Brian Wampler
Activating Democracy in Brazil: Popular Participation, Social Justice, and Interlocking Institutions (2015)

J. Ricardo Tranjan
Participatory Democracy in Brazil: Socioeconomic and Political Origins (2016)

Tracy Beck Fenwick
Avoiding Governors: Federalism, Democracy, and Poverty Alleviation in Brazil and Argentina (2016)

Alexander Wilde
Religious Responses to Violence: Human Rights in Latin America Past and Present (2016)

Pedro Meira Monteiro
The Other Roots: Wandering Origins in Roots of Brazil *and the Impasses of Modernity in Ibero-America* (2017)

John Aerni-Flessner
Dreams for Lesotho: Independence, Foreign Assistance, and Development (2018)

Roxana Barbulescu
Migrant Integration in a Changing Europe: Migrants, European Citizens, and Co-ethnics in Italy and Spain (2019)

Matthew C. Ingram and Diana Kapiszewski
Beyond High Courts: The Justice Complex in Latin America (2019)

Kenneth P. Serbin
From Revolution to Power in Brazil: How Radical Leftists Embraced Capitalism and Struggled with Leadership (2019)

Manuel Balán and Françoise Montambeault
Legacies of the Left Turn in Latin America: The Promise of Inclusive Citizenship (2020)

Ligia Castaldi
Abortion in Latin America and the Caribbean: The Legal Impact of the American Convention on Human Rights (2020)

Paolo Carozza and Clemens Sedmak
The Practice of Human Development and Dignity (2020)

Amber R. Reed
Nostalgia after Apartheid: Disillusinment, Youth, and Democracy in South Africa (2020)

For a complete list of titles from the Helen Kellogg Institute for International Studies, see http://www.undpress.nd.edu.

For Bill and Ursula.
Fondly.
Jim

MAKING A
MODERN
POLITICAL ORDER

The Problem of the Nation State

JAMES J. SHEEHAN

University of Notre Dame Press
Notre Dame, Indiana

University of Notre Dame Press
Notre Dame, Indiana 46556
undpress.nd.edu

Published in the United States of America

Library of Congress Control Number: 2022951796

ISBN: 978-0-268-20537-9 (Hardback)
ISBN: 978-0-268-20539-3 (WebPDF)
ISBN: 978-0-268-20536-2 (Epub)

To those who have given me the gift of their friendship,

with enduring gratitude and affection

Order is the exhausting Sisyphean labor of mankind, against which mankind is always in a potential state of conflict.
—Guglielmo Ferrero, *The Principles of Power* (1942)

Underlying the questions we raise about order among states there are deeper questions, of more enduring importance, about order in the great society of all mankind.
—Hedley Bull, *The Anarchical Society: A Study of Order in World Politics* (1977)

I do not know why this need for order exists. It is not simply a need for an instrumentally manageable environment, though this is part of it. It's more like the need for a rationally intelligible cognitive map, but it is obviously more than cognitive. There is a need for moral order—for things to be fit into a pattern which is just as well as predictable.
—Edward Shils, *The Constitution of Society* (1982)

CONTENTS

ILLUSTRATIONS

ACKNOWLEDGMENTS

This book began as a series of lectures delivered at the University of Notre Dame in April 2015. I am grateful to Thomas F. X. Noble for the invitation, to Robert L. Dilenschneider for endowing the lectures, and to all of those who made my time in South Bend both stimulating and enjoyable. Engaging conversation, excellent food, and gracious hospitality combined to make this a wonderful experience.

Like many other things I can think of, the passage from lecture notes to book turned out to be much harder than I had expected. Peggy Anderson, my ideal (but by no means uncritical) reader was my companion on this long journey from beginning to end: she listened to the lectures, encouraged me, and was the first to read an earlier version of this manuscript. Gerhard Casper, David Kennedy, Frances and Randy Starn, Don Lamm, Jerry Muller, and Keith Baker were all sympathetic readers and, as always, loyal friends. I am especially grateful to John Connelly, who read the manuscript with great care, pointed out a number of errors both large and small, and gave me the benefit of his deep knowledge of Eastern Europe. The two anonymous readers for the University of Notre Dame Press were extraordinarily helpful—because of them, this is (I hope) a better book. My thanks to the Workshop on Political Theory at Stanford, whose participants discussed a selection from the manuscript and offered many helpful comments. Special thanks to Karen Offen, who pointed out deficiencies in the book's treatment of the woman question. On several occasions, I have had the privilege of teaching courses with David Kennedy and Keith Baker, who will, I hope, recognize in the following pages how much I have learned from them both. At the University of Notre Dame Press, Eli Bortz skillfully steered the manuscript through the publication process. Elena Kempt did excellent work proofreading and organizing the final draft. Scott Barker was an exemplary copyeditor.

I am fortunate indeed to have been given so much encouragement and advice, but I must admit that although I accepted all of the former, I took only some of the latter. The errors and infelicities that remain, therefore, are entirely my own.

Berkeley, California
April 2022

Introduction

Horizons of Expectation

Alfred North Whitehead regarded organized society as a "standing miracle," which must somehow find a way to "bend its individual members to function in conformity to its needs." Michael Walzer had the same thing in mind when he defined politics as "an art of unification; from many, it makes one."[1] The art of unification is at once the purpose and the prerequisite of that complex set of ideas and practices that constitutes every political order.[2] There is nothing natural or inherently stable about political orders. All of them contain tensions; if it is to endure, an order must manage these tensions, preventing them from causing paralysis or collapse. Every order, therefore, is a work in progress or decline, which is why I titled this book "*Making* a Modern Political Order" rather than "*The* Making" or simply "The Modern Political Order." Despite the enduring millenarian myths that promise ultimate cohesion in a community without conflict, the art of unification never ends; it is always under construction, inherently imperfect, constantly at risk.

The political art of unification necessarily involves the capacity to use violence to make individuals' wills conform to social needs. But in the long run, a political order's coercive power must be legitimate, that is, it must rest on a set of shared assumptions about how the political order should and does work. These assumptions are an essential part of the habits of domination and obedience on which a political order depends. Since they are at once descriptive and normative, our assumptions have a complex, un-settled relationship to political theory and political practice. Both models and mirrors, our assumptions shape and reflect the way people think and act. And even when they do not conform to the way people think and act (which is, of course, sadly true in many of the world's states), these shared assumptions are an essential part of the political order's ability to trans-form, in Rousseau's famous formulation, "force into right, and obedience into duty."

These assumptions about the political order's legitimacy define our "horizon of expectation," which, as the philosopher Stephen Toulmin writes, establishes "the field of action in which, at the moment, people see it as possible or feasible to change human affairs, and so to decide which of our most cherished practical goals can be realized in fact."[3] The *horizon*, from the Greek word *horos* ("limit or boundary"), defines what we can ex-pect from our political world, what we can do or even imagine as doable.

Our expectations must be reaffirmed by our experience, including our political experience and our experience of the nonpolitical norms and habits that govern our public and private lives. As Charles Merriam notes, "Unless the practices of government were closely akin to the social prac-tices of the social group in which they are found, successful political action would be impossible."[4] These common social practices—expectations about how society should and does work—at once sustain and are sustained by the political order. They give the order what has been described as its "inherent imaginative plausibility."[5]

Although they depend on our experience of the world, our expecta-tions also require faith. Faith is necessary because there is always some-thing self-referential and circular about the principles at the core of every political order. Legitimacy, therefore, involves a belief in a transcendent source of value. For most of human history, this belief was part of people's faith in some kind of divine order from which political authority ulti-mately derived its legitimacy. But even in our secular world, the political order requires what Edmund Morgan regarded as the capacity to "make believe."[6] In the old regime, the symbols and rituals of power were designed to reveal its sacred source; in the modern world, they usually conceal those leaps of faith on which the order depends. However it is expressed, faith is always essential.

Because our expectations about politics combine the way we think things are and what we believe they ought to be, they contain a certain tension between perception and judgment. The need to live with, manage, and perhaps overcome this tension produces the political order's most important myths and rituals. This tension is also the source of the endemic discontent and sporadic conflict with which every order must live. People's expectations, therefore, are both a source of cohesion and of conflict, necessary for the order to survive but also inherently contestable. At times of crisis, and especially as one political order gives way to another, the internal tensions within people's expectations become especially intense.

There is a constant connection between political expectations and political practice. Charles Taylor put it this way: "If the understanding makes the practice possible, it is also true that it is the practice that largely carries the understanding."[7] Even when those in power often insist (perhaps *especially* when they insist) that they are motivated by timeless ideals or rational calculations of utility, their behavior is shaped by their expectations about how the political order can and should work. Indeed, without these expectations, neither ideals nor interests would have intellectual substance or practical relevance.

The stability of a political order requires that these expectations are widely shared by ordinary men and women.[8] Sharing occurs through the communication of political ideas and images and, even more significantly, by collective political practices, that is, through common action, including both conflict and collaboration. In the *Laws,* Plato writes that the *polis* is a dramatization of the good and noble life (notice that he does not say that the *polis* is *like* a dramatization, but rather that it *is* the enduring enactment of a script based on good laws).[9] People's expectations are what enable them to understand, participate in, and accept, endure, or seek to replace this political drama.

Because our expectations about the political order occupy an intermediate space between thought and action, they are most vividly expressed in documents that are close to political practices, such as treaties, law codes, constitutions, pamphlets, party programs, parliamentary debates, and maps. There is a great deal to be learned from the work of the great political theorists who see the world of politics more clearly than their less gifted contemporaries. But political ideas often anticipate rather than reflect the theorist's world. We are, therefore, frequently better off looking for expectations about the political order in the rougher, less polished texts that have been created by political actors, forged in the course of political conflicts, designed to guide or advance a particular policy. Here we are most likely to find those tensions, ambiguities, and inconsistencies that are deeply rooted in every political order.

This book is about the origins and character of the underlying expectations that enable us to understand and manage the contemporary political order. For purposes of analysis, I divide them into three groups. First, there are expectations about the definition and character of political space, which in the modern era are connected to the emergence of a new kind of state. Second, expectations about the nature of political communities, that is, about how people relate to one another and to their governments, which, I will argue, is best understood as the development of nations. Third, expectations about the international system, that is, about how states interact in a society of nation states. Although I shall treat these three dimensions of the political order separately, it should be clear that they are closely bound together, each dependent on—and reinforcing—the others.

There is a distinctly modern set of expectations about the political order. "Modern," as Bishop Creighton wrote in his introduction to the *Cambridge Modern History*, first published in 1902, refers to "the period in which the problems that still occupy us came into conscious recognition, and were dealt with in ways intelligible to us as resembling our own."[10] In other words, "modernity" simply means the world in which we live, here and now. Precisely because the modern political order is our own, because it so clearly conforms to our expectations, it can be difficult to see.[11] One of the purposes of historical analysis is to make the distinctive features of the present visible by taking us to the other side of time's horizon, to a period when people's expectations about the political order were radically different from our own. This should help us to avoid anachronism, which reads the past in terms of the present, and teleology, which regards the present as the natural and permanent product of the past. Both come from a failure to recognize the importance of historical horizons, one separating our experience from the past, the other, from an unknown and largely unknowable future.

Chapter 1, therefore, provides the starting point for our effort to understand the modern political order by examining people's expectations about political space, community, and international society in the premodern European world that came to be called the *ancien régime*. The next three chapters—on states, nations, and the society of nation states—trace the development of a modern political order that slowly and unevenly replaced the ancien régime in Europe and eventually spread throughout the world. These chapters are thematically organized, but each also has a certain chronological focus. Chapter 2 emphasizes the eighteenth and early nineteenth centuries. Chapter 3 begins in the eighteenth century but concentrates on the nineteenth and early twentieth. Chapter 4 begins at the end of the eighteenth but then carries the story to the present. The conclusion will briefly speculate about the horizon ahead of us, the horizon beyond which lies a future order that may someday replace our own.

The European experience is at the center of this story. In part this is a reflection of my own background and limitations. I think a case can be made for the European origins of the modern political order, but I recognize that scholars with a different set of skills and assumptions could tell the story in a different way. I hope it will be clear that my emphasis on Europe implies historical priority, not moral or cultural superiority.[12]

This is a work of synthesis, necessarily derivative from and dependent on the work of other scholars. I have tried to indicate my debts in the notes, but the attentive reader will recognize the pervasive influence of Alexis de Tocqueville. Like Tocqueville, I believe in both the primary importance of political institutions and in their inseparable connection to other aspects of our common life. On the following pages, I will have several occasions to quote his insight: "In the long run political society cannot fail to become the expression and image of civil society."[13] Most important, I share Tocqueville's conviction that the key to understanding the modern political order is "democracy," by which he meant the creation of a society of equals, that is, a society composed of people "like oneself." This extraordinary project, so deceptively easy to invoke but, as we learn anew every day, so endlessly difficult to achieve, is the source of our highest aspirations and deepest fears. From it flow the unprecedented potential for both freedom and tyranny that characterizes the modern political order.

Tocqueville knew that it was useless to argue for or against democracy. However imperfect it is in practice, the yearning for democracy is rooted in the experiences of our common life and sustained by assumptions of which we are only partially aware. This is true even in those parts of the world where democratic institutions are no more than a façade for authoritarian rule. Nevertheless, as long as we remain within our contemporary horizon of expectations, our choice is how, not whether, we live in and with a democratic political order. Living with democracy may be easier if we remember, as Alan Ryan remarked, that although democracy "is the modern ideal of life," it "is everywhere realized in extremely inadequate ways."[14] Democracy, like growing old, reveals its advantages most vividly when it is compared to the alternatives.

CHAPTER ONE

The Ancien Régime

The concept of an *ancien régime* emerged in the early days of the French Revolution of 1789. It was defined by its historical location rather than its antiquity, that is, it was not just the "*old* regime," it was the immediately preceding (the *former*) regime that had supposedly been swept away by the Revolution. The ancien régime was both a social and political order; it combined, in Claude Lefort's words, "the idea of a type of constitution with that of a style of existence or mode of life."[1] In the ancien régime, people's expectations about politics were deeply imbedded in their "modes of life," the social, economic, and cultural ideas and institutions that created their world.

To understand this premodern regime, we must keep in mind that language usually changes more slowly than practice.[2] It is, therefore, easy to overstate the continuities in the way politics has been organized and imagined. Frozen in printed texts and treatises, words such as *state* and *nation* travel through the ages, inviting us to overlook those fundamental changes that have redefined their application to the world. The definition of political space, for example, has always been important for political orders, but its nature has changed, from the crude barriers built by our distant ancestors to discourage predatory intruders, to the finely calibrated lines on a modern map. Like the definition of space, membership in the political community has always mattered, but how membership is defined, acquired, and affirmed varies greatly, evolving from biological bonds of kinship to legal definitions of citizenship. And then there is the question of power. The significance of power runs like a red thread through the history of political thought and action, which is why Thucydides and Machiavelli still speak to us across the centuries. But even though Max Weber's definition of power as "the ability of an individual or group to achieve their own goals or aims when others are trying to prevent them from realizing them" might seem to have enduring validity, its meaning is determined by the different ways power is deployed, by the character and relative strength of those "others" against which it must struggle, and, most importantly, by the changing nature of the "goals or aims" it seeks to achieve.[3]

The purpose of this chapter is to prepare the ground for our examination of the modern political order by providing a brief and necessarily schematic account of the regime that it gradually and unevenly replaced.

COMPOSITE STATES

Let us begin our examination of premodern expectations about the organization of political space by looking at the map that Vermeer depicted in *The Art of Painting*, which he completed around 1667 (fig. 1). The map's prominence in this picture, and in many others by Vermeer and his contemporaries, suggests the significance of cartography for early modern visual culture. Vermeer based his map on a work by an Amsterdam craftsman, Claes Visscher, originally done in the 1630s and then published by Claes's son, Nicholas, in the 1650s. It shows the Seventeen Provinces of the Netherlands (Germania Inferior), portrayed here with the north to the right of the chart. The map's iconography and design affirm the Netherlands' spatial unity and historical identity. In Visscher's version (but not in Vermeer's), there were eighteen portraits of famous political and military leaders across the top of the map; their presence recalled the Netherlands' recent past and thus served to fix its identity in time and in space. But the map also acknowledges the state's composite nature: around the margins are twenty panels showing local centers of power and authority, including the major cities and the courts at Brussels and The Hague. In the cartouche toward the center left, Visscher states the theme of his work: "The tremendous wars waged in these lands [in dese lande] in the past, and still being waged in the present, bear witness to their strength, power, and wealth."[4]

Figure 1. Vermeer, *The Art of Painting* (Google Art Project)

Visscher's use of the plural *lande* reflected the obvious fact that the Netherlands were composed of distinct political units. This was most apparent in the division between north and south, to which Vermeer gestures with the fold that he skillfully places in the center of his map. The northern provinces were themselves highly decentralized, with locally powerful urban and regional institutions. These local authorities sent representatives to the States General, which, often with considerable difficulty, made decisions about common foreign and military policy. Executive power resided in the office of stadtholder, a kind of elected monarch, whose position, though not formally hereditary, was traditionally held by a member of the House of Orange. Historians sometimes emphasize the anomalous character of Dutch institutions.[5] In fact, the Netherlands were unusually wealthy and powerful, but their composite character appears anomalous only if viewed in the light of our own expectations about territorial states. In the premodern world, the decentralized, regionally diverse "lande" that appear on Visscher's map conformed to most people's expectations about how states should look. Vermeer's contemporaries would not have found anything unusual about his map.

To cite another example of a composite state, consider the territories belonging to the elector of Brandenburg, which would eventually become the Kingdom of Prussia in a process that is often cited as the locus classicus of early modern state-making. In the seventeenth century, when this process is conventionally thought to begin, the elector's possessions were scattered across central Europe; they all belonged to him but did not necessarily belong together. In 1650, when Elector Frederick William asked the estates of Brandenburg to assist him in the defense of Pomerania against Sweden, they refused to come to the aid of "foreign provinces."[6] Fifty years later, when Frederick William's son Frederick sought to enhance his authority and prestige by having himself made a king, it was not clear what he could be king of. It was not possible for him to be king *of* Prussia, since part of that duchy remained formally tied to the king of Poland.[7] Finally, in an expensive and elaborate ceremony, Frederick became king *in* Prussia, while remaining elector, margrave, and duke, the titles that connected him to his other lands. The Hohenzollern did not become kings *of* Prussia until 1772. Even then residues of the state's composite character remained. As we will see in chapter 2, the *Allgemeines Landrecht*, the codification of Prussian laws published in the 1790s, was applied to the Prussian "states," territories that were better integrated than at the beginning of the century, but still diverse enough to be referred to in the plural. Traces of Prussia's composite character lingered into the nineteenth century. The Hohenzollern lands did not become completely contiguous until 1866, when the annexation of Electoral Hesse finally bridged their eastern and western provinces.

Everywhere we look in premodern Europe, we find states that were composed of diverse pieces.[8] Like the Netherlands, Poland had an elected monarch who ruled over a fragmented, institutionally divided terrain. Like the Hohenzollern in Prussia, the House of Savoy drew its royal title from one piece of its patrimony (Sardinia); the king's possessions included a variety of other territories (Savoy, Piedmont, Montferrat, Aosta, and Nice) that were held under different titles. Nor were small states necessarily more cohesive than large ones. Eighteenth-century Venice controlled about 30,000 square kilometers on terra firma, some of it directly, some leased or rented. Even though Venice's economic viability and political security depended on its access to these territories, no single agency in the Serene Republic was responsible for administering them.[9] To the Venetian elite, and to many other European leaders in the old regime, it did not seem either necessary or possible to create the sort of spatial cohesion and institutional uniformity that would become part of people's expectations about states in the modern political order.

We are accustomed to thinking about premodern empires as collections of loosely connected entities. These empires, Lauren Benton points out, "did not cover space evenly but composed a fabric that was full of holes, stitched together out of pieces, a tangle of strings."[10] The same could be said about most premodern states, small and large, which were also "stitched together." Braunschweig-Wolfenbüttel, for example, a state with a population of about 180,000 on the eve of the French Revolution, occupied about 3,700 square kilometers that were scattered across a fragmented political landscape that also contained a variety of autonomous ecclesiastical and secular principalities as well as a number of semisovereign monastic orders and imperial cities.[11] Empires and states differed in scale and geopolitical weight, but not in the way they occupied and imagined political space. It may be misleading to think about early empires as big states, but it makes a certain amount of sense to think about premodern states as small empires.

The composite states that dominated Europe's political order in the ancien régime were the products of a long, uneven process of consolidation. We will have more to say about this when we turn to the premodern society of states at the end of this chapter, but for now it is enough to point out that after the Roman Empire's collapse in the West, Europe's institutional landscape was fragmented but not disorganized. European state-making did not take place in sparsely populated, loosely organized territory, as was the case, for example, with the expansion of the United States on the North American plains or of Russia on the Central Asian steppes. Nor were European states imported ready-made, as they would be in much of the colonial world. Instead, these states were constructed by absorbing, transforming, and sometimes destroying the dense network of the tribal kingdoms, Byzantine colonies, and hundreds of episcopal districts, small cities, and rural communities that had gradually emerged to provide people with security, sustenance, and salvation in the wake of Rome's slow and fitful disintegration. The composite character of European states, and their characteristic institutional hybridity, was built into their historical DNA.[12]

Patriotic historians conventionally depicted the formation of their states as the necessary fulfillment of the nation's authentic territorial identity, just as patriotic geographers claimed to discover their nation's "natural frontiers."[13] No state evolved according to a predetermined plan. Most are the product of complex and contingent processes, driven by the fortunes of dynastic marriage, diplomatic bargaining, and, most of all, military conquest. "All European states," Michael Oakeshott wrote, "began as mixed and miscellaneous collections of human beings precariously held together, disturbed by what they had swallowed and were unable to digest, and distracted by plausible or fancied irredenta."[14] Modern governments constantly had to struggle in order to swallow and digest their territories.

State-making was driven by many different motives. Hobbes located the essential wellspring of political action in humanity's insatiable acquisitive desires: a man, Hobbes believed, always wants more "because he cannot assume the power and means to live well, which he hath at present, without the acquisition of more. And from hence it is, that kings, whose power is the greatest, turn their endeavors to assuring at home by laws, or abroad by wars; and when that is done, there succeedth new desire." A ruler's desire for more, Hobbes realized, can have many different objects. Some longed for "fame from new conquest," others "ease and sensual pleasure," and some "being flattered for being excellent in some art."[15] Since the ruler's desire for the glory and rewards of conquest played such a major part in the making of most European states, there is a good deal of truth in Charles Tilly's lapidary comment that "states make war, and vice versa." But the capacity to wage war was not the only, and sometimes not the most important, goal of state-making.[16]

In order to mobilize the resources necessary to fulfill their desire for power at home and abroad, rulers did not have to create, indeed they could not have imagined, the kind of territorial cohesion and institutional uniformity that we expect to find in states. Sometimes, the expansion of state power did involve some degree of consolidation, but it was never an end in itself. Rulers had no model of the modern state to which they aspired. Cohesion and uniformity might not even be desirable. In his *Della Ragione di Stato* (1589), the Italian theorist Giovanni Botero argued that unified states were often at a disadvantage since unification invited corruption, while the disparate pieces of a composite state might cooperate and assist one another.[17] Power, as Helmut Koenigsberger pointed out in his pioneering study of composite states, did not require uniformity.[18] There is no better illustration of Koenigsberger's insight than the Habsburg Empire, Europe's greatest and longest-lived composite state. In the sixteenth century, Emperor Charles V claimed seventy-two dynastic titles, giving him authority over 28 million people, who lived in twenty-seven kingdoms, thirteen duchies, and twenty-two counties and other principalities.

Even had they wanted to impose cohesion and uniformity on their domains, few rulers could have done so.[19] Projecting power in an age when roads were poor, travel hazardous, and distances hard to overcome was usually beyond the capacity of even the most energetic and efficient monarch. It might have been easier when the land was flat, rivers navigable, harbors deep and defensible. But local communities could defend their autonomy in mountainous terrain, or on vast spaces, such as deserts and steppes, where people could resist outsiders' efforts to organize them. In the making of political orders, geography is not destiny, but it did decisively limit the size and shape the character of institutions in the ancien régime—it continues to do so, even after technology has loosened the physical environment's grip on human life. State-making is, after all, still a problem in the mountains of Montenegro and in the Arabian desert.[20]

Given the means of projecting power available to them, successful rulers had to come to terms with their territories' institutional diversity. Of course, a prince could use force to arrest a recalcitrant bishop, suppress a rebellious town, or raze the castle of a disobedient vassal. But once the din of battle had ceased, the ruler usually had neither the ability nor the will to govern without the cooperation of municipal, ecclesiastical, or aristocratic authorities. In most of Western and Central Europe, the day-to-day business of raising revenues, settling disputes, and enforcing laws involved a network of preexisting institutions—the representative bodies, religious authorities, and local notables—on which Europe's political order ultimately depended.[21] *Managing* seems like an appropriate term for the process of state-making: management requires leadership and control, but also the art of husbanding resources and successfully mastering a task; to manage something demands a capacity to inspire and persuade as much as to command and coerce.[22]

The classic analysis of political management in premodern Europe is Machiavelli's *The Prince*. Machiavelli was acutely aware of the problem of institutional hybridity. In chapter 5, for example, he considered how best to rule newly acquired polities that had "once lived by their own laws." There are, he advised his prince, three ways of dealing with them: you can destroy their institutions and impose your own, you can try to rule them directly, or (and this was the alternative he preferred) you can "let them continue living under their own laws, levying tribute on them, and creating a government of a few people who will keep the state friendly to you."[23] The best way to manage hybridity, in other words, was to make new territories distinct parts of a composite state.

There were more than Machiavelli's three ways of dealing with established laws and institutions. Many of them involved a more complicated mixture of coercion and compliance than he described. In places where local elites remained obdurately opposed to their new rulers, they might have to be repressed and replaced, but often they could be bribed or flattered or intimidated into entering the ruler's service, enticed to his court, or recruited into his officer corps. Some corporate assemblies were dissolved by the conqueror, others were transformed into instruments of the central authority, a few survived as bastions of regional interests and allegiance. Institutional hybridity was the norm in most of premodern Europe; how it was managed varied enormously. Since our attention is naturally drawn to incidents of conflict and contestation, we tend to underestimate the enduring structures of negotiation and compromise on which most states depended. Success in the premodern world depended more on managing diversity than on imposing uniformity.

Scholars disagree about what people in the premodern era had in mind when they talked about *states*.[24] What was it, for example, that the prince acquired when, in Machiavelli's words, he took over "a state that had lived under its own laws"? One thing is clear enough: Machiavelli and his contemporaries did not mean those impersonal, clearly defined territorial units that we expect states to be.[25] For many people, the state was the ruler's legitimate right to exercise power over the community. In Bodin's influential formulation, "a commonwealth may be defined as the rightly ordered government of a number of families, and of those things which are their concern, by a sovereign power."[26] For Bodin, states were essentially a certain

way of exerting authority, governed by law (what Bodin called "rightly ordered"), concerned with the community as a whole (which set them apart
from local authorities), and possessing distinctive rights and obligations
(Bodin's "sovereign power"). Although states occupied territory, they were
not primarily territorial entities, but rather a set of relationships between
rulers and those they ruled.

In the often quoted opening sentence of *The Prince*, Machiavelli stipu-
lates that "all the states and governments [*dominii*] that have ever had or
now have power over man were and are of two sorts: republics and princely
states [*principati*]." The latter, he adds, were either hereditary, "where the
family of the ruler has been in control for a long time," or they were newly
established (which, Machiavelli knew, created special problems of political
management).[27] This typology of states obviously reflected the turbulent
and varied geopolitical landscape of early modern Italy that informed
Machiavelli's political expectations, but for a majority of his contemporaries the range of political possibilities was more limited. In most of Europe, a republic was regarded as an unusual form of government that was
only appropriate for small entities. "It is," Montesquieu was convinced, "in
the nature of a republic to have only a small territory; otherwise it can
scarcely continue to exist."[28] For most people, some kind of monarchy was
the norm. A few states—Poland, the Papal States, Venice, the Netherlands—
elected their rulers, but in the majority, sovereign power was hereditary. In
this regard, Shakespeare, who was deeply concerned with the problem of
dynastic legitimacy, is a much better guide to premodern political expectations than Machiavelli.[29]

For most of human history, in most parts of the world, kinship, in one
form or other, was both the source and substance of legitimate rule. The
connection between kinship and power is nearly universal, but it is important to recognize how premodern European dynastic states created pervasive and historically significant forms of hereditary rule, notable for their
quantitative and qualitative domination of public life from the late Middle
Ages to the nineteenth century.[30] The number of political units in Europe
dramatically declined after 1500, but the relative importance of dynastic
states significantly increased as monarchies absorbed their various competitors. All of Europe's major states began as hereditary monarchies.
Other ways of imagining and organizing power, including imperial city-
states, such as Venice, or elected monarchies, such as the Polish Commonwealth, diminished in importance before they eventually disappeared.[31]

The great advantage of these hereditary monarchies was that, better than any other way of organizing and imagining political power in the pre-modern world, they were able to manage "the art of unification." No one put this more clearly and forcefully than Hobbes: "A multitude of men, are made one person, when they are by one man, or one person represented. . . . For it is the unity of the representer, not the unity of the represented, that maketh the person one."[32] The famous frontispiece that Hobbes helped design for *Leviathan* conveys the essential interdependence of sovereign and subject: the sovereign contains the bodies of his subjects, without him there is nothing to unite them, just as without them, he would not exist (see fig. 2).[33]

Monarchs unified the separate pieces of their composite states by holding them under different titles. As king, prince, duke, and elector, the monarch literally personified his realm. Like the king's body, the realm was both one and many. In his sacred person, a composite state could be represented as a unity without surrendering its diversity. The ruler represented the state literally and symbolically: he made it present, gave it a collective existence it would not otherwise have.[34]

Monarchs could add a newly acquired territory by assuming another title or, as Emperor Charles V did in 1555, they could hand over pieces of their realm one by one, thus easing the burden of transition to their heir.[35] Monarchs managed the institutional hybridity of their states in their royal courts, the symbolic and practical arena in which elites were co-opted, contained, or accommodated, allies recruited and rewarded, rivals isolated and punished. With the possible exception of military service, the court was the single most important political institution in most premodern states, the center of power and source of prestige on which almost every government depended.[36]

One of the reasons why dynastic rule met premodern Europeans' expectations about the political order was that it conformed to their assumptions about other aspects of their lives. For the prince, as for most of his subjects, the principal source of wealth and power in society was the possession of agricultural land. Rulers were themselves great landholders, whose domains often contributed a significant share of their own and their state's income. In the 1740s, for instance, a quarter of the Hohenzollern territory (and as much as a third of the arable land) was in the royal domain, which provided roughly half of the state's revenue.[37] The transition from domain to taxation was an essential part of making states modern, just as

Figure 2. Frontispiece, Hobbes, *Leviathan* (Library of Congress)

the relative decline in the importance of landed wealth would eventually help to undermine the assumptions supporting dynastic rule. This was another illustration of Tocqueville's insight that "political society cannot fail to become the expression and image of civil society."

Landholding was also a model for how power could be acquired and exercised. Great landowners usually held many pieces of property, often under different titles and with different rights and duties.[38] Most proprietors, and certainly every owner of a great estate, could understand the tangle of diverse privileges and obligations that characterized a monarch's relationship to their composite states. Landed property was more than legal possession: it was not simply a commodity that a person *had*, it defined who he *was*; it was a source of identity, status, authority—and income. The bond between property and identity is captured by the titles of nobility—"von" or "de"—in which the particle represents the fusion of an individual, a family, and a place.[39]

At every level of the social order, the primary locus of authority was the household. This was the basic unit from which states were built and, as Bodin and many others argued, the best model for how states should be organized.[40] With its elaborate hierarchy, ornate rituals, and magnificent spaces, the prince's court was set apart from the quotidian world in which most people lived, but it was nonetheless recognizable as a household. At court, as in thousands of other households, there were complex rankings based on kinship, gender, age, and function, rankings that nevertheless might sometimes be disrupted by people's unusual strengths and weaknesses. The sort of intrigues and scandals that punctuated courtly life were not unknown in more modest venues, where unfaithful spouses, domineering parents, disappointing children, and disloyal servants could also be found.

Although princes possessed extraordinary powers that could alter the lives of their subjects in dramatic ways, many of a ruler's hopes and fears resembled those of ordinary men and women. Every family knew how important it was to have progeny, someone to inherit the title, take over the land, carry on the trade. For a ruler, the failure to produce an heir raised the specter of political upheaval and civil strife; for a farmer or a craftsman, to be childless brought the risk of poverty and abandonment. Everyone understood why the constant search for strategic marriages preoccupied royal families. Whereas kings schemed to get the alliances and resources an advantageous union might provide, peasants yearned for the adjacent field or fertile pasture that might come into the family with a new wife or daughter-in-law. "A princely marriage," Walter Bagehot wrote, "is the brilliant edition of a universal fact."[41] For prince and commoner alike, the bonds of kinship offered sources of security and enrichment in a world full of uncertainty and danger. As Pierre Bourdieu noted, "The family and the family way of thinking is always with us, in the very logic of functioning of the social world."[42]

Royal domains, royal households, and royal marriage strategies were familiar, but they were also extraordinary, not simply for their possible impact on the fate of the realm but also because they had a distinctive place in the divine order of the universe. Europeans did not believe that their kings were divinities, but they were convinced that their authority came from God. In St. Paul's oft-cited formulation from Romans: "For there is no power but of God: the powers that be are ordained by God." The sacred source of royal power set kings apart from other authorities. Shakespeare's Richard II proclaims: "Not all the water in the rough rude sea / Can wash the balm from an anointed king; / The breath of worldly man cannot depose / The deputy elected by the lord."[43]

The ruler's role as God's deputy had to be constantly reaffirmed by religious symbols and rituals, especially the foundational rite of coronation, but also the ceremonies that marked royal marriages, births, deaths, victories in battle, and recovery from an illness. As A. M. Hocart, whose pioneering anthropological studies of kingship are still unsurpassed, pointed out, in traditional societies (and this would include premodern Europe), politics and religion were not simply mixed together but were like the elements in air or water, which can be analyzed individually but were essentially and inseparably fused.[44]

Because they were indispensable for affirming the legitimacy of dynastic rule, religious institutions and rituals were a political necessity. The relationship between political and religious authorities, therefore, though often disrupted by conflicts over jurisdiction and resources, was shaped by mutual dependence. Rulers had to be anointed, their weddings blessed, their children baptized, their triumphs celebrated with appropriate rites of thanksgiving. Churchmen could frequently be hard to live with, but throughout the premodern era few rulers risked exercising power without the sanctions that religion alone could provide.

The central importance of religion in the premodern political order was what made the division of Christendom in the sixteenth century so disruptive, both within and between dynastic states. It was particularly disruptive when the ruler's religious identity differed from the majority of subjects. Sometimes this could be resolved by a monarch's conversion: Paris, Henry of Navarre, soon to be King Henry IV of France, famously declared, "is worth a Mass." Occasionally, a complex accommodation was possible (as was worked out between the elector of Brandenburg, a Calvinist, and his Lutheran subjects). Most serious of all was a situation where religious affiliation became tied to the problem of dynastic succession, which happened—with disastrous consequences—in seventeenth-century England.

The "imaginative plausibility" of the dynastic order depended on the way monarchs combined in their person the sacred and everyday nature of political authority. They were at once God's anointed instrument of legitimate power and an example of the sort of authority that existed throughout premodern society. In the family, on the farm, and in the workshop, power was embodied by particular individuals, usually but not always male. *Herrschaft*, as the German term for authority suggests, was an extension of *Herr*, a term that might refer to God as well as to the man who, as ruler but also as father, proprietor, or master, at once embodied and exercised power. The monarch, therefore, was a link in a "chain of leadership in society" that was comparable to the great chain of being "that connected the lowest inorganic substance to God."[45]

"All precepts concerning kings," Francis Bacon wrote in 1612, "are in these two remembrances: that he is a man, and that he is God's representative." This duality of kingship, the subject of Ernst Kantorowicz's classic study of the king's two bodies, has been vividly portrayed by generations of royal portraitists from Hyacinthe Rigaud to Cecil Beaton.[46] As a human individual, the monarch represented—that is, made present—legitimate authority, gave it substance, specificity, physical presence. In and through the body of the monarch, power could be seen, heard, and even, under certain circumstance, touched. Nowhere was this more dramatically expressed than in the coronation, the ceremony in which the monarch's dual nature was at once expressed and transcended. The ruler's human body is at the very center of the ritual: the observers never forget that here is a human being like themselves; at the same time, the whole point of the ritual—the clothes, symbols, carefully choreographed acts of homage—transport this

Figure 3. Rigaud, *Louis XIV* (Google Art Project)

human person to a higher realm, giving him or her a new identity (and sometimes a new name).[47] Being a monarch was not only an office to be held or occupied, it was an inseparable part of the ruler's person. Rigaud's great portrait of Louis XIV captures this perfectly: Louis's humanity is subtly suggested in the display of his legs and casual position of his arm, but he is above all a king (see fig. 3). *Being* a king is all that he is doing here, nothing more, but also nothing less.[48]

The ruler's dual character was the source of monarchy's persistent power and of its inherent vulnerability. Every monarch was, of course, mortal, but the fact of mortality could be transfigured in the rituals of renewal on which the dynastic order depended. Other frailties of the flesh were more difficult to overcome: the failure to produce an heir to the throne, mental instability, or physical incapacity—all might result in domestic unrest or international catastrophe. The same expectations about the legitimating power of kinship that gave monarchies their cohesive power could then become the source of political conflict both within and between dynastic states. As we shall have occasion to remark several times in the following pages, this tension between cohesion and conflict characterizes the principle of legitimacy that is at the core of every political order, including our own.

COMMUNITIES: EXPERIENCED AND IMAGINED

It has frequently been remarked (no one seems to know who said it first) that there are only two master plots: someone goes on a journey; a stranger comes to town. These are, of course, not two plots but one, the same story told from different perspectives: the first from that of someone who leaves their community, the second, from that of the community confronting an outsider. Together the plots' universal appeal reminds us that for most of history, people expected to live in small worlds that would be dangerous to leave and difficult to enter. Outsiders were always viewed with suspicion, and often with enmity; to be an outsider was to be vulnerable and exposed, a condition to be avoided if at all possible. As always, these expectations have left their traces in our language. The English word *hostile*, for example, comes from a Latin noun (*hostis*) that means both "enemy" and "foreigner"; *Elend*, the German word for "misery," has its roots in an archaic term for "being without a place."

Even in the era of jumbo jets, cell phones, and the World Wide Web, face-to-face communities still matter. Most of us live surrounded by people we know and who know us; strangers can still make us uneasy; travel is often attended by anxiety. But in some important ways, our social worlds have become bigger, more loosely knit, and increasingly diverse. Our social and political identities have become more portable: a plastic card, for instance, frees us from the personal connections upon which getting credit once depended. Ties of kinship or patronage are less important when we have a passport to validate our identity and an insurance card to get access to medical care. As a result, membership in a community is, or at least we expect it to be, easier to change; people have, or at least we expect them to have, more choices about where and with whom they will live, work, and play. But just as the number of possible communities has grown, their tensile strength has declined, as has their relative importance for the conduct of our lives. The extension and subsequent loosening of communal bonds have powerful implications for our expectations about the nature of political communities.[49]

To recapture premodern expectations about the political order, therefore, we must remember that people then assumed that most communities were relatively small and familiar. Because the language of politics rarely registers changes in scale, it is easy to overlook this fundamental aspect of "the world we have lost."[50] That is why we so often misread premodern political thinkers, from Plato to Rousseau, when we assume that the polities they discuss are entities the size of modern states rather than the intimate communities that they assumed to be the norm. Such communities were as essential for their members' lives as the air they breathed, but, like air, they could easily be taken for granted, unless they were threatened by internal conflict or invasive attack.

The premodern political landscape is best understood as an "archipelago of communities"—villages, manors, landed estates, towns, and cities—in which most people lived (or hoped to live) their lives.[51] Just as the modern state was created by absorbing or replacing existing political institutions, so modern society was an accumulation of insular communities. In the ancien régime, these communities were usually clearly separated from one another, often by visible barriers, the stone fences, city walls, rivers, or moats whose physical presence pervaded the premodern order. Communities were separate, but rarely self-sufficient; almost all of them needed goods and services that had to be imported from elsewhere. This was especially true of cities, even very small ones, that had to have ties to their environs, in which they could buy supplies and market their products and from which they could import the people necessary to replenish a population in which deaths almost always exceeded births.

In the ancien régime, some people were continually on the move: during the 1590s, for example, between five hundred and a thousand outsiders entered the Italian city of Mantua each month. We know these numbers because in Mantua, as in most premodern cities, visitors had to register before entering, giving their place of origin, the purpose of their stay, and where they would lodge. This ritual took place at the city gates that were always guarded and locked after dark. Here both insiders and outsiders were reminded of the community's identity, the essential distinction between who belonged and who did not, and of the need to keep a watchful eye on strangers, however necessary their presence might be for the city's existence. Once again, we are struck by the physical presence and personal nature of premodern boundaries.[52]

It would be a mistake to overestimate either the stability or the cohesion of these communities. They could easily be disrupted by natural or man-made disasters—crop failure, plague, fire, civil strife, or a marauding army—that left in their wake deserted fields, ruined houses, broken lives. Nor was everyone fortunate enough to have a place. Across the archipelago of communities wandered a rootless collection of servants without masters, peasants without land, children without parents, men and women too old or infirm to work, mercenaries no longer fit for battle. Some of these people were dishonest or dishonorable, but most were just unfortunate, the victims of circumstances over which they had no control. An illness or injury, a family quarrel or unwanted pregnancy brought ruin, disgrace, and expulsion from the community. In retrospect it might seem that the premodern world was relatively stable because the lives of its inhabitants changed much more slowly than our own, but in fact our ancestors often experienced sudden, unpredictable upheavals that were far greater than most of us can imagine or could easily endure. We expect the larger world to be constantly changing but our own lives to be relatively predictable; the reverse was true for most people in the premodern world.

Not everyone belonged to, or could remain in, a face-to-face community, and not every community was able to provide the security and sustenance its members might need, but these communities did represent the kind of social world that most people devoutly hoped would be theirs. The lingering influence of these hopeful expectations can be seen in the longing for an intimate common life that is such an important part of modern sensibilities. We are fascinated by, and some of the time long to return to, those small, confined collectivities that seem to have provided a degree of security and stability absent from the present. Nostalgia always points us toward what we have lost and would like to have again, or at least to what we think we would we like to have again.

Our language invites us to speak of community as an agent, a person, or, most misleading of all, as a thing. In fact, communities are best understood as a particular pattern of behavior, a set of institutionalized practices that are produced by a complex blend of choice and compulsion, individual desire and collective obligations. What E. P. Thompson wrote about class is true of most forms of social action: "Class is not this or that part of the machine, but the way the machine works once it is set in motion—not this or that interest, but the friction of interests, the heat, the thundering noise . . . class itself is not a thing, it is a happening."[53] Not every community involves a friction of interests, nor do they all create heat and noise, but communities, like classes, *happen*. They are not agents or objects, but are created as people relate to one another in a sustained but constantly changing process of cooperation and competition.

All communities happen: *how* they happen varies enormously because the practices that produce them are inevitably shaped by those material conditions and institutional arrangements that establish the possibilities and set the limits of social action. We will return to this point in chapter 3 when we consider the nature of communities in the modern era. For our present purposes, it is important to emphasize that in premodern Europe, the same material conditions and institutional arrangements that shaped the way people organized and imagined political space encouraged the primacy of locally focused, relatively small social units. First of all, there was the difficulty of movement, what the great nineteenth-century historian Jules Michelet called "the tyranny of distance"—travel was possible, but usually demanding and sometimes dangerous. Except for the very rich or truly adventuresome, people traveled either because they had no choice or because they hoped for some significant reward, perhaps wealth from a successful voyage or the spiritual benefits acquired by visiting a pilgrimage site. Most commercial transactions, units of measurement, and monetary systems were locally defined and not easily transferable.

The localism of premodern society was also reinforced by the fact that most communication was oral. There were, to be sure, people who could read and write, but like those who specialized in long-distance trade, these literate groups formed an elite, whose power and prestige derived from skills that most of their contemporaries did not have. Because communication was difficult, most supralocal institutional ties were thin, their power and influence intermittent at best. In order to settle a dispute, borrow money, or get aid in times of need, there was usually nowhere to turn except to the people nearby, who were, for better or worse, enmeshed in a web of mutual dependence. Most social units, therefore, were small and familiar, their rules and procedures directly transmitted, shaped by custom, deeply rooted in the accepted practices of everyday life.

In addition to communities that were small enough to be immediately experienced, people also belonged to groups that were too large, distant, or vaguely defined to be apprehended directly. These communities were the products of imagination, the mental capacity that Kant called *Einbildungskraft*, by which he meant the ability to project from what we know firsthand to what we do not, often cannot, know directly.[54] Ever since the publication of Benedict Anderson's influential book, imagined communities are often identified with nations and nationalism. In fact, most communities have dimensions beyond their members' immediate experience. Even the inhabitants of small, cohesive tribal societies imagine their connections to ancestors who exist in a realm outside everyday experience and therefore must be represented by ceremonies and symbols. Among the most important things to understand about any political order is the way in which its participants imagine their common life, and the necessary but complicated relationship between what they imagine and what they experience.[55] In that realm where imagination and experience uneasily coexist we find the myths and rituals with which people try to manage the strains and contradictions that can be found in every political order.

In the premodern world, the most important imagined community was spiritual, another example of the fusion of religion and the political order. As with every imagined community, people's conception of their religious identity blended experience and faith, what they did in their everyday lives and what they believed about a transcendent realm they could not see. People practiced their religion within a local community. At its center was the parish church, which was usually the only building large enough to hold the entire community. At the church's baptismal font, infants became members of the church on earth; in the churchyard's consecrated soil, the remains of the faithful departed waited for their final resurrection. Here in this sacred space, where present, past, and future came together, people's faith was affirmed in ceremonies that marked the milestones in their individual and common lives—births, marriages, deaths, the feast days of patron saints, and the recurring celebrations of the liturgical year. These ceremonies provided a bridge between the congregation and a greater community of believers that included the pilgrim church on earth and the saints in heaven. The church's rituals and symbols were designed to close the gap between experience and imagination by expressing the congregation's commitment to the immediate life of the parish and the larger community of the faithful, both on earth and in paradise.[56]

Religious affiliation was not a matter of choice. Both as experience and imagination, the church was not a consensual community; like the family, it was a community into which one was born. As the eminent nineteenth-century student of religion William Robertson Smith once remarked, people did not choose to be religious, but the orthodoxy and intensity of their faith might vary: "To practice religion was to be a member of a community and only by abandoning the community could one abandon religion."[57]

Precisely because religion and community—like religious institutions and political authority—were so closely intertwined, the shattering of Christian unity in Catholic Europe during the sixteenth century reverberated throughout the social and political order. In the next section, we will see what this rupture meant for the relationship among dynastic states; now it is enough to point out how religious differences inevitably divided communities, creating sources of conflict that reached deeply into people's everyday lives. In some places, communities acted together, accepting a common confessional identity. When they could not, conformity had to be imposed, usually by excluding the weaker elements or forcing them underground. Only in some cases—parts of Poland, Hungary under the Ottomans, and a few cities such as Augsburg—were people able to create institutions that enabled them to remain a single community with more than one confession.[58]

Although we should not overlook the diversity within and between spiritual communities in the premodern world, social and political pressures for religious conformity were powerful and difficult to evade. Individual heretics were punished or excluded, deviant communities isolated or destroyed. Throughout Christian Europe, the most prominent outsiders were the Jews. Unlike the other religious groups in the ancient world, most Jews had resisted conversion, often at great cost; they remained an enduring challenge to Christians' universalist aspirations. Although Jews were invited to settle and given rights in the Polish Commonwealth, in many other places they were not permitted to reside; even where they were tolerated, they lived as a people apart in separate, carefully restricted communities that were imperfectly, often unreliably protected from their potentially hostile neighbors. In most of Europe, these insular Jewish communities were an especially vivid expression of the characteristic fragmentation of the premodern social order, just as in the nineteenth century the gradual dissolution of these communities would be a sign of modernity's promise and perils.[59]

Christians, St. Paul wrote, belonged to a mystical community represented by Christ and united by divine grace. In the famous passage from Galatians, Paul proclaims that among the baptized was "neither Jew nor Greek, slave nor free, male nor female." All would become one in Christ Jesus (Gal. 3:29). Paul does not say that these categories, the essential building blocks of the contemporary social order, would disappear; he promises spiritual, not social equality. In the community that Paul asked his readers to imagine, people would retain their ethnicity, legal status, and gender, but these distinctions would be transcended by another, more powerful source of unity. Just as the belief in Christ's dual nature (both human and divine) helped people to understand the king's two bodies—the king was at once a mortal individual and the personification of an immortal state—so their membership in a spiritual community beyond the one they could directly experience reinforced premodern expectations about other kinds of imagined communities in the social and political order.

Political communities, like spiritual ones, were primarily small, familiar, and personal. "Only power on the spot [*sur place*] was effective power," wrote the great medievalist Marc Bloch.[60] Power was usually exercised "on the spot" by local elites and their representatives, landlords, urban patricians, the leaders of a guild, and, sometimes, the parish priest. The sites where political power was exercised—the church, manor house, guildhall—were embedded in the life of the community, inseparable parts of people's everyday world. The rules that established how people should behave, how crimes were punished and disputes resolved were most often based on custom and tradition, communicated orally, enforced by and on people who knew one another.

Some of these political communities—independent city-states and some isolated villages—were autonomous, but most of them were connected to wider webs of obligation, linked in a complicated set of overlapping hierarchies to what we have described as composite states. The representatives of these states—sometimes outsiders, more often local elites—collected revenues, extracted services, and enforced the rules. How much these representatives of the state affected the life of the community varied widely, depending on how much the state needed resources—money, men, material—and on its capacity to extract them.[61]

Both the needs and capacity of states increased during the premodern era, but until the eighteenth century the contact between most communities and their state was usually intermittent and uneven. The ceremonies that characterized the premodern political order—such as the celebrations of dynastic births, marriages, and burials, the rulers' ritual progresses through their realms, and the brutality of public punishments and executions—were designed to represent the power of the state. These representations of the state were supposed to direct the way people imagined their connection to distant sources of authority, and thus to reaffirm the customs, habits, and beliefs on which the political order's legitimacy depended. The extravagance of these events, perhaps above all their often vivid cruelty, were an indication of the practical limitations on the ability of most political institutions to project power across time and space. Beyond the local community, away from where control could be imposed *sur place*, political power was usually expressed by symbols and ceremonies rather than the government's capacity to manage their subjects' lives. Membership in these larger political communities, therefore, was more often imagined than experienced.[62]

Did the nation exist as an imagined community in premodern Europe? Students of nationalism disagree sharply about this issue. Some stress the ancient origins of nations, others insist that nations and nationalism are a distinctly, indeed uniquely, modern phenomenon.[63] We will return to this question in chapter 3, which is about how and why national communities became so significant in the modern political order. In that respect, my analysis will support the "modernist" position. But for now, a few words should be said on behalf of the "perennialists." If we take Walker Connor's definition of the nation as "a human grouping whose members share an intuitive sense of kindredness or sameness, predicated upon a myth of common descent," then there is no doubt that nations existed well before the modern era.[64] For evidence we need look no further than chapter 11 of the book of Genesis, which describes how God created different nations by dissolving humanity's linguistic unity, thus establishing a connection between language and nationality that would be of lasting significance.

After the account of the tower of Babel, the focus of the biblical narrative shifts from mankind to Abraham and his progeny and thus becomes the history of the Jews as a people. It is hard to think of a better—or more influential—illustration of Connor's definition of the nation than the story of the Jews, whose association of kindredness, common origins, and political destiny could serve as a template for modern nationalism. In premodern Europe, however, a sense of ethnically based "kindredness"—and, no less important, of ethnically based difference—usually had less to do with myths of common descent than with particular character traits, such as temperance and drunkenness, hygiene and its absence, industriousness and laziness, courage and cowardice, that were commonly associated with national communities. To cite one example among many, recall how the description of Portia's suitors in *The Merchant of Venice* reflects national stereotypes (the nephew of the elector of Saxony is usually drunk, the prince of Morocco flamboyant, etc.) that would have been easily recognized by Shakespeare's audience.[65]

National differences were most visible when viewed from the outside, as people moved from one place to another. At the beginning of the seventeenth century, for instance, a traveler noted that "immediately outside the gates of Trent one enters Germany."[66] By "Germany" he seems to have meant a place where people had a particular language, manners, and customs that set them apart from the citizens of Trent and, of course, from the traveler himself; in other words, Germany was where people who acted like Germans lived. Only rarely did these national units coincide with territorial or jurisdictional boundaries; most people experienced and imagined them as cultural rather than political communities.

National identities could acquire a particular significance in times of crisis. We see this in the image of England evoked in the great speech that Shakespeare gives to Henry V on the eve of the battle of Agincourt, when the king invokes his comrades' common heritage. But note how this image is entwined with religious sentiments, family honor, and dynastic loyalties: "Follow your spirit and upon this charge / Cry 'God for Harry, England, and Saint George!'" For Henry—and for Shakespeare—England is a source of inspiration because it has a shared past and promised future that was personified by its monarch and patron saint.[67]

National loyalties were strongest when ethnicity overlapped with dynastic or religious antagonisms, as happened, for example, when Spanish troops invaded the Netherlands or Germans crossed the Alps. This kind of animosity prompted Erasmus, writing in 1516, to lament that "nowadays the Englishman generally hates the Frenchman, for no better reason than that he is French. The Scot, simply because he is a Scot, hates the Englishman, the Italian hates the German, the Swabian the Swiss, and so on; province hates province, city hates city."[68] It would, however, be a mistake to read Erasmus in the light of modern national conflicts: he clearly has in mind a wide range of communities, including kingdoms such as England or France, politically fragmented territories such as Germany or Italy, regions such as Swabia or Switzerland, along with cities and provinces. All of them, he believes, create "ridiculous labels" that can alienate Christians from one another.

In premodern Europe, a complex skein of imagined communities—religious, political, ethnic, and linguistic—was superimposed on the archipelago of small social worlds in which most people lived. Nations, which would become the most important form of imagined community in the modern era, certainly existed, but they could become an important source of cultural identity or political allegiance only when they were fused with other sources of identity and allegiance. For most people, most of the time, national loyalties had a limited relevance for the exercise and distribution of political power. Nor did nationhood provide an essential linkage between domestic and international politics as it would in the modern era. This linkage, as we shall see in the next section, came from the dynastic loyalties and conflicts that shaped expectations about the foundations of the political order both within and among premodern states.

A SOCIETY OF DYNASTIC STATES

In the previous two sections we examined premodern expectations about the organization of political space and the nature of community. We turn now to the environment in which premodern states engaged in a complex combination of coexistence and competition. Here too we must be alert to the terminological anachronisms that make it hard to see the fundamental differences between the premodern order and the one in which we live.[69] The difficulties begin with naming the object of our inquiry. It is a mistake, I think, to assume there was an "international order" or an "international system" in Europe before the second half of the eighteenth century. The term *international*, which was used for the first time by Jeremy Bentham in 1789, suggests a group of clearly defined, sovereign political units that match our expectations about what a state should be. But premodern states were usually not clearly defined, nor were many of them truly sovereign in the modern meaning of the word. Instead, states were a complex composite of different kinds of jurisdictions held together by dynastic claims and personal loyalties. Our modern expectations about international affairs are the product of a long historical process that slowly and unevenly transformed what I have decided to call, for want of a better alternative, the "society of dynastic states."

The first and usually most important question to ask about any society is, Who belongs? This is not an easy question to answer about the society of dynastic states. It has been estimated that there were five hundred "states" in Europe at the beginning of the sixteenth century.[70] This figure seems plausible enough, but it is necessarily imprecise. We don't really know how many states there were in the year 1500 because we can't be sure what should count as a "state."

Consider, for example, the duchy of Savoy, a characteristic composite state on the frontier between what is now Italy and France. The dukes of Savoy ruled part of their territory directly, part as the feudal lords of local nobles; they were themselves vassals of the Holy Roman emperor and, as late as 1530, were deeply concerned about where they stood in the imperial hierarchy. Was Savoy one state, or several, or perhaps not a state at all? And what about a city such as Bologna? It had once been a powerful, independent actor in northern Italy (around 1300 it was the fifth largest city in Europe). After Bologna was conquered by Pope Julius II in the early sixteenth century, it became part of the Papal States. But since Bologna retained partial autonomy and continued to exchange ambassadors with some other states, it remained something more than a papal possession.[71] And even though the political landscape in northern Italy may have been unusually fragmented, it was not fundamentally different from much of Europe.

Given the tangled mixture of autonomy and dependence that existed almost everywhere, maps of premodern Europe are always oversimplified and misleading. An accurate representation of the hundreds of imperial cities, ecclesiastical entities, and semisovereign aristocratic properties that were scattered across the Rhineland in the eighteenth century would have been beyond the capacity of even the most meticulous cartographer.[72] There was, to anticipate our discussion of political space in chapter 2, something fundamentally "illegible" about the ancien régime. The distinguished geographer Norman Pounds's assessment that by the early fourteenth century "the political map of Europe had assumed a form which, with minor changes, it was to retain into modern times" may be roughly accurate for some of Europe, especially in the west and north, but it is deeply misleading for Italy, the German lands, and territories along the Ottoman Empire's border.[73]

Before the end of the eighteenth century, much of Europe's political landscape was not only fragmented and complex, it was also structurally unstable and extremely volatile. Perhaps because this world did not experience the kind of tectonic shifts that we identify with the great revolutions of 1789 and 1917, the ancien régime might seem relatively inert, a time when institutions changed slowly and tomorrow seemed much like today. But in fact, although premodern society may not have been revolutionary in the modern sense, it was anything but stable: endemic violence and frequent crises persistently disrupted the lives of both individuals and their communities. Genoa, for example, which was famous for its civic volatility, endured seventy-two rebellions and regime changes between 1300 and 1528. Many European territories moved from one ruler to another, sometimes with bewildering rapidity: Sardinia, which was given to Spain by the Treaty of Utrecht in 1713, went to Austria a year later before ending up with Savoy in 1720. To acquire Sardinia, the dukes of Savoy had surrendered Sicily to Austria; the Austrian Habsburgs, in turn, passed Sicily on to a branch of the Spanish Bourbons fifteen years later.[74] When states changed rulers, they frequently changed their status. For example, after France picked up a complex collection of polities in Alsace in 1648, the nature of French rule over these lands remained unsettled, generating a series of controversies that would last until 1789.[75] In Alsace, as in many other parts of Europe, the line between domestic and foreign dominion—and therefore what should be defined as a state—was very difficult to establish.

By the middle of the seventeenth century, around 150 of the 500 states that had existed in 1500 had been erased from the political landscape; many more would disappear in the following decades.[76] Some of these territories retained vestiges of their former identity by becoming distinct parts of a composite state; others were totally absorbed into a larger entity. Most people accepted these territorial changes as a normal—if perhaps regrettable—ingredient of political life. In the premodern era, therefore, though there was no shortage of celebrations and lamentations about territorial gains and losses, it is hard to find those enduring expressions of national outrage that would be provoked, for instance, by Germany's annexation of Alsace-Lorraine in 1871 or Israel's occupation of the Golan Heights a century later.[77]

There were a number of reasons for the premodern order's inherent instability, but the most important was the ubiquitous desire of rulers to expand their domains. Princes were always prepared, in the words of an Italian diplomat, to "cut and pare states and kingdoms as if they were Dutch cheeses."[78] These acquisitive impulses were an essential element in people's expectations about how politics worked. For Machiavelli, the rapaciousness of princes was rooted in human nature: "It is perfectly natural and ordinary that men should want things; and always when men do what they can, they will be praised and not blamed."[79] Although Machiavelli's fascination with how territory could be acquired and retained reflected the distinctive character of an Italian environment in which weaker states constantly fell victim to their predatory neighbors, his expectations about the unsettled nature of the society of state were widely shared throughout the ancien régime, even when they were expressed in a more subdued fashion and with a different moral tone. More than two centuries after Machiavelli, Montesquieu, for example, still believed that "war and expansion are the essence of monarchy."[80]

War *and* expansion: Montesquieu recognized that the expansive impulses of states were tied to the violent realities of warfare. People may have longed for a serene world in which they could travel, trade, and celebrate as do the figures in the magnificent fresco *Allegory of Good Government* that Ambrogio Lorenzetti painted for Siena's town hall in the 1330s. But the citizens of fourteenth-century Italian cities knew all too well that peace was precious because it was so rare, while war was a persistent and pervasive fact of life.

By twentieth-century standards, the scale of combat in the old regime might seem limited. Armies were relatively small, campaigns usually brief, major battles comparatively infrequent. But premodern warfare was endemic; it was a chronic condition, not a violent interruption in the normal course of events. In the sixteenth and seventeenth centuries, the major European states were at war two-thirds of time.[81] This surprised no one; just as most people expected states to try to expand, they accepted that war and conquest were fundamentally important for a state's existence, an unavoidable feature of human affairs, two of the four terrible horsemen (the others were famine and death) whose hoofbeats echo in the book of Revelation. "A prince should have no other object, no other thought, no other subject of study than war," Machiavelli insisted. "The quickest way to lose a state is to neglect this art, the quickest way to get one is to study it." Jean Bodin, writing a few decades later, admitted that "reason and commonsense alike point to the conclusion that the origin and foundation of commonwealths was in force and violence."[82]

Considering the "force and violence" that beset the premodern society of states, we can understand why some people yearned for a universal order that would bring peace and stability. This yearning helps to explain the remarkable hold that the Roman Empire continued to have on Europeans' political imagination. In the sixteenth century, the Roman model shaped the aspirations of rulers as different as Emperor Charles V and Sultan Suleiman the Magnificent, both of whom dreamed of creating a new universal imperium. For them, and for scores of lesser rulers, Roman symbols, rituals, and architectural forms were the best way to express political power. In Mantua, the Gonzaga family commissioned the court painter Andrea Mantegna to produce a series of frescos celebrating Caesar's triumphs, thereby illuminating their own modest domain with the reflected light of imperial glory.[83] Long after the empire's decline and fall, which Edward Gibbon called "the greatest, perhaps, and most awful scene in the history of mankind," memories of Rome's glorious achievements continued to be a part Europe's political imagination.[84] Although Gibbon may have lamented Rome's decline, he, together with many of his contemporaries, celebrated what he called the "great republic" of European states that he saw taking shape around him, a republic composed on different states united by common values and practices.[85]

Dreams of a universal order have never entirely vanished from Europe; they recur again and again as people continue to hope that they might be able to banish instability and violence from the society of states. By the fifteenth century, however, some theorists and practitioners had begun to abandon hopes for a universal order and to recognize the political primacy of separate states. A more peaceful society of states might be created by regulating its members' interactions rather than transcending them. Few believed that violence could be perpetually banished, but some did hope that it could be contained. This would require working within what François Guizot, writing in the nineteenth century, called European civilization's "agitated but fruitful diversity."[86]

One sign of these changing expectations about the society of states was the evolution of diplomatic norms and procedures. Governments had always dispatched envoys, exchanged messages, and signed agreements, but by the fifteenth century these interactions began to be more durable and formalized. We should not overestimate the linear, irreversible direction of these changes; like the scholarship on other elements of the political order, historical accounts of diplomatic practice have a tendency to be both anachronistic and teleological. Nevertheless, around 1500 some familiar features of international relations, such as the exchange of permanent ambassadors, diplomatic immunity, conventions governing treaties, and declarations of war, were clearly taking shape.[87] Behind these innovations in diplomatic practice was the slowly emerging assumption that there was something distinctive about the relationships among states. In the society of states, Bodin argued, the participants were equal, which meant that one sovereign could make an alliance with a stronger partner without becoming his subject, a situation that would not be possible between a lord and his vassal.[88] In chapter 4, we shall see that this assumption would become a key element in the theory and practice of sovereignty.

Although Bodin believed that the norms and practices in the society of states had a special character, he continued to think of them in terms of individual human interactions. Bodin acknowledged that a corporate body might sometimes hold sovereignty, but he assumed that sovereign authority would usually be exercised by individual rulers, who acted for their subjects and the territory in which they lived. Ambassadors were emissaries of the prince, sent to represent him (or, rarely, her). That is why François de Callières titled his widely used instructional manual for diplomats, first published in 1716, *On the Manner of Negotiating with Sovereign Princes.*[89]

The royal court, so centrally important for managing the competing elements within composite states, was also the site where the prince and his advisors conducted foreign affairs. As Norbert Elias noted, the art of what we call diplomacy was "cultivated in the everyday life of court society," where the aristocratic representatives of foreign princes mixed with their counterparts (who were sometimes their relatives) in the monarch's retinue.[90] The court's importance for diplomatic forms and functions can be seen in the Ambassadors' Staircase at Versailles (built for Louis XIV and demolished in the mid-eighteenth century), which provided a carefully arranged setting in which the king, surrounded by his courtiers, could receive the representatives of his fellow princes.[91] We can still find residues of these premodern expectations about the personal nature of international relations in the way contemporary ambassadors present their credentials to the head of state when they take up a new post. Treaties are still signed by heads of state in ceremonies that recall how agreements between states were once regarded as contracts between individual rulers, based on their personal connection and, when possible, reinforced by some familial bond.[92]

War, like diplomacy, was viewed as an extension of dynastic relations. A prince declared war against another ruler, which is why so many of the causes of war mentioned in the formal declaration of hostilities have to do with points of honor, betrayed trust, and broken friendships.[93] Personal valor and heroic virtue, a willingness to accept the risks and revel in the glory that only war could bring were important elements in the myth of monarchial authority. The long line of warrior-princes that extends from ancient times and continued through the old regime included such distinguished figures as Gustavus Adolphus of Sweden and Frederick the Great of Prussia before culminating in the extraordinary career of the last great warlord, Napoleon Bonaparte. Even when the nature of both monarchy and war was transformed in the nineteenth century, the connection between dynastic legitimacy and military virtues continued: with few exceptions, modern monarchs wore (and many still wear) uniforms, members of their family did military service, and some of them occupied important posts in the army's high command.

During the ancien régime, dynastic institutions became an increasingly important element in the political order. In the fifteenth century there were many dynastic states ruled by scores of ruling families scattered across the European continent. These rulers intermarried, but they also competed with one another, driven by those acquisitive urges that played such an important part in the works of theorists, such as Machiavelli and Hobbes, and in the history of their states. Between the fifteenth and eighteenth centuries, a few of these dynasties began to separate from the pack; good luck (especially genetic good luck), an occasional ruler of unusual ability, and the capacity to seize opportunities for expansion enabled these dynasties to win decisive victories and, usually more important, to avoid catastrophic defeats. Over time, many European ruling families died out, lost their lands, or were driven to the margins of the political stage. A few—the Habsburgs, Bourbons, Romanovs, and Hohenzollern—survived and flourished.

In the world of states, legitimacy was, to quote Martin Wight's useful formulation, "the collective judgment of international society about rightful membership of the family of nations; how sovereignty may be transferred, how state succession is to be regulated, when large states break up into smaller, or several states combine into one."[94] Until the nineteenth century, and in some places, into the twentieth, legitimacy was founded on heredity. Dynastic connections gave princes the right to rule, conferred full membership in the society of states, and justified the transfer of territories from one state to another. Successful ruling families, such as the Habsburgs, skillfully chose marriage partners for their offspring who could bring lands, wealth, and political support.[95] Throughout the ancien régime, virtually every attempt to seize new territories—by the French when they invaded Italy in 1494 or by Prussians when they grabbed Silesia in 1740—was done in the name of dynastic rights. Such claims were, to be sure, often made with a cynical disregard for authenticity; it is hard to imagine that many contemporaries believed Frederick the Great's justification for annexing Silesia. Nevertheless, the ubiquity and persistence of dynastic claims affirmed their salience as a foundation for political authority.

The same expectations about dynastic legitimacy that encouraged cohesion and stability were also, essentially and unavoidably, a source of disruption and conflict. Because the fate of dynasties, like the fate of every family, was subject to the vagaries of biology, there was always the chance that biological accidents would undermine the established order of things. A ruler's early death or incapacity, a failed royal marriage, or—above all—the inability to produce an heir to the throne offered opportunities for domestic upheaval and foreign intervention. The premodern period is marked by a series of wars in which rivals attempted to take advantage of a dynasty's reproductive misfortune.

When we recall the central role of religion in the premodern political and social order, it is easy to understand why the division of Western

Christendom in the sixteenth century marked a turning point in the society of dynastic states as well as in the life of many communities. Conflicts of interest between rival states—England and Spain, for instance—were now intensified by confessional enmity.[96] Internal unrest based on social, regional, or ethnic antagonisms was now fed by religious antagonisms and thus could become a struggle over people's immortal souls. Since both Protestants and Catholics were willing to kill and to die for their faith, martyrdom became an all too familiar occasion for violence within and between states.[97]

Like the ideological conflicts of the twentieth century, religious quarrels crossed state boundaries and created the basis for both foreign and domestic alignments. "Formerly," an Italian diplomat remarked in 1565, "friends and enemies have been distinguished according to frontiers and states. . . . Now we must say Catholics and heretics, and the Catholic prince has to have as his allies all Catholics in all countries, just as the heretics have for their allies and subjects all heretics, whether at home or abroad."[98] In practice, of course, things were rarely this simple. Protestants and Catholics could cooperate, just as Christian princes had once enlisted the aid of "infidels" when it was to their advantage. Nonetheless, confessional conflict undermined domestic legitimacy and encouraged foreign disputes again and again in the sixteenth and seventeenth centuries, most prominently in France, the Netherlands, the British Isles, and Bohemia, where religious conviction, regional identity, and dynastic ambitions were especially volatile and contentious.

To step back from the abyss of international anarchy, the condition that Bodin regarded as "worse than the cruelest tyranny," Europeans sought to find ways to limit the disruptive role of religious conflict.[99] For Bodin in France and, a century later, for Thomas Hobbes in England, this meant strengthening the sovereign's claim to control both religious and secular affairs. For Hobbes, "Temporal and spiritual government are but two words brought into the world to make men see double, and mistake their lawful sovereign."[100] In the frontispiece to *Leviathan*, the sovereign is portrayed as holding both a sword and a bishop's crook, symbols of his political and ecclesiastical authority. In 1555, the Treaty of Augsburg attempted to stabilize the existing confessional order by allowing German princes to determine the religious affiliation of their own territories and exhorting them to refrain from intervening elsewhere. At the end of the century, France's Henry IV, having become a Catholic in order to gain the throne, sought to dampen religiously motivated unrest by guaranteeing the rights of the Protestant minority in the Edict of Nantes.

The best-known and in some ways the most influential attempt to manage the political upheavals created by confessional divisions occurred in 1648, when, following thirty years of intense civil and international strife, European rulers agreed to the so-called Peace of Westphalia (contained in the treaties of Münster and Osnabrück). These documents set out an elaborate if not entirely consistent set of regulations that gave religious minorities certain limited rights and established some measure of confessional parity within the territories of the Holy Roman Empire. The practical effect of these agreements was limited. Like the Augsburg settlement of 1555, the treaties of Münster and Osnabrück were part of a long, uneven process of change that would continue for decades. Of course the agreements of 1648 were significant, but the conventional view of a "Westphalian order" that supposedly created a system of sovereign and secular states in 1648 is a myth, a projection backward of our own expectations about the world.[101] For more than a century after 1648, wars were still provoked and justified by dynastic succession, religious alignments continued to influence the relations among states, and institutions such as the Holy Roman Empire remained intact.

A modern society of states was not created in 1648; it emerged gradually and unevenly as part of a larger set of changes within the political order. We will return to this new international system in chapter 4, but first it is necessary to examine the development of new expectations about states and communities. These expectations gradually and unevenly transformed the way people organized and imagined the domestic and the international order.

CHAPTER TWO

Making States Modern

"L'état n'est jamais donné: il est toujours <u>forgé</u>" (The state is never a given, it is always forged).[1] Lucien Febvre's use of *forgé* seems just right. By evoking the blows of the smithy's hammer and the scratch of the <u>counterfeiter's</u> pen, Febvre's verb nicely captures the complex blend of violence and artifice with which states are made. In this chapter we will see how Europeans began to forge states that were significantly different from their premodern counterparts and, as a result, fundamentally transformed people's expectations about the territorial, legal, and institutional dimensions of the political order. This was a gradual and uneven process that began in the late seventeenth century, intensified in the eighteenth, and was fully developed in the nineteenth.

The process of state-making was driven by a variety of social, economic, cultural, and political forces. Monarchs and eventually governmental agencies competed with one another to build elaborate palaces (usually inspired by Versailles), build collections of art or other precious objects, and sometimes even to improve the lives of their populations. Above all, states competed to acquire the capacity to make war. War was, and would long remain, the state's most important function, and the only one on which its very existence might depend. Beginning in the <u>late seventeenth</u> century, there was a <u>revolution in military affairs</u> that involved larger and more complex armies and, no less important for some states, a new kind of navy that transformed war at sea. These innovations demanded that states command more resources and create more effective organizations than ever before.[2]

In this chapter, we will primarily be interested in *how* rather than *why* states became modern.[3] How were they able to organize and deploy resources in new and more effective ways? How did they acquire what Michael Mann referred to as "infrastructural power," that is, "the capacity to actually penetrate civil society"?[4] Infrastructural power required new kinds of knowledge about the state's territory, population, and resources. States also had to create more extensive and uniform bodies of rules that would enable them to manage people's lives in ways earlier governments could not have imagined. And states had to build an administrative apparatus that was no longer staffed by members of the ruler's household or local notables, but rather by agents of state power. These officials became the human face of the state's territorial and legal identity; they were fully committed, at least in theory, to carrying out the thousands of quotidian tasks that made up the process of state-making.[5]

Histories of the modern state often emphasize the work of a few heroic individuals—Peter the Great, Frederick II, Napoleon—and the impact of a few great events, especially wars and revolutions. About the significance of these individuals and events for the development of states there can be no doubt. But states were made not only according to the plans of some great political architect or in response to the epic challenges of a major crisis; also important was the work of tens of thousands of ordinary men and women who used state institutions to mobilize resources, settle disputes, protect their communities, and, of course, to enhance their own wealth and power. The significance of these everyday acts of state-making is harder to see, not simply because their historical footprint is lighter, but also because their overall effect is cumulative, producing slow, almost imperceptible changes in people's political imaginations and practices.[6] State-making was not a sudden revolution but, like changes in maritime technology, it was a process of incremental evolution in which one source of energy was gradually displaced by another.

The cumulative changes in the state's infrastructure eventually transformed expectations about what states were and should be. People now expected a state's spatial dimensions to be clearly defined and assumed that its population could be accurately counted and systematically classified.

People also expected that there would be a uniform set of rules and regulations that described and sometimes limited the power that the state's agents claimed over their lives. We saw in chapter 1 that in the ancien régime, most states had been embodied in, and represented by, their rulers. By the beginning of the nineteenth century, legitimacy was no longer inseparable from the sacred person of the king, but was becoming increasingly secular and impersonal, institutionally embodied and represented by bound volumes of legal codes and written constitutions. Until the second decade of the twentieth century, most European states still had monarchs, who sometimes had a good deal of power and always fulfilled important ceremonial functions, but by then most monarchs had become the first servants of the state.

KNOWLEDGE: THE GROWTH OF THE LEGIBLE STATE

"Bureaucratic administration," Max Weber wrote, means "domination through knowledge." In fact, every political order depends on knowledge.[7] Governments have always had to know about their territory and population, but the nature of this knowledge and how it is produced and communicated constantly changes. In premodern Europe, most political knowledge was immediate and personal, best acquired directly, through practice and experience. Machiavelli, for example, recommended that princes devote a great deal of time to hunting, not simply because it was good exercise, but also because it was the most efficient way to learn about their realms. Erasmus agreed about the kind of knowledge rulers needed: he urged them to get to know their kingdoms the way a physician knows the bodies of his patients or a farmer the contours of his lands.[8]

In the modern political order, immediate and personal knowledge still matters, but it is not enough. We now expect governments to have extensive information about their environments, information that they can organize systematically and access easily. We can see an early example of this kind of knowledge in a memorandum written in 1680 for Duke Ernst August of Braunschweig by Gottfried Wilhelm Leibniz, who was then serving as the duke's librarian and political counselor. Leibniz advised Ernst August to prepare what he called political tables, *Staats-Tafeln*, which were brief, written summaries of vital information about the state that would be readily at hand and thus—in Leibniz's words—could "provide a convenient instrument of praiseworthy self-government."[9] Like Machiavelli and Erasmus, Leibniz was concerned with the knowledge necessary to rule, but for him it was written, comprehensive, and available. He believed that knowledge about the state, and therefore the state itself, should be legible.

Let us, once again, begin by considering some maps, not only because they represent how territory was organized and imagined, but also because mapmaking illustrated the cultural and institutional aspects of the state-making process. We have seen how maps played an important role in early modern visual culture; they were both symbols and instruments of political authority. Toward the end of the seventeenth century, new sorts of carto-graphical projects began to produce maps with unprecedented levels of precision, comprehensiveness, and uniformity. These maps aspired to de-pict with great accuracy the dimensions and topography of the state's entire territory, whose features were represented with clearly defined, uniform symbols. To meet these standards, a map could not be the work of a single craftsman, such as Claes Visscher's map of the Netherlands that we dis-cussed in chapter 1. The new sort of map had to be produced by organi-zations able to enforce common practices and support projects over a long period of time. Such organizations were usually funded by states, but the results of their work eventually became available to the public. The repre-sentation of political space, therefore, was expected to be comprehensive, precise, and accessible.[10]

The first family of this cartographical movement was the Cassini clan, four generations of which produced an increasingly elaborate and detailed set of maps for the kings of France. In the late seventeenth century, the French Academy of Sciences hired Gian Domenico (soon to become Jean Dominique) Cassini, an Italian astronomer and expert on the calculation of longitude, to lead an ambitious new cartographical project. Cassini es-tablished a team that began to map all of France, using the recently devel-oped technique of triangulation that measured spatial dimensions with remarkable precision. Making maps like this took time. The meridian ex-tending north to south through Paris, which represented both the geo-graphical and political foundation of the project, was not completely mea-sured until 1718. Efforts to map the entire kingdom began in 1733; eleven years later, an eighteen-sheet map of France was published to great acclaim (see fig. 4).

Figure 4. Cassini, Map of France, 1756 (Library of Congress)

In cartography, as in many other eighteenth-century projects, the appetite for ever-greater coverage and accuracy was insatiable. In 1744, therefore, a new generation of Cassini set out to produce an even more elaborate set of maps, which would include 180 separate sheets by the time it was finally finished in 1793.[11]

Most European states started similar cartographical projects in the late seventeenth and eighteenth centuries. Peter the Great, for instance, returned from his famous journey to Holland in 1697 with a collection of maps and great admiration for Dutch cartographical technique. He and his successors sponsored efforts to measure their expanding territories and thus to create, at least on paper, the kind of integrated state for which they yearned.[12] The Habsburgs commissioned a survey of their monarchy in 1764. This took twenty-three years to complete and finally produced a vast number of maps—about 5,400—of varying size and format, which were substantially less expensive and less accurate than the Cassini maps that were finished about the same time.[13] The British Ordnance Survey began in 1791, when the king formally approved a comprehensive cartographical project to be run by the army's Ordnance Department. The first product of this enterprise, a map of Kent in four rectangular sheets, was published in 1801. The final ordnance map, number 108, did not appear until January 1870.[14]

Brian Harley, one of the most influential modern historians of cartography, remarked that "much of the power of the map as a representation of social geography is that it operates behind a mask of seemingly neutral science."[15] Everything about a map—and this is especially true of comprehensive projects like the Cassini maps of France or the British Ordnance Survey—encourages us to see them as precise, neutral representations of the physical world. In fact, as Harley insisted, "maps are preeminently a language of power."[16] That is why mapmaking had a special significance in those areas where territorial boundaries remained contested. In Poland, for example, old maps of the vanished Commonwealth were carefully preserved and sometimes republished by exiled patriots; in Ireland, where locals resisted the British Ordnance Survey team when it began its work in 1824 (hampered by bad weather, rough terrain, and popular animosity, the Irish ordnance survey took two decades to complete); and, most significantly, in Europe's overseas possessions where creating maps of newly acquired territories was an essential element in the process of colonial appropriation.[17]

Scholars have often noted the similarity between mapmaking and census-taking. The cultural anthropologist Arjun Appadurai, for example, wrote that "statistics are to bodies and social types what maps are to territories: they flatten and enclose."[18] There was, of course, nothing new about counting people. Like maps, the census has ancient roots and, in various forms, remained an important tool of premodern statecraft. By the early eighteenth century, however, both mapmakers and census-takers were motivated by unprecedented aspirations for comprehensiveness, precision, and uniformity.[19] For this, governments had to establish institutions that could ensure uniformity and continuity. Census-taking eventually served both the public and the state, and thus, like mapmaking, became another example of the state's increasing legibility.

Census-taking turned out to be a more complicated, time-consuming, and expensive enterprise than mapmaking. Because the physical landscape, complex and sometimes inhospitable, is relatively inert, cartographical surveys could proceed gradually, adding new territories year by year until they had completed their mission. The census, on the other hand, was supposed to be taken everywhere simultaneously, preferably on the same day, certainly within a brief period of time. Moreover, human beings can be difficult to count because they move around, go missing, and can intentionally mislead. Census-takers were sometimes driven away by angry crowds who realized their connection with tax collectors and the recruiting officers, both unwelcome agents of state authority.[20] In 1789, the Chevalier des Pommelles wearily concluded that "an enumeration of individuals which, at first glance, seems such an easy thing, not only would be expensive but, when one considers it, presents so many difficulties in carrying it out that one must doubt even the possibility."[21]

Even without resistance, an accurate census required an elaborate organizational structure. Britain, although the richest and probably the most cohesive European state, needed a century to create the institutions necessary to count its population. In 1753, the House of Commons passed a bill calling for a census to be taken the following year: in every community the overseer of the poor was supposed to go from house to house and record every inhabitant, listing them by age, gender, marital status, and whether or not they received alms. The bill was defeated in the House of Lords, where a majority had no desire to become what one critic called "the numbered vassals of indiscriminating power."[22]

Uncertainty about the size and development of the British population continued through the eighteenth century. Thomas Malthus's essay of 1798 is only the most famous example of a large literature devoted to the question of whether the population was growing (as Malthus maintained) or declining (as some people feared). Until the first national census was held in 1801, both positions had to be based on estimates and speculation. Even then the data on the British population were woefully incomplete and inaccurate. Finally, in 1837 a central registry was established for England and

Wales (1844 for Ireland, 1854 for Scotland). The first truly effective British census was held in 1841. In 1853, the *Manchester Guardian* called the results of this census one of the wonders of the world: "Imagine a pile of schedules, seven millions in number, and forty tons in weight, and who will say that Egypt or Greece, Palmyra or Rome, ever reared a superstructure more imposing?"[23]

In many other European states, the national census began earlier than in England, but everywhere its administration turned out to be challenging.[24] There was, for instance, a complete national census taken in Iceland as early as 1703, but the results were not systematically analyzed. The Danish census of 1769 was done, very badly, by a private firm. The government set up a Tabulating Office to carry out censuses in 1787 and 1801; the first was unreliable, the second still unfinished by the time the office was disbanded in 1819. Some progress was made by a new Tabulating Commission in the 1830s and 1840s, which was finally replaced by a Statistical Bureau in 1850.[25] The most efficient censuses under the old regime were in Sweden, where a law of 1748 established the registration of vital statistics in every parish. In France, the importance of statistical data was widely recognized. For instance, Jacques Necker, the Swiss banker and French finance minister, had devoted a chapter to the subject in his 1784 book on financial administration. In 1791, as part of the Revolution's campaign to reform state and society, the National Assembly called for an annual census throughout the country. The response was, to say the least, unenthusiastic. The first truly effective national census did not take place in France until 1831.[26]

What Brian Harley said about maps is equally true of the census: both are powerful because they operate "behind a mask of seemingly neutral science." There is something inherently persuasive about those long columns of numbers that appear to capture the complex contours of the social landscape. The census, like a map, both creates and describes the objects it is supposed to represent. As with cartography, the relationship between counting and conquest is most apparent in colonial settings. As the American anthropologist Bernard Cohn demonstrated in his classic article on the Indian census, colonial administrators imposed categories of caste and religious affiliation and thus contributed to what Cohn called "the objectification of Indian society."[27] In Europe, something of the same happened in those areas, such as the Habsburg monarchy, where the census confronted the problem of fitting fluid and sharply contested national identities into precise categories, a problem to which we will return in chapter 3. Those familiar maps of the monarchy's ethnic composition, based on national censuses taken in the late nineteenth and early twentieth centuries, are the result of bitter political struggles over how (and even whether) "nationalities" should be counted.[28] In the United States, the census was also the product of complex struggles for political power; throughout the nineteenth century, some people were simply not counted, which was yet one more way of denying their civil rights and identity.[29]

Mapmaking and census-taking were both part of a larger European project to measure, classify, and record the social and natural world. Governments everywhere gradually adopted what one contemporary observer called "the statistical gaze," a way of looking at the world that involved precise calculation, classification, and systematic analysis.[30] Statistics, a French expert declared in 1800, provide "the facts, the basis for calculation, the real picture of wealth and strength of the state."[31] Originally *statistics* referred to all kinds of descriptive material about states, but by 1800 it had acquired its modern, quantitative meaning. Eventually the statistical gaze began to generate what Theodore Porter has identified as "a great explosion of numbers" that measured an expanding list of political, social, and cultural activities.[32]

In the nineteenth century, most European states established a Statistical Office to collect and manage these numbers: Prussia in 1805, Bavaria in 1808, Württemberg in 1820, Austria in 1829, Britain in 1837. By the end of the century, agencies at every level collected data about their communities: in 1900, there were more than one hundred urban statistical offices in Europe.[33] In addition to these official agencies, Europeans created a wide network of nongovernmental organizations that produced and circulated knowledge about nature, society, and politics. By connecting the worlds of scholarship and statecraft, these local, national, and international societies helped to transform the way knowledge was acquired and deployed.[34]

A necessary lubricant of its administrative machinery, knowledge was an essential part of the state's expanding power. Improving the state's fiscal capacity obviously depended on the government's ability to have access to information about its citizens' wealth and property. Similarly, mass-conscript armies could not have existed without data on the age, location, educational level, and physical condition of the male population. Elections,

another characteristic nineteenth-century enterprise, compelled governments to gather information about voters, how many there were, where
they lived, and if they met the requirements for eligibility. Taxes, military
service, and electoral participation—three critical elements in the creation
of a modern political order—all required the collection, classification, and
storage of information far greater than had ever before been necessary or
possible.[35]

Almost everything states did to penetrate civil society depended on
an increase in their store of useful knowledge. Consider, for example, the
rather undramatic matter of accident insurance for workers. One of the
state's first attempts to provide social services, accident insurance was established in the German Empire in the 1880s and then adopted in the
Austrian part of the Habsburg monarchy a few years later. In order to administer this program, officials had to know a good deal about who was
covered, how much compensation had to be paid for various injuries, and
how the cost should be shared among the participants. This all turned out
to be a complicated and often contentious exercise. In the Prague office, a
young lawyer named Franz Kafka was among the most efficient and competent experts in these matters.[36]

In 1855, Ernst Engel, who was head of Saxony's Statistical Office and
would eventually move to an even more prominent position in Berlin,
wrote that his organization's ultimate objective was "the creation of the
most complete and accurate anatomical portrait of the cultural condition
of Saxon politics and society." Statistics, he continued, "is not only the scale
held by Justice, it is also the sword. . . . Knowledge is power."[37] As critical
students of modern statehood, such as James Scott, have eloquently argued,
by gathering the knowledge that made states legible, governments greatly
increased the ability to control their population.[38] Scott is certainly right.
But knowledge could also be used to challenge the state, calibrate the distance between its aspirations and achievements, and reveal corruption and
injustice. The same data that were meticulously published by and for the
British government provided Karl Marx with the empirical basis for his
radical critique of capitalist society.

Whether it served as an affirmation or a critique of the political order,
the power of this new knowledge came from its cumulative quality. Once
the information had been assembled—the maps drawn, the population
counted, the statistics collected—it could be preserved in archives and

offices, administrative files and publications. Some of the most important technological instruments of state-making served this process of accumulation, including machines such as printing presses, typewriters, and eventually computers, and even more modest innovations, such as steel pens, standardized forms, and file boxes.[39] Because these new techniques of data-gathering and classification developed slowly and unevenly, it is easy to underestimate their significance for the creation of a modern political order.

The accumulation of knowledge about states and society gradually transformed the way people experienced and imagined the political order. This transformation is vividly illustrated by the image of France that is represented on the Cassini maps. By portraying the state's territory with great precision, representing its topographical features and settlement patterns with a uniform set of symbols, these maps encouraged people to imagine a political space that was both clearly defined and visually accessible.[40] Geography, the enlightened French scientist Nicolas Desmarest wrote in 1757, replaced images of the world as a "pile of debris" with one in which "order and uniformity" prevailed.[41] In the modern world, people came to expect states to be orderly, bounded units rather than the scattered debris of which composite states had been composed. No wonder that conservatives such as Edmund Burke recoiled from this new vision of space that he regarded as "a malady of a geometrical and arithmetical constitution."[42]

The "statistical gaze" helped to create the expectation that "order and uniformity" should prevail in the state. The complex process of information-gathering, conducted by an expanding corps of public officials, encouraged people to believe that the true dimensions of the state could be known and therefore mastered. The creation of categories with which this information could be ordered and analyzed encouraged people to imagine a political community that, like the space it inhabited, was bounded and coherent. More important than the precise nature of the classifications that the statisticians created was the practice of classification itself, the division of the state's population (the term itself is a statistical artifact) into uniform categories that promised to make society more clearly visible and widely accessible. Those who lamented the passing of the old order regarded the new statistical knowledge with undisguised hostility: the exemplary reactionary Joseph de Maistre, for example, ridiculed the belief that "you could count grains of sand and think the sum total is a house."[43]

Among the classifications created by modern states, none was more significant than the distinction between those who belonged and those who did not. In the ancien régime, belonging was most often defined by communities. To be an outsider was a perilous condition to be avoided at all costs. In the modern world, the state gradually replaced the community as a source of support and identity.[44] Citizenship, which would eventually be inscribed in the documents vital to every state and to every individual, became a legal, social, and usually cultural category.[45] Citizens were able (or at least should be able) to count on the legal protection of a state. And, of course, both the legal and social definition of citizenship was powerfully gendered; the ideal citizen was male (and often males of a particular ethnicity and with a certain amount of property). Even though rights were unequally distributed in most states, statelessness was to be without a claim to having any right, to confront borders that excluded rather than protected, and, like the homeless refugees in the ancien régime, to be dependent on the often unreliable charity of strangers. Anyone who has lost their passport experiences a brief and mercifully temporary sense of the anxiety that statelessness can engender.[46]

During the ancien régime, people experienced and imagined the state as embodied by the ruler and governed by his agents and local representatives. The premodern state was represented in symbols and ceremonies of monarchical rule, and also in those rituals that vividly affirmed its power of life and death. The modern state was experienced and imagined in quite different ways—as lines on a map, columns of numbers in the census, and, as we will see in the next two sections of this chapter, in law codes and bureaucratic practices.

Public spaces, like private property, were divided by often invisible but compulsively precise boundaries rather than the stone walls and physical barriers that had once marked jurisdictions and possessions.[47] This was part of a process through which institutions that had once been tangible and immediately apparent became more abstract and impersonal. Courts, markets, and cabinets began as physical entities; in the modern world, they became institutional abstractions. Status, which originally meant where someone literally stood in relationship to a more powerful person, was now a more general and also more elusive measure of a person's social position.[48] Ownership of stock in a modern corporation, as represented by a printed document, is very different from owning a plot of land that could be occupied, or from having a share in a Venetian galley, whose departure and return could be directly experienced.

Just as people shape the natural landscape to meet their economic needs, Lucien Febvre wrote, they rearrange the political world, breaking up "the natural units . . . to construct other political ones from the detached pieces."[49] Composite states were made up of different pieces that retained some measure of their former institutional and cultural identity. In the modern political order, these pieces tended to become parts of a cohesive whole. Now they are supposed to be united, not by dynastic ties and personal loyalties, but by cartographical conventions, statistical categories, legal documents, and administrative authority. Like so much else in the modern political order, we find a vivid and influential example of this process in revolutionary France where the traditional division of the country was replaced by intentionally abstract units called "Departments."[50] No longer imagined as an organic living thing, both unified and diverse, the institutional presence of the modern state became more uniform, but also more abstract; it seemed like a machine rather than a body.

New ways of knowing the state helped to dislodge political power from its place in a sacred order of meaning and devotion. Official cartography and statistical analysis belonged to a world that was secular and scientific, a world that was affirmed by a variety of similar enterprises throughout eighteenth- and nineteenth-century Europe. For example, the mapmakers' and census-takers' search for precision was clearly part of a broader scientific campaign to observe and measure natural and social phenomena.[51] The same aspirations for comprehensiveness that moved cartographers and statisticians can be found among the founders of the great encyclopedic projects that sought to bring together all useful knowledge, fix the meaning of terms, and compile grammars for the world's languages. Similarly, their aspirations were part of what one historian of science has called "the heroic age of classification," an appropriate name for the age of Buffon, Linnaeus, and Alexander von Humboldt.[52] Because classification is a way of imagining *and* organizing the world, it always both theoretical and practical.[53] As in the process of state-making as a whole, the theory and practice of classification were inseparable from the accumulation and exercise of power over information, things, and people.

In the modern world, states became legible, which meant that it was possible to know them in new ways. But this new knowledge did not displace what Edmund Morgan called the need "to make believe," the element of faith that had always been part of people's political expectations. And if this faith was still necessary, from what could it be constructed? How could it be represented and enacted? These questions will continue to occupy us as we examine other aspects of the new political order that slowly emerged from the wreckage of the ancien regime.

RULES: CODES AND CONSTITUTIONS

We sometimes say that "states *have* laws," as if states existed apart from their legal foundations. In fact, the two are inseparable; one could not function without the other. The state, as Ernest Barker, one of the state's most astute twentieth-century students, has written, "exists for law, it exists in and through law, we may even say that it exists as law. . . . The essence of the state is a living body of effective rules; in that sense the state is law."[54] The key phrase in Barker's statement is a "living body of effective rules," which describes the institutions that make, interpret, and enforce the law. These institutions enable people to settle disputes, legitimize the exercise of power, and operate the machinery on which social life depends. Law, therefore, is at once the product and the source of the political order's identity and cohesion.

States make laws, and vice versa. And different kinds of states make different kinds of laws, and vice versa. Every political order, from the smallest tribe to the greatest empire, has norms and practices that are supposed to regulate its members' relationships to one another, establish their duties and obligations, and define the scope and limits of political authority. How these norms and practices work, in other words, the nature of what Barker called law's "living body," varies widely across time and space. In this section, we will see how changes in the law's living body helped to reshape Europeans' expectations about what states were and should be.

The evolution of these expectations about the law resembles the growth of those new forms of knowledge that we examined in the preceding section. Both had the same rough chronological development, beginning in the seventeenth century, expanding in the eighteenth, and then becoming fully developed in the nineteenth. Lawmakers, like cartographers and statisticians, aspired to draw clear boundaries and define useful categories of analysis; they wanted their work to be precise, comprehensive, and systematic, at once mirrors and models of an orderly world. Lawmakers wanted what they produced to be legible, captured, contained, and communicated in the publicly accessible world of print. Maps, censuses, codes, and constitutions, therefore, were all part of that long, immensely significant sea change that marked the shift from an oral to a written culture based on print, the same change that produced not only new political expectations but many other familiar features of modern life, such as novels, newspapers, and printed parliamentary debates.[55]

For state-makers, as well as for ordinary men and women, the legibility of both knowledge and rules became an increasingly indispensable source of legitimation. After 1789, when the revolutionaries in France demanded "accountability" from their governments, they realized this required written records available to the public.[56] In 1858, John Stuart Mill (who earned his daily bread dealing with the East India Company's correspondence) claimed that the most important reason why India was so well administered was that "the whole Government of India is carried on in writing." As one German jurist put it, "Quod non est in actis, non est in mundo" (what is not in the documents, is not in the world).[57]

Like many expectations about the modern political order, new ways of experiencing and imagining the law had their roots in the ancien régime. Beginning in the second half of the seventeenth century, a number of monarchs issued decrees that provided a legal (and therefore secular) basis for dynastic legitimacy and thus for the territorial integrity of their composite states. Among the first were two Danish laws from 1665 that established the right of dynastic succession and the indivisibility of their "provinces and *Länder*, islands, fortresses," and also such royal possessions as "regalia, jewels, moneys, furniture, and weapons."[58] In 1701, the English Parliament passed an "Act of Settlement" that ensured that only Protestants could inherit the crowns of England and Ireland. Six years later, the Parliaments of Scotland and England agreed to the Acts of Union, in which the crowns of the two states would be united, thereby establishing the foundation for what would become one of Europe's longest-lasting composite states.[59] The Pragmatic Sanction, issued by the Emperor Charles VI in 1713, sought to secure not only the integrity of the Habsburgs' diverse possessions but also the right of Charles's daughter (and only heir) to inherit them.[60] In Russia, Peter the Great issued a Fundamental Law in 1722 in order to legitimize the Romanovs' dynastic succession. Unlike his contemporaries, however, he did not link legitimacy to biology but allowed the emperor to choose his successor, thereby preparing the way for political turmoil later in the century. Although these dynastic documents were clearly enmeshed in the premodern political order, they also represented the growing conviction that the right to rule and the identity of the state required a formal, written declaration.

Closer to our modern expectations than these decrees on dynastic succession were the projects carried on in most European states to create uniform, comprehensive, and systematic legal codes. These projects, like other attempts to make states more legible, required the coordination of local knowledge and central authority. But even more than its territory and population, an ancien régime state's complex mix of unwritten rules, regional customs, and competing jurisdictions resisted the codifiers' efforts at orderly and uniform representation. Premodern Europe was governed by an extraordinarily diverse and complex set of laws, drawn from several different sources and adjudicated by many overlapping institutions. A man traveling through eighteenth-century France, Voltaire complained, "changes laws almost as many times as he changes horses."[61]

The most prominent characteristics of law in the old regime, David Bell has written, "were duplication, ambiguity, and competition."[62] Given the arduous task confronting codifiers everywhere, it is not surprising that the first systematic compilations of laws were produced in relatively small states: Denmark in 1683, Norway in 1687, Sweden in 1734, Bavaria in the 1750s.[63] Codification in larger states could take decades. In Russia, for example, Catherine the Great convened a commission to reform the legal system in 1767; it was sixty years before a code was finally completed. In Austria, reform of the civil law began in 1753 (the same year as the first national census); a draft was finished in 1766 but was derailed because of bitter conservative opposition. A new code was eventually published in 1811.[64]

Like his contemporaries Catherine the Great and Maria Theresa, Frederick the Great wanted a unified code for his composite realm. After a failed attempt at comprehensive reform at the beginning of his reign, he set the process in motion again in 1780. It was completed, eight years after his death, in 1794, which was breathtaking speed by codification standards. With a title that captures both the code's universal aspirations and the Prussian states' fragmented condition, *Das Allgemeine Landrecht für die*

Preussichen Staaten fills almost seven hundred closely printed pages. It is organized into nineteen parts, each divided into sections and then paragraphs. A recently published index runs to 130 doubled-columned pages, listing provisions from A to Z, beginning with an entry on *Abbreviations*, which the code recommended avoiding in drafting wills, and ending with one on *Zwillinge* ("twins"), whose birth order was to be established by lot if witnesses could not remember which one emerged from the womb first. With this bewildering collection of provisions, the Prussian code tried to contain the underlying tensions in enlightened absolutism between universal rights and special privileges, centralized authority and local power, legal equality and traditional hierarchy.[65]

Around the turn of the eighteenth to the nineteenth century, at the same time that there was significant progress in cartography and statistical analysis, a new chapter opened in the history of codification. Here too France was in the forefront. Legal reform had begun under the ancien régime and then became a goal of the revolutionary governments after 1789. It entered a new era in 1800, when Napoleon, then still first consul, set up a commission to prepare a new Civil Code. Driven by his own formidable energies and drawing on his growing prestige and unquestioned authority, Napoleon and his legal experts eventually completed five separate codes: a civil code, codes of civil and of criminal procedure, a penal code, and a commercial code. A sixth, regulating rural society, was drafted but never became law.[66] These laws were the emperor's most powerful and enduring legacy, not only in France but throughout Europe and eventually much of the world.[67]

Whether they adopted the French model or one of its competitors, most states set out to compile and systematize their laws. Common law states such as Britain did not codify, but they also took steps to collect and classify legal decisions, beginning with Blackstone's famous *Commentaries on the Laws of England* (1765–69).[68] In both civil and common law, these projects were part of what one scholar has called "the vocation of the century" that sought to make a unified system of laws an essential part of a well-regulated, stable, and orderly society.[69] The "uniformity" to which legal reformers aspired, wrote the influential Swiss liberal thinker Benjamin Constant in 1814, is "the key word" of today: "The same code of law, the same measures, the same regulations . . . this is what is proclaimed to be the perfection of organization."[70] Every central government, Tocqueville noted, "adores uniformity" because it relieves the government from the need to make different rules for different people. "Underlying the ardor to codify," the political theorist Pierre Rosanvallon has recently argued, was "a veritable utopia: to govern the world flawlessly by remaking it through abstraction so as to achieve absolute comprehensibility."[71] Codes, maps, and statistical surveys belonged to the same set of expectations about states, each dependent on the other: a unified legal community required clear territorial and demographic definition, just as a state's territorial integrity and clearly defined population required uniform rules and conventions.[72]

There is an obvious historical connection between codes and constitutions. But though both are clearly the products and instruments of the same political process, there are some important differences between them. Codes are extensions and amplifications of a tradition of legal reform that reaches into the ancient world. The genealogy of constitutions is more difficult to trace. Some scholars link them to the dynastic decrees that were issued in the old regime. Wolfgang Burgdorf, for example, has recently emphasized the paradigmatic importance of the Holy Roman Empire's Electoral Capitulations of 1519 for later constitutional projects.[73] Nevertheless, there seems to be something distinctly modern about those eighteenth-century constitutions that set out to provide the foundation for a new political order rather than merely to digest existing laws or affirm traditional rights and duties. Like so many other aspects of the modern era, constitutions rest on the conviction that it was possible to make a new beginning, that time was an arrow moving forward, not a series of cycles. The association of constitutions with innovation, and especially with the necessity to encourage (and often to control) revolutionary aspirations is an important reason why, as Germany's leading legal historian has written, "for two hundred years, every fundamental political debate has been engaged with the magic word *constitution*."[74]

Constitutions, the eminent constitutional scholar K. C. Wheare argued, "were drawn up and adopted because people wanted to make a fresh start."[75] In fact, constitution-making combines the aspiration to make a fresh start with the aspiration to establish an enduring order. The dual desire for innovation and stability is reflected in the word itself: the verb to *constitute* refers to an action that establishes, initiates, or creates something; as a noun, *constitution* refers to an existing condition, that is, the makeup, composition, or structure of something (including a form of government).[76]

An enduring tension in the modern world was created by people's expectations that both innovation and stability are necessary elements in the political order.

In the eighteenth century, when constitutions first began to be part of some Europeans' political expectations, the search for both innovation and stability can be clearly seen. Perhaps the earliest example was the constitution written by Pasquale Paoli and approved by the Corsican Diet at the start of the island's brief period of independence in November 1755. Issued in the name of the "People of Corsica," Paoli's constitution was designed to provide the basis of "a durable and constant form of its government."[77] Before it was terminated by the French annexation of the island in 1769, Corsica's political experiment attracted wide attention (including praise and encouragement from Rousseau, an admiring account by James Boswell, and a town named in Paoli's honor in the far-off province of Pennsylvania). The constitution itself, however, remained unknown until the twentieth century.

On the western side of the Atlantic, another crisis of colonial rule produced a more famous and influential attempt "to make a fresh start." In May 1776, a year after the American rebellion had begun, the Continental Congress called upon Britain's individual colonies to write constitutions that could provide the basis for their new governments; eleven of the thirteen complied. Eleven years later, an assembly in Philadelphia, acting in the name of "the people of the United States," established a constitution "in order to form a more perfect Union, establish Justice, insure domestic Tranquility, provide for the common defense, and secure the Blessings of Liberty for ourselves and our Posterity." The U.S. Constitution, therefore, was both a break from the past and the foundation of a union that would prevail, so its authors hoped, "for ourselves and our posterity."

Although the Constitution would become one of the most influential texts in world history, for most contemporaries the constitutional projects that really mattered were not in Britain's American possessions but in Paris, the center of European politics and culture. Unlike the U.S. Constitution, the constitution passed by French National Assembly in September 1791 and then reluctantly accepted by the king did not set out to proclaim the existence of a new state. Yet like revolutions against foreign rule, the Constitution of 1791 did seek to "make a fresh start." The nation for which the men in 1791 spoke may have already existed, but it needed to be purged and reconstructed. The Constitution of 1791, therefore, begins by calling for the abolition of "institutions which are injurious to liberty and the equality of rights." The section devoted to "Public Powers" provides an ambiguous statement on what should replace these institutions: "Sovereignty is one, indivisible, inalienable, and imprescriptible"; it belongs to "the nation" but can only be exercised by the nation's representatives, that is, by "the legislative body and the King."[78]

The unstable compromises reflected in this formulation did not survive the violent pressures of the revolutionary moment. The Constitution of September 1791 marked the first of fifteen constitutional projects over the next two centuries. Not all of these constitutions were "fresh starts," but they all attempted to create a stable basis for political authority in France: radical democracy in the early 1790s, an authoritarian constitution of 1799 (eventually revised to establish the Napoleonic dynasty), the Charter of 1814 that was decreed by the restored Bourbons, a new monarchical constitution following the July revolution of 1830, several midcentury constitutions that ended with a second Napoleonic empire, and finally the documents that created the Third, Fourth, and Fifth Republics.[79] For our purposes, the most important thing to notice about this complex, contentious, and sometimes violent history is that from 1791 to the present, the legal status of political institutions, whether they were republican, monarchical, or imperial (or some combination of the three), required a constitutional foundation. The source of legitimate government changed, but every regime was expected to be legible, its character described and ultimately legitimated by a written document.

At the beginning of the nineteenth century, the expectation that states should have a constitutional foundation was clearly incompatible with that extraordinarily long-lived survivor of the premodern order, the Holy Roman Empire. In 1802, G. W. F. Hegel, a thirty-two-year-old philosophy instructor in Jena, captured the empire's difficulties when he began his analysis of the German situation by commenting that "Germany is a state no longer," by which he meant that the empire had lost the capacity to defend or support itself, dissolving instead into nothing more than "a congress of independent states."[80] Four years later, the empire disappeared with remarkably little fanfare; it was replaced in 1815 by a Confederation of German States, whose identity and institutions were defined by a constitutional document, the "Deutsche Bundesakte," drafted by the Great Powers at the Congress of Vienna and issued on behalf of Germany's sovereign princes and free cities. Article 13 of the Bundesakte declared that all of the Confederation's member states should have a representative constitution (*Landständische Verfassung*).[81] The practical implications of this were by no means clear. The two major German powers, Prussia and the Habsburg monarchy, along with some smaller states, did not have written constitutions until after midcentury. Nevertheless, most of the empire's middle-size successor states did issue constitutional documents that provided a legal basis for their governments and defined their territorial identity.[82]

"This is clearly the era of the constitution," wrote the prominent German liberal Karl von Rotteck in 1830, a pronouncement that was at once descriptive and normative, an expression of the conviction, shared by many nineteenth-century liberals, that history was on their side.[83] There were, to be sure, some bumps in the road ahead, but there was good reason to believe that Rotteck was right. By 1830, the year when a new, more progressive constitution was adopted in Paris, constitutional governments were to be found in many European and American states. Their origins and character were carefully recorded in handbooks, such as the four-volume survey edited by Karl Heinrich Pölitz that was published in Germany between 1817 and 1825.[84] In the course of the nineteenth century, the number of constitutional regimes created in Europe steadily increased, either in response to revolutionary pressures (for example, in Prussia and the Habsburg monarchy at midcentury) or when newly created states sought to legitimate their existence with a legal foundation (Italy in 1859 and Germany in 1871, and also the successor states of the Ottoman Empire).[85]

Like other aspects of the modern political order, in the twentieth century constitutionalism became a global phenomenon. As was often the case, Japan played a critically important part in the spread of European institutions: the Japanese constitution of 1889 was closely modeled on the German example.[86] Between 1905 and 1911, revolutionary movements introduced constitutions in Mexico, Persia, the Ottoman Empire, China, Portugal, and Russia—territories inhabited by about one-fourth of the world's population. Another wave of constitution-making followed the two world wars: after the first, among the successor states of the European empires, after the second, in Europe's former colonies.[87]

These constitutions continued to combine that characteristic mix of innovation and stabilization, the need for a fresh start, and what the

Corsican constitutionalists called the creation of a "durable and constant" basis for the political order. The historical record suggests that many of these efforts failed. A recent study of the 935 constitutions issued by about two hundred states between 1789 and 2005 concludes that the average life for a constitution is nineteen years; some last much longer, others are swept away in a few weeks or months.[88] Of course, many constitutions are hastily contrived fictions that set out a legal framework that has little or nothing to do with the true nature of the political system. And yet, despite their often ephemeral and sometimes fictional character, constitutions have become an essential part of what it means to be a state. We expect states to have one, and, in fact, almost all of them do.

Codes and constitutions are just the most prominent elements in an expanding network of laws with which states try to regulate increasingly complex social and economic activities and fulfill the growing list of tasks people expect them to perform. A few of these laws were created as amendments to the state's constitution (almost always a difficult process). Others were the work of legislative bodies that, as we will see in chapter 3, provided the consensual foundation that political legitimacy began to require. Some came from the judicial courts themselves or were issued by the expanding ranks of state or local officials.

The legal network essential for modern states defined and, at least in theory, limited the power of governments. Laws regulated social relations and economic activity, determined how people behaved, who could marry and when, how long children had to stay in school, who was obliged to do military service, who could vote and hold office.[89] Central to every legal system was the question of citizenship, no longer determined by localities, but among the most significant, and sometimes the most contested, prerogatives of the state. The more rights and obligations citizenship conveyed, the more it mattered who was or could become a full member of the political community. The closely connected development of democracy and nationhood made the question of citizenship at once more urgent and more difficult.[90]

In addition to governmental regulations, the nineteenth century produced a small library of written rules about how people should behave in factories, playing fields, private clubs, and school rooms. To take just one example, in 1876 Henry M. Robert, then a major in the U.S. Army, published his *Rules of Order*, which became a durable classic that is still the standard guide to conducting a public meeting. When we survey the wide array of regulations that attempted to impose order on people's public and private lives, we are once again reminded of Tocqueville's insight that "in the long run political society cannot fail to become the expression and image of civil society."

In both public and private institutions, most rules are enforced with the threat of some kind of sanction, but in the modern political order only states have the right to use violence to compel obedience to their laws.[91] Modern states have access to remarkably efficient and effective instruments of violence, which enable them to exercise a degree of control over their population far beyond what their predecessors could have imagined. Precisely because states have become more powerful, however, their use of violence has become less visible and more discreet. In most states, most of the time, the capacity to use violence is a source of strength, its actual use, a symptom of weakness.[92]

In a well-ordered state, authority depends on compliance, backed by the threat of coercion. "Coercive power is a criterion of the state," the political scientist R. M. MacIver observed in 1926, "but not its essence. . . . The primary fact of the state is not force but a universal order constituting a foundation of all social activities." And in the modern world, the substance of this universal order is the law, which remains essential for any legitimate exercise of political power.[93] It is in this sense, to return to the formulation by Ernest Barker that I quoted earlier, "the state is law."

As with many other aspects of the modern political order, people often have mixed feelings about the law. It is significant that when writers as different as Victor Hugo, Charles Dickens, and Franz Kafka needed metaphors to represent the oppressive uses of power, they chose the legal system. Jean Valjean, the litigants in *Jarndyce v. Jarndyce*, and the unfortunate Josef K. confronted quite different legal problems, but they shared a similar predicament: all of them were caught in a dense and implacable web that they could neither fully understand nor successfully evade. In these works of literary imagination and in the lives of many ordinary men and women, the law could embody the dark side of the modern state.

But the law can be liberating as well as oppressive, an instrument of both emancipation and repression, a means of asserting an individual's rights, limiting the government's arbitrary powers, protecting the weak from the strong. Innocent defendants are sometimes acquitted; disputes over property and inheritances can be fairly resolved; people's freedom to speak, assemble, or vote is often reaffirmed by the courts. Among our most important expectations about the political order is the belief that laws should be legible and uniform, administered honestly and impersonally, responsive to the popular opinion and designed to serve the public good. Of course, we recognize that even the best legal system has ambiguities and defects that make it difficult to fulfill these expectations. Nevertheless, the aspiration to live under "the rule of law" remains one of the modern political order's most cherished goals.

AGENTS: THE DEVELOPMENT OF BUREAUCRATIC STATES

The purpose of the Massachusetts Constitution, John Adams wrote in 1780, was to create "a government of laws not men."[94] It is clear enough what Adams wanted: a government that would be subject to enlightened rules rather than the capricious will of powerful individuals. Yet taken literally, Adams's well-known phrase is certainly misleading since laws must be made, interpreted, or enforced by organized individuals. Every government is a government of men (and women).[95]

Like the other aspects of the state's infrastructure that we have examined so far in this chapter, the social composition and political function of the state's agents began to be transformed in the eighteenth century. Eventually these agents would grow in number and significance until they became the personification of the modern state. They were essential for its survival and the most important instruments of its influence on the lives of its citizens. Often as benignly familiar as the postman's daily visit, sometimes as burdensome as the tax collector's bills, and occasionally as intrusive as the policeman's knock on the door, the interactions of most Europeans with their state involved the expanding ranks of its officials. Among the various experiences that shape people's expectations about their political order, interactions such as these are usually the most common and often the most significant.

In constructing an administrative apparatus, European states took different paths to the same destination.[96] The source of these differences is not hard to see. European states were motivated by different aspirations, deployed different resources, and faced different challenges at home and abroad. Moreover, each had its own way of managing the institutional hybridity that was part of every state's historical experience. In some, local elites lost their political power to agents of the state. Elsewhere, local notables—landowners, clergymen, urban patricians—continued to keep a significant amount of administrative authority in their own hands. Sometimes they remained autonomous actors; often they served as partners of the central government. Britain had more laymen involved in government than most other modern states; German states had a substantial corps of trained civil servants, but also—as in urban government, for example—had institutions where professionals and laymen worked together.[97]

To get some sense of this diversity, we need only consider the different roles played by religious institutions in the state-making process. In most of Protestant Europe, the clergy were, legally and practically, employees of the state. In Catholic countries, where the ecclesiastical authorities often tried to defend some measure of their traditional autonomy, church and state engaged in prolonged jurisdictional disputes that remained a central feature of public life throughout the nineteenth and early twentieth centuries.[98] The outcome of these disputes—over such matters as clerical appointments, educational authority, church property, and marriage laws—varied widely, but nowhere in Europe was there a clear separation of religious and political institutions and influence. Catholic clergy continued to be what they had been for centuries, that is, both the agents and the rivals of state power.

Although they acted at different times and used various methods, the central authorities in every European state eventually tried to abolish or co-opt competing institutions. At the same time, states—once again, unevenly but universally—took on new tasks as they tried to meet people's changing expectations about how states should regulate their expanding and increasingly complex societies.[99] This dramatic growth of the state's role in people's everyday lives was an essential element in the modern political order.

Because the structure of the administrative apparatus varied so widely among European states, its precise dimensions are impossible to measure; this is the reason why Brian Chapman, a leading historian of administrative institutions, decided not to include statistics in his excellent survey of European public services.[100] Nevertheless, the direction of governmental growth is clear enough. Britain had 17,000 civil servants in 1841; 81,000 in

1881; 153,000 in 1901; and 644,000 in 1911. In France, the numbers were larger, but the trajectory was the same: 90,000 in 1841; 379,000 in 1881; 451,000 in 1901; and 699,000 in 1911. In 1881, there were 452,000 civil servants in the German Empire; 1,187,000 in 1911. By the eve of the First World War public employees were slightly more than 7 percent of the workforce in Britain and France, 10.6 percent in Germany.[101]

One of the first attempts to measure the growth of the state apparatus was by a young scholar named Adolf Wagner, who eventually became one of Germany's most influential political economists. In 1863, he formulated "Wagner's Law," which stated, "Overall, the scope of the state's activities will always expand; the more the idea of the state develops and the higher the level of a nation's civilization and culture, the more new demands will be made on the state."[102]

The growth of bureaucracy was inseparable from the other aspects of state-making we considered earlier in this chapter. The increasing legibility of states, their expanding legal framework, and the development of a professional corps of administrators are entwined like the braids of a rope, each one connected to and strengthening the others. The essence of a modern bureaucracy's power was its capacity to gather and manage the flow of written information about territories, people, material resources, and, needless to say, itself. The management of information was both prerequisite and product of the state's legal system, whose operation was among the administration's most significant tasks. On the Continent, future civil servants studied law before entering either the judicial or administrative branch. The British system was different: administrators studied the classics and the judiciary was not a branch of the civil service. But everywhere, the agents of the state were charged with enforcing the expanding network of regulations that modern societies needed to function.[103]

The bureaucratic apparatus had its own elaborate rules that regulated the recruitment, organization, and conduct of its personnel. Administrative law, which set norms and disciplinary procedures, was among the fastest-growing sectors of the legal system. Of course, habits from the old regime lingered: in every bureaucracy, kinship, patronage, and personal connections continued to widen the path to promotion. And yet the influence of these personal connections had to coexist with, and was often mediated by, the institution's formal rules and procedures. Equally important, whatever their social origins, civil servants gradually acquired those shared values and manners, ways of dressing, speaking, and writing that create a collective identity in every effective organization.[104]

People expect a good deal from civil servants, but often do not much like them. As a student of the French bureaucracy put it, "one of the strongest elements of continuity in the history of the French administration has been the continuing criticism with which it has been faced." In the nineteenth century, the radical social critic Pierre-Joseph Proudhon gave an extreme version of this criticism when he complained about being "watched, inspected, spied upon, directed . . . by creatures who have neither the right nor the wisdom nor the virtue to do so."[105] Such "creatures"—Tolstoy's dutiful but dull Alexei Karenin, the listless denizens of Dickens's Circumlocution Office, and the various dim policemen who provided foils for Sherlock Holmes—were familiar features in contemporary literature. In many languages, including English, the term "bureaucratic" still retains a pejorative coloration.

There were, of course, always those who regarded the growth of administrative capacity as essential to effective statecraft. In the early nineteenth century, the Prussian reformer Karl von Hardenberg believed that a good administration (*Verwaltung*) was more important than a good constitution (*Verfassung*). Indeed, Hardenberg thought that the main function of a constitution was to secure the administration's role in the life of state and society.[106] The most elaborate theoretical defense of the bureaucracy's significance is in G. W. F. Hegel's *Philosophy of Right*, which argues that civil servants are a "universal estate," uniquely able to pursue the common good because their origins, training, and values freed them from the conflicts of interest that necessarily divided the rest of civil society.

Even when they did not adopt Hegel's complex philosophical justification, a number of nineteenth-century thinkers argued that modern social and economic life required an honest and effective administrative organization. By the end of the century, British reformers were prepared to abandon their country's reliance on part-time officeholders in favor of a professional body of civil servants. At the same time, some European theorists maintained that administrative efficiency would make it possible for the rest of the state to disappear. When this happens, wrote Leon Duguit, a leading French scholar of public law, "the notion of public power is replaced by the notion of public service; the state ceases to be a power which commands and becomes a group which works."[107]

As administrations grew in size and importance, the nature of bureaucratic organizations became a centrally important issue for both theorists and politicians. Max Weber—and many of his contemporaries—recognized that the evolution of governmental infrastructure was just one example of how bureaucratic modes had spread across every social institution. Like governments, many enterprises had to manage an increasing body of information and enforce an increasingly complex set of rules. To do so, firms, schools, churches, trade unions, political parties, and interest groups all needed full-time specialists. Like Hegel, Weber set his analysis of bureaucracy within a densely woven theoretical context. Bureaucracy, he argued, was the institutional expression of the process of rationalization that provides the key to understanding modernity.[108]

Weber realized that although bureaucratic modes of organization existed throughout society, the state played a distinctive role in the modern world. According to his famous definition, a "ruling organization" can be called "political" if it exists within a "given territorial area." Such an organization can be called a state "insofar as its administrative staff successfully upholds the claim to the monopoly of the legitimate use of physical force in the enforcement of its order."[109] "Territorial area," "administrative staff," "monopoly," "legitimate use of physical force"—each of these terms reflects significant aspects of the modern political order that we have examined. We should also pay attention to the phrase "successfully upholds the claim." Here Weber emphasizes that a state is not defined philosophically but practically, not by its inherent nature, but by its behavior. To understand the state, we must determine not just what it should do, wants to do, or claims to be doing, but what it actually does.

For centuries, most Europeans believed that the state's most important capacity (and its most important use of legitimate political force) remained the ability to wage war. In his classic study of European institutions, the Prussian historian Otto Hintze may have somewhat overstated the case when he wrote that every political organization has its origins in organized warfare ("Alle Staatsverfassung ist ursprünglich Kriegsverfassung, Heeresverfassung"), but at least until the second half of the twentieth century this formulation fits the evolution of European states better than any other.[110] We will return to the changing relationship of states and war in chapter 4, but now it is enough to emphasize once again how the need to prepare for, and, if necessary, to conduct a new kind of warfare was the single most significant impetus for the growth of a new kind of state.[111]

Throughout the nineteenth century, the military was the largest item in every state's budget. And the total amount spent on armaments increased dramatically: in Britain, which had the world's largest navy but a relatively small professional army, expenses for the military grew from 12.8 million pounds in 1838 to 29 million in 1889 to more than 61 million in 1909.[112] Although in every European state there were often bitter political debates about the quantity and deployment of these resources, few political leaders doubted that national defense was the state's most important purpose.[113] In the nineteenth century, as national security became a state's primary and exclusive responsibility, the military gradually dissolved its ties to semiprivate institutions, such as licensed privateers at sea or the mercenary armies like the one fielded by the British East India Company until 1858. Together with the outlawing of duels and the suppression of clan feuds, the decline of these institutions was one more example of the state's increasingly successful claim to a monopoly of legitimate violence.[114]

Whether they liked it or not, most people expected that states had the right and, equally important, the capacity to call upon their male citizens to fight and die in their defense. There was, therefore, no more emblematic institution for the modern political order than the mass-conscript army. Military service required both the information and rules that were such important parts of the state's new infrastructure. Mass armies also needed an administrative apparatus to process and train draftees and provide them with uniforms, weapons, food, shelter, and medical care. All this required an organizational capacity that would have been beyond the comprehension of even the most effective military establishment in the ancien régime.[115]

Creating a mass-conscript army was only the beginning. In order to be effectively deployed, modern armies had to make use of another exemplary nineteenth-century innovation, the railroad. This too required great organizational skill and an elaborate infrastructure—timetables, maps, plans, and personnel—that had not been necessary when armies marched or rode into battle, as they had for millennia. One illustration of the immensity of this enterprise will suffice: in the first nine days of the war in August 1914, the French army needed 4,300 trains to move 1.5 million troops to the German frontier. (This part of the operation went well, what happened next did not.)[116]

The modern army has often been seen, and rightly so, as the symbolic representation of the nation; it was also, and perhaps more accurately, the most significant expression of the modern state's administrative capacities.[117]

The state's monopoly of legitimate violence had a domestic dimension. People expected their governments to defend them from both external threats and dangers close to home, pirates, highwaymen, cutpurses, and drunken brawlers. Like raising a conscript army, meeting these expectations required states to collect information about how people behaved (in the nineteenth century every state gathered statistics about crime and other forms of deviant behavior), enact rules that regulated social conduct, and, most importantly, establish those familiar agents of domestic order, the police.[118]

The evolution of European police forces was another illustration of how states took diverse paths to a common destination. Some—France, Italy, Spain, Portugal, and several German states—had centralized police forces; others—Sweden, Holland, England—retained a mixture of central and local jurisdictions. In England, each county had its own police, except for London, whose metropolitan police were under the home secretary and could also be called in to assist local forces.[119] In most of Europe, police power was concentrated in large cities, especially capitals, rather than in small towns and the countryside where policemen were thin on the ground. In Berlin, for instance, there were 1,025 policemen in 1862; 8,858 in 1910. Dortmund, which had 40,000 inhabitants in the 1870s, had just a dozen police officers.[120] Compared to the twentieth century, the effective power of the police was still relatively insubstantial, but compared to agents of public order in the old regime, the nineteenth-century police represented a new set of expectations about what states could and should so.[121]

People expected the streets of their cities not only to be safer but also to be cleaner and more accessible. State-initiated projects that provided better sewer systems, streetlights, and pedestrian walkways made possible the kind of urban public life we find so vividly depicted in nineteenth-century art and literature. At the same time, public transportation—at first drawn by horses, later electrified and on rails—changed the way urban communities were organized, enabled them to expand, and encouraged their commercial vitality.[122]

Governments also began to take greater responsibility for their citizens' health. Under the ancien régime, states had used crude measures to contain the plague; now they went beyond closed borders and enforced quarantine with attempts to prevent the diseases that had once made most cities lethal places to live. Sanitation, waste management, clean water supplies, and other regulations improved the quality of life for some, if by no means all, the population. As usual, these efforts required information, regulation, and trained personnel. Like the rest of the state's infrastructure, the extent and effectiveness of public health initiatives varied widely; by twentieth-century standards their effectiveness remained modest, but it represented a substantial improvement over the ancien régime.[123]

In traditional society, the central governments did little or nothing to protect their citizens from life's inevitable vicissitudes, such as sickness, accidents, unemployment, poverty, and the infirmities of old age. These sources of human suffering were addressed, if at all, by families, local authorities, or charitable institutions. The hope that they might claim some small relief from their suffering bound people to their immediate communities; unless they were rich, those who could not make such claims were one misfortune away from destitution and misery. Beginning in Germany in the 1870s, states began to introduce insurance programs that provided some security and support for selected social groups.[124] In the twentieth century, programs like these would become an important part of people's expectations about the political order. At first, these insurance systems were limited in scope, but they clearly anticipated the sort of safely nets that modern states are expected to provide. For a modest but informative example of this process, let us return to the Workmen's Insurance Office in Prague, where Franz Kafka worked from 1908 to 1922. One of seven institutes charged with administering the Austrian government's accident insurance law of 1887, the Prague office employed more than two hundred people in 1908, including lawyers like Kafka, statisticians, medical professionals, and engineers, along with scores of clerks and typists who processed the enormous quantity of paper generated by the thousands of claims that had to be investigated and settled.[125]

How did states pay for the new tasks that they were expected to perform? In an often cited formulation, Sidney Finer described what he called the extraction-coercion cycle: "To secure its taxes, without which it had no army, the center tried to coerce. To coerce, it needed an army."[126] Finer's proposition can be extended beyond the relationship between revenue collection and military organization to include a reciprocally reinforcing relationship between all of the state's infrastructure and its extractive capacity. Gathering information, making laws, and regulating social life cost money, but at the same time these activities enhanced the state's ability to identify and extract the resources it needed. A good example of this process is the expanding network of communication—postal service, telegraph, and especially the railroad—that placed added administrative burdens on the state and at the same time greatly increased the state's ability to penetrate society.[127]

In his 1863 account of the growth of state activity, Adolf Wagner postulated that in advanced states the need for public revenue [*Staatsbedarf*] would constantly expand as governments responded to the ever-increasing demand for their services. As Wagner predicted, throughout the nineteenth-century European state expenditures amounted to a growing share of the Gross National Product. By the eve of the First World War, the cost of government represented 9.7 percent of France's GNP, 7.1 percent of Britain's, and 15 percent of Germany's, figures that would substantially grow in the decades ahead. Governments' demand for resources took bigger and bigger pieces of a larger and larger pie. By the 1970s, public expenditures would amount to more than 40 percent of GDP throughout the European Economic Community.[128]

Europe's extraordinary economic expansion in the nineteenth century transformed every aspect of people's lives, including the way they experienced and imagined their states. Scholars debate whether the modern state was the cause or the outcome of economic development, but there can be no question that the growth of the European economy produced an unprecedented amount of wealth. States everywhere converted some of this wealth into instruments of political power, most obviously military power but also the power to control their populations. Britain, Europe's richest and most powerful state, collected 52.6 million pounds in 1843; 87.3 million in 1883; and 198.2 million in 1913.[129] The Habsburg monarchy, the weakest of the five great powers, was also the poorest, with fewer resources and a cumbersome system of taxation. Everywhere the redistribution of relative economic power among states reordered the hierarchy of power within the international system. We will consider the consequences of this in chapter 4.

When we examine the different mechanisms with which governments extracted their society's increasing resources, we find another example of how states used different means for the same ends. In the eighteenth century, Britain, often thought to be a relatively weak state, was actually the first European power to develop an effective fiscal system, one that enabled the government to extract a share of the economy's growing resources and thus to finance the global projection of the nation's military, commercial, and cultural influence. In order to survive, every state had to erect—often with great difficulty—a system of taxation (some balance between imposts on imports, consumption, income, property, financial transactions, and inheritance), regulate the money supply, and establish ways of borrowing funds.

Taxation required the sort of infrastructure we have just described—information, rules, and agents.[130] Everywhere, one product of these efforts was the expectation that government finances were public, that is, the realm of the state, not the monarch. In Prussia, for example, where the royal domain once provided a substantial part of the state's revenue, the king issued a decree in January 1820 that defined the government's outstanding debts as "*Staatsschulden*," which meant that they were "burdens of the state and its institutions." Speaking for himself and his heirs, the king accepted the dynasty's responsibility for these debts and transferred the income from all of the Hohenzollern properties to the state, except what was necessary to support the royal family and its court.[131] Similar steps were taken in most European states. The significance of these new laws is clear: the dynasty's property was now at once guaranteed and limited by law (often, but not in Prussia until midcentury, by a constitution). Both practically and symbolically, this was an important step in the separation of the state from the person and property of its ruler.

The shift away from royal domains as a major source of the government's income was just one of a series of displacements through which tasks once performed by the ruler's servants were taken over by agents of the state.[132] For example, ambassadors continued to be received at court and diplomats were expected to participate in its social activities, but the real business of international relations was now conducted by the still small staff of professionals in the foreign office.[133] Monarchs made state visits (usually accompanied by their ministers), but when they tried to set the direction of policy—as in the famous "Willy-Nicky" correspondence between the emperors of Germany and Russia in 1905—it rarely amounted to much.[134] Monarchs could still have some effect on political decisions, but when they attempted to exert a sustained influence on public policy, they had to work with, and sometimes against, civil servants who could devote all their time and energy to the business of government. William II, the last of the Hohenzollern, talked a great deal about his own importance, but the significance of his "personal regime" was fitful at best. Few of his innumerable plans, suggestions, and bombastic pronouncements actually shaped political practice.[135] More prudent rulers accepted their place as part of the state's complex apparatus: Franz Joseph of Austria, for example, who embodied the traditions of dynastic rule much more effectively than his younger German counterpart, listed his occupation in the 1910 census as "self-employed chief official."[136]

Behind the pomp and ceremony that still surrounded dynastic institutions was the inescapable fact that, like so much else in modern life, monarchical power had been what Weber called *entzaubert*, a term usually translated as "disenchanted," but more accurately rendered as "deprived of its magic."[137] Monarchs were no longer seen as God's representatives on earth, the crucial link in the chain of legitimate authority that reached from God the Father in heaven down to the head of the most modest household. As we can see in this portrait of the ninety-year-old emperor William I by Franz von Lenbach, monarchs were now recognized as human beings who, like the rest of us, had to face the frailties of old age and physical decline (fig. 5).

Like William, the other popular rulers of the nineteenth century, such as Queen Victoria and Emperor Franz Joseph, were admired for their dignity, sense of duty, and personal fortitude, not for the way they represented divinely ordained power.[138] By embracing their humanity and compromising with the political currents of their time—administration, constitutionalism, and nationalism—monarchs were able to survive the modern transformation of the political order until the First World War.

The price of survival was to weaken—and in some states to abandon—the sacred element that had always been at the core of dynastic legitimacy. The result of this *Entzauberung* was suddenly revealed between 1917 and 1922 when, with remarkable speed and relatively little violence, the rulers of the Russian, German, Austrian, and Ottoman empires lost their thrones.[139] Stefan Zweig, an Austrian writer with the knack of being in the right place at the right time, happened to be at the frontier train station when Emperor Charles, the last Habsburg, left the country his ancestors had ruled for centuries. Zweig noted that among the officials who watched the emperor depart there was neither hostility nor sorrow, but only an embarrassed uncertainty about how they should respond to this moment of

Figure 5. Franz von Lenbach, *William I* (Bridgeman Images)

imperial extinction.[140] In 1793, the French revolutionaries had thought it necessary to execute their king; at the end of the Great War, it was sufficient to provide him transportation and a safe refuge.[141]

By the time these last representatives of the old order left the political stage, people's expectations about their states had been transformed. In the course of the late eighteenth and nineteenth centuries, European states had acquired capacities that are far beyond anything the most ambitious pre-modern ruler could have imagined. These capacities depended on new technologies of power that freed governments from the limitations of a political order that rested on the locally rooted, kinship based, oral cultures of the ancien regime. The modern state's great strength was its ability to reach into, and project its power beyond, those small worlds in which many people still lived. The essence of the premodern state had been personal relations, those familial, face-to-face communities that were sustained by the weight of custom, religious belief, and practical necessity.[142] The modern state aspired to be impersonal and thus could claim, to modify John Adams's aspiration, to be a government of institutions rather than of men.[143]

In the new political order, people began to expect that states were separate from "society." Among the recurring questions in modern political theory and practice, therefore, was how state and society should relate to one another. Did the state stand above the social landscape, acting as the ultimate custodian of the public interest? Or was it, as some liberal thinkers argued, no more than a source of the rules that ensured that the productive forces in society could adequately function? Or, as radical critics insisted, was the state merely an instrument of repression and an agent of economic inequality? Would the state "wither away" or was it the new Leviathan whose shadow darkened all of human affairs? These questions reflected profoundly different views of the political order's past, present, and future, but they all rested on the assumption that modern states stood apart from the social landscape.

Because the state stood apart, it was in some respects more visible than its old regime counterparts. James Scott has rightly insisted that modern states try to expand their ability to *see* their world so that they can control it more effectively.[144] But states could also be *seen* in new ways: their borders were now precisely defined on more and more accurate maps, their populations counted and classified by increasingly effective statisticians, their laws codified and collected by an expanding legal system, their will enforced by a growing corps of professional civil servants.

States were also visible in the public buildings that could be found in every European city. Under the old regime, most public structures were connected to the monarchy, the church, or municipal governments. In the nineteenth century, states erected buildings that had few if any counterparts in traditional society: post offices, railroad stations, court houses, schools, museums, police departments, prisons, armories, and a variety of administrative offices. Architecture, Spiro Kostof once noted, is "the material theater of human activity."[145] These new governmental structures provided the stage on which people enacted the rituals of the modern state. Because the rituals of the ancien régime seem so exotic and remote, they have been carefully examined; we are less aware of the equally important but familiar and mundane rituals with which we create and affirm our expectations about the political order.[146]

The modern state might have been easier to see than its old regime counterpart, but it could also be harder to imagine. In the early nineteenth century, when this process had just begun, Benjamin Constant worried that "we have lost in imagination what we have gained in knowledge."[147] As its infrastructure expanded, it became increasingly difficult to imagine the state as a unified whole. Those "everyday practices" that people enacted in government buildings—posting a letter, catching a train, obtaining a marriage license, paying their taxes, serving on a jury, taking their preinduction physical examination—were disconnected from one another, different pieces of an elusive unity. People had once imagined the state to be like a body, whose varied parts were joined in a familiar organism that was represented by the king. The modern state was disembodied, impersonal, ever present but hard to comprehend.[148]

Throughout the nineteenth century, the makers of modern states emphasized the value of uniformity and unity. "Since as long as the state remains a mere aggregation of diverse components," the Bavarian Constitution of 1808 maintained, "it can never attain the full measure of strength that its potential might provide. We are seeking to establish a uniform system." But the unity of the state that was so often emphasized by its champions and assumed by its citizens was and is a fiction. And fictions, as David Runciman wisely noted, "function by having attributed to them as inherent the one thing they inherently lack."[149]

The linguistic expression of the state's fictive unity is our tendency to speak of it a thing, to make *the* state into a singular agent. "All sentences that have the state as a subject are theological sentences," wrote the sociologist Pierre Bourdieu, "which does not mean that they are false, inasmuch as the state is a theological entity, that is, an entity that exists by way of belief."[150] A belief in what? The state may be a theological entity, but in this desacralized world, it is a theology without a divine presence. Without this divine presence, as Marcel Gauchet pointed out, the world is no longer "presented" as something whose existence can be taken for granted, it must be "constituted," that is, it must be made and this means it must be made by ourselves. The burden of constituting our world is why Hegel believed that it was "a monstrous blunder" to separate religion and the state. "Political mysticism," Ernst Kantorowicz wrote, "in particular is exposed to the danger of losing its spell or becoming quite meaningless when taken out of its native surroundings, its time and place."[151] Exactly this happened to the political mysticism that sustained political power in the ancien regime.

The modern state, the great nineteenth-century German institutional historian Otto Gierke recognized, was "no longer derived from the divinely ordained harmony of the universal whole; it was no longer explained as a partial whole that was derived from, and preserved by, the existence of a greater: it was simply explained by itself."[152] And this brings us to the question that haunts the modern political order: Is that enough? Can the state's enormous power be explained and legitimated "by itself"? Can states find a way to fill the gap left by the disappearance of sacred kingship? Now that they are free from the inevitable uncertainties of hereditary rule and are no longer willing or able to invoke divine sanctions, could states find a new foundation on which to base their vast, impersonal authority? The modern political order's most influential attempt to answer these questions is the subject of chapter 3.

CHAPTER THREE

Nations

In this chapter, our attention shifts from state structures to political communities. Instead of viewing the emergence of the modern political order from the top down, we will try to see it from the bottom up by examining how people defined their political identity and obligations rather than how governments penetrated their societies. These two stories are closely connected, but each has left a somewhat different evidentiary trace in the historical record. The growth of government can be examined by looking at printed sources, such as maps, statistics, laws, administrative directives, and tables of organization. Products of both imagination and action, political communities are less stable and more porous than bureaucratic and military organizations. The evidence about them is often more elusive and indirect, imperfect reflections of popular attitudes and opinions.

In the modern world, the most significant political community is the nation. We should not overestimate the power or pervasiveness of national communities, but it is clear that "nation-ness" has become "the most universally legitimate value in the political life of our time."[1] Like the emergence of the modern state, modern nationhood happened first in Europe and North America and then spread throughout the world.

"But what are nations?" Walter Bagehot asked in 1867. "What are these groups which are so familiar to us, and yet, if we stop to think, so strange?"[2] Always a perceptive observer of his political world, Bagehot was right about both characteristics of nationhood: by 1867, nations had indeed

become a familiar part of many Europeans' expectations about how to define political communities, but at the same time there was (and is) something strange about people's attachment to their nation. An awareness of
this strangeness has been a pervasive feature of the scholarly literature on
nations and nationalism. In the introduction to his influential book about
nations, Benedict Anderson wrote that his purpose was "to offer some ten-
tative suggestions for a more satisfactory interpretation of the 'anomaly' of
nationalism."[3] Both the modesty of Anderson's aspirations and his use of
the term "anomaly" point to an uneasiness about their subject that we often
find among those who study nations.

Bagehot tried to explain away the nation's strangeness by suggesting
that "national character is nothing but successful parish character." The
equation of nation and parish, however, merely underscores the problem.
We know very well why the face-to-face world of the parish was important; for many people it was the primary source of sociability and support.
But the nation was composed of individuals whom one did not, indeed
could not, know. Why should we feel a sense of kinship and connection
with them? Eric Hobsbawm, one of the nation's most astute critics, was
clearly perplexed by this question: "Why and how," he wondered, "could
a concept so remote from the real experience of most human beings as
'national patriotism' become such a powerful political force so quickly?"[4]

Nations are, by definition, too big to be experienced directly. But this
does not mean they are necessarily remote from people's "real experience,"
that is, from their ordinary expectations and practices. Hobsbawm's per-
plexity, therefore, rested on a false premise: in the modern era, most human
beings' experience made it possible, desirable, and perhaps even essential
for them to imagine belonging to a "remote" national community. There is
nothing mysterious about the appeal of nationalism. As Robert Wiebe
argued, "Nationalism thrived because it addressed basic human needs."[5]
Understanding these needs is the central task of this chapter.

These needs, I will argue, are closely connected to the growth of democracy. Modern nationhood and democratic politics were born together
in the late eighteenth century, when people's expectations about the origins
and character of the political order were transformed by the idea that they
should be governed by people like themselves. A nation, Bagehot wrote,
"means a like body of men, because of that likeness capable of acting together . . . and inclined to obey similar rules."[6] The most influential and

compelling source of the "likeness" that made common action possible was the sense of belonging to the same national community. That is why Raymond Aron believed that "to deny the modern nation is to reject the political advent of the eternal claims of equality."[7]

The modern nation, therefore, provided the most influential answer to democracy's essential question: What is the *demos*? The nation gives the *demos* historical roots by blending past, present, and future; it also provides a sense of emotional connection and the promise of political solidarity. In this way, nationhood transforms the abstract idea of a "people" into an apparently cohesive, enduring source of commonality. "Whether we like it or not," Ghia Nodia writes, "nationalism is the historical force that has provided the political units for democratic government." "'Nation' is another name for 'we the people.'"[8]

The first section of this chapter examines the origins and development of democracy in eighteenth-century Europe. We will pay particular attention to the Revolution in France, not only because of its global resonance, but also because the French experience so vividly illustrates the persistent power and enduring difficulty of a democratic political order. We then turn to the expansion of democratic politics in the nineteenth century and to its complex relationship to national communities. In the chapter's third section, we will consider how, like so many of our foundational expectations about the political order, nationhood was both the basis for political cohesion and the occasion for political conflict. Just as dynastic relations had been the source of some of the old regime's most destructive domestic and international antagonisms, so too could divisions about the definition of national communities be the source of bitter domestic and international strife. As the bridge linking domestic and international politics, the problem of nationhood leads us to this book's final chapter in which we examine the emergence of a global society of nation states.

FROM KINSHIP TO CONSENT

A community, Emile Durkheim once remarked, "is not made up merely of the mass of individuals who compose it, the ground which they occupy, the things which they use, and the movements which they perform, but above all the idea which it forms of itself." What Durkheim called the "idea" is based on the expectations that the members of a community have about what their community is and should be.[9] For most of human history these expectations about community had to do with kinship, the familial rights and obligations that shaped the lives of individuals, households, villages, and states. People expected that property, status, and authority were hereditary and, so far as the unpredictable fortunes of reproduction would allow, should, like physical traits, be passed from generation to generation.

The importance of kinship has by no means disappeared from the modern political order, but it has slowly and unevenly been displaced by the expectation that communities should be based on consent. As with kinship, the political role of consent is reinforced by its presence in other aspects of life, both public and private. Because what Pierre Manent called "the empire of consent" keeps expanding, we have come to expect that "all relations and all bonds are voluntary."[10] Our ancestors saw their public lives in familial terms and understood them with familial metaphors; we tend to see even the most intimate parts of our private life in terms of contract and consent.[11]

Even when kinship was dominant, consent usually had some significance for the European political order.[12] Cicero, for example, defined the commonwealth as "the coming together of a considerable number of men who are united by a common agreement upon law and right and by the desire to participate in mutual advantages."[13] The Danish historian Jørgen Møller has recently emphasized the importance of consensual politics in medieval ecclesiastical institutions, which he maintains are the roots of modern representative institutions.[14] In the eighteenth century, Blackstone described the state as "a collective body, composed of a multitude of individuals, united for their safety and convenience, and intending to act together as one man."[15] Words such as "agreement," "desire," and "intending" point to the widespread assumption that a political community can only exist where "a considerable number of men" willingly accept its laws and obligations.

In the ancien régime, the most important political institutions for expressing consent were the representative bodies that could be found in many cities, provinces, and states throughout Western and Central Europe.[16] The significance of these institutions varied widely; some rarely met, others were largely ceremonial, but a few exercised substantial power by providing an essential connection between rulers and ruled. Participation in these bodies might be ex officio, linked to membership, for example, in a cathedral chapter or clerical estate. More often, participation was connected to hereditary status, as was the case with the closed caste of families that dominated Venice's public life. Everywhere, however, these institutions were *representative* in two meanings of the term: they acted for society, and they reflected its fundamental divisions. Nowhere were they equal and widely accessible.

In the modern world, consent is not just one element in the successful operation of a political community; it has become the *primary* source of legitimate authority and obligation: what Alexander Hamilton called the "pure, original fountain" from which all legitimate authority should flow.[17] Like most foundational principles, consent is so deeply embedded in our expectations about the world that we can easily take its pervasive significance for granted. And like other principles, consent remains important despite its persistent theoretical and practical difficulties. To cite Edmund Morgan again, the existence of a consensual community demands a certain amount of "make believe."

The transformation of consent from a desirable to an essential feature of the political order is a good illustration of the philosopher R. G. Collingwood's observation that the "history of political theory [and, I would add, of political practice] is not the history of different answers to one and the same question, but the history of a problem more or less constantly changing, whose solution was changing with it."[18] The new problem that the foundational role of consent sought to answer is not how the political order should operate but how it is possible to have such an order at all. For an increasing number of European political thinkers, this question was posed by the waning significance of divine authority: if the political order was not created by God, it had to be constructed and its origins had to be explained. In theory and practice, the concept of consent became the most compelling answer to how this process was to be understood and justified.

The idea of consent may have helped answer questions about the origins of the political order, but at the same time it raised questions of its own, questions about when and why consent occurred and, even more important, about whose consent mattered. Kinship is a given, part of the natural, divinely ordained social order. Consent is an event, something that happens or happened (in fact, something that must happen again and again) in a particular way and at a particular time. Kinship is a condition, consent is a practice; one depends on biology, the other on history. This is why consensual societies are by nature historical; they are communities that exist in time, which means they have a beginning and must live with the possibility that they might have an end.[19]

We can find a vivid and influential formulation of the foundational role of consent in the work of Thomas Hobbes. There was, Hobbes believed, nothing natural about a political order. In their natural state, humans' lives were "nasty, brutish, and short"; the weak were at the mercy of the strong; insecurity was endemic because everyone, even the strongest, was a potential victim. A political order became possible when, in order to escape this condition of perpetual insecurity, "men agree amongst themselves, to submit to some Man, or Assembly of men, voluntarily, on confidence to be protected by him against all others." This primordial act of consent created the sovereign, who in turn made a community possible. Consent, therefore, established the people's open-ended obligation to obey, but at the same time it is "more than consent, or concord; it is a reall unitie of them all."[20] Only under quite exceptional circumstances, could the commonwealth's foundational act of consent be reversed, thereby risking a return to that terrifying condition in which there is a war of all against all.

Like Hobbes, Jean-Jacques Rousseau began from the premise that the political order was not natural: "No man has received from nature the right to command others."[21] Where does this right come from? It cannot, Rousseau argues, come from force alone: "The strongest is never strong enough to be always the master, unless he transforms strength into right, and obedience into duty." The right to command, that is, the existence of a political order, is only possible when individuals freely join a collectivity: "Each of us puts his person and all his power in common under the supreme direction of the general will, and in our corporate capacity, we receive each member as an indivisible part of the whole."[22]

Rousseau shared Hobbes's view that consent established the political order, but he revised the Hobbesian model in two ways that would have lasting importance for the theory and practice of democracy. First, Rousseau's primal consent is the foundation of continuing political activity, not of perpetual obligation and obedience. Second, this activity takes place within an enduring consensual community that joins "each of us" to "the general will." This community of active individuals has unlimited power. If necessary, it can revoke any law and even the social compact itself.[23] Here again we are struck by the contrast between a natural order based on kinship and a constructed order based on consent. In the former, a reproductive misfortune could threaten the stability of a regime but not the existence of the political order; in an order based on consent, both stability and survival depended on the community's ongoing ability to act together.

The ideas of seminal thinkers such as Hobbes and Rousseau (and many others who could be added to the list) anticipated rather than reflected their contemporaries' expectations about the importance of consent for the origins and character of the political order. The path from ideas to expectations is usually long and indirect because expectations are produced by the experiences through which ideas are applied, tested, and reinterpreted as people try to use them to understand and influence the world. There is, to borrow a useful distinction from the historian Peter Lake, a difference between political thought and thinking about politics. In the latter, ideas and experience are bound together, each shaping and shaped by the other.[24]

In the late seventeenth and eighteenth centuries, more Europeans were thinking (and talking and writing) about politics than ever before. An expanding network of institutions—formal organizations such as Masonic Lodges and Reading Societies, informal ones such as salons and coffee houses—provided the setting for extended conversations about public life. The culture of print expanded to feed people's appetite for information and to provide them with an opportunity to debate the issues of the day. Newspapers, periodicals, pamphlets, and philosophical treatises became a part of more and more people's daily lives. Taken together, these various institutions and publications created a "public sphere" outside of the established order of the old regime. The ideas and actions within this open and accessible realm were diverse and often disconnected, but they represented a growing belief that opinion—that is, *public* opinion—had an important political role to play by connecting rulers and ruled.[25]

The rise of a political public helped to prepare the way for the great upheavals of the late eighteenth century, when, for the first time in human history, the foundational role of popular consent became part of the world of political practice. In chapter 2, we saw how constitutions were an essential instrument in establishing modern states. We can now turn to their importance for the nation, that is, for the creation of a political community whose consent provided the irreplaceable source of legitimate authority.

In 1776, the authors of the American colonies' "Declaration of Independence" justified their rebellion by invoking a universal principle: in order to secure mankind's inalienable, God-given rights, they wrote, "governments are instituted among men, deriving their just powers from the consent of the governed." This consent is conditional and can, therefore, be withdrawn. When the government no longer fulfills its duties, "it is the right of the people to alter or abolish it."[26]

The Declaration of Independence asserted that there was a "people" that its authors represented. But who exactly were these people? Surely not all those living in the thirteen colonies, whose number included Native Americans, African slaves, a substantial minority who remained loyal to the British crown, and, of course, all females. An "American people," although still strictly limited by restrictions of race, ethnicity, political conviction, and gender, gradually emerged, in part as a result of the colonies' struggle against British rule. These were "the people of the United States," in whose name a representative convention issued a constitution for the new nation.[27] In the 1850s, Leopold von Ranke, one of Europe's most influential historians, called this "the greatest revolution" that had ever taken place because "hitherto it was the king, graced by God, around whom everyone grouped themselves; now the idea emerged that power should come from below."[28]

Although it is often overlooked in the celebratory histories of American democracy, the founders of the republic were uneasy about this power "from below." The Constitution was issued in the name of "We the people," but it was drafted behind closed doors and was full of provisions designed to limit the influence of direct democracy.[29] We should probably not make too much of Hamilton's remark that "your people, sir, are a great beast," but there is no doubt that he regarded a "pure democracy" as a corrupt and potentially tyrannical form of government. In his famous Farewell Address, George Washington expressed his anxiety about the domestic factions and foreign entanglements (in his mind, closely connected maladies) that could divide and perhaps destroy the young republic. Anxiety about the *demos* would remain an enduring feature of the democratic political order in the new United States.

As in America, the revolutionary process in France originated with a question about consent. Here the question was posed by the government itself when, in a desperate attempt to overcome a severe financial crisis, the king and his advisors decided to convene the Estates General (*États généraux*), a nationwide representative body that would, or so they hoped, give its consent to a reform of the state's ramshackle and ineffective taxation system. Unintended consequences are an enduring part of political life, but rarely have consequences been less desired or more momentous than those that followed the decision in 1788 to summon what would turn out to be the ancien régime's last representative body. This decision set in motion a revolutionary process that was experienced, over a long period of time and with varying degrees of intensity, by millions of people, first in France and then throughout Europe and the world. As a historical memory, the Revolution lasted well after its original flames had been extinguished. It may be, as François Furet famously asserted in 1978, that the French Revolution is finally over, but it persisted long enough to leave a lasting imprint on people's expectations about the power and problems of a political order based on consent.[30]

In preparation for the meeting of the Estates in 1789, the king ordered electors in each community to compile statements of grievances that could inform the proceedings. More important than the contents of these *cahiers de doléances* was how the enterprise itself implicitly acknowledged the legitimacy of a public whose collective opinion mattered, even when it was critical of the government. The 40,000 *cahiers* collected in 1788 and 1789, together with the flood of pamphlets and broadsides that followed, are another example of the growing legibility of public life that was so central to the emergence of a new political order. "Writing and reading the commentary on events," a student of the revolutionary public has recently noted, "plays a part in learning democratic life, bearing witness to a space suddenly opened to all eyes."[31]

The Estates General was a curiously hybrid institution. The first two estates, representing the clergy and nobility, reflected the ancien régime's assumptions about a social order based on rank and hereditary privilege. Their membership was ascriptive and therefore largely predictable (although some effort was made to represent the lower clergy in the First Estate). The Third Estate, by contrast, was elected by a relatively large and diverse sector of the population. In effect, the Third Estate represented a different kind of society, one that was not a hierarchy of corporate orders, but of unattached individuals who were supposed to act both for themselves and for the common good. From the start, the delegates in the Third

Estate demonstrated their distinctive character, not only in the contrast between their somber clothes and the splendid attire of those in the First and Second Estates, but also by their refusal to sit according to their regional origins.

The first act of the revolutionary drama, conducted in an atmosphere of intense political agitation and deepening social crisis, was dominated by a debate about the meaning of representation, that is, about who had the right to belong to a consensual community. Perhaps the most influential contribution to this debate was a 127-page pamphlet published in January 1789 by Abbé Emmanuel-Josef Sieyès, then an unknown clergyman but soon to become one of the Revolution's most important thinkers. Sieyès's title pointed to the central issue: "What is the Third Estate?" His reply was—or at least seemed to be—incandescently simple: the Third Estate was, unlike the First and Second, not just one part of the whole, it was "everything" and therefore the only legitimate representation of a society of free individuals. Because they continued to cling to their ancient rights and hereditary privileges, the members of the other two estates were no longer a legitimate part of the nation.[32]

By mid-June, the government's original plan to have the three estates function separately had collapsed. On the 17th, in a statement drafted by Sieyès, the members of the Third Estate constituted themselves as a *National* Assembly. Three days later, after having been locked out of their regular meeting place, they gathered in the royal tennis courts where they swore an oath not to disband until a new constitution had been written. This was a decisive step toward replacing an institution that represented separate parts of the social order with one that represented the "people," that is, a unified, cohesive community of equals.

Unlike Rousseau, who was suspicious of the idea that the general will could function through representatives, Sieyès realized that the expanding scale of political and social institutions meant that the people would have to select agents to act in their name. In a country as large as France, a consensual polity had to be based on representation. This representation had to reflect the equality of ruler and ruled: "Citizens enjoy the right to be represented by virtue only of the qualities they share in common and not those which differentiate them."[33] Representative government, therefore, rested on the conviction that political power was exercised by and for people who were, in some important ways, alike. Because equality is not just the legal condition of individuals, but also the essential foundation of a consensual community, defining and sustaining social equality has always been a crucially important and deeply problematic part of the democratic project.[34]

In the first months of its existence, the revolutionary regime confronted a dilemma that would continue to trouble every democratic political order. On the one hand, the members of the National Assembly drew their authority from the nation that was, as Sieyès wrote, "prior to all, it [was] the source of everything."[35] But at the same time, the revolutionaries realized that the nation that they claimed to represent had to be created. This meant, as William Sewell wrote, they needed to construct "a new kind of state and society around the key legitimizing concept of 'the nation.'"[36] As Sewell's formulation makes clear, the Revolution had to create both "a new kind of state," that is, a state based on popular consent, and a new kind of society, that is, one that was based on equality. This was the extraordinary task that the representatives of the Third Estate, joined by some renegade delegates from the First and Second, set out to perform in the summer of 1789.

The key document in this revolutionary enterprise was the "Declaration of the Rights of Man and the Citizen," adopted by the National Assembly in late August 1789. The most important article was the first, which defined a new kind of society: "Men are born and remain free and equal in rights. Social distinctions may be founded only upon the general good." About the nature of "the general good" the members of the Assembly were, and would remain, divided, but it was clearly no longer to be determined by the distinctions of birth (with the obvious, but unspoken exception of gender) and corporate identity that had structured the old regime. The Declaration then defined a new kind of state by asserting that this society of equals was the source of all legitimate power: "The principle of sovereignty resides essentially in the nation. No body nor individual may exercise any authority which does not proceed directly from the nation." A product of intense debate and hasty compromises, the Declaration was filled with ambiguities and evasions about what kind of a society it wanted to create. Nevertheless, it captured the fusion of social and political aspirations that gave the Revolution its distinctive character and historical significance.[37]

A revolutionary transformation of the ancien régime had begun even before a final version of the Declaration of Rights was formally issued. During a dramatic session that lasted through the night of August 4/5, the Assembly abolished "the feudal system," which included the seigneurial rights and privileges of noble landowners and the tithes paid to support the Catholic Church.[38] Within a few hours, a number of institutions, some of them centuries old, were demolished. What would take their place, both as a source of order in people's lives and of loyalty in people's hearts?

The revolutionaries knew that to answer this question it was not enough to demolish the ancien régime. The conditions for a new society had to be created—quickly, ruthlessly, and from the center outward. This required an expansion of the infrastructure we described in chapter 2. The National Assembly, for example, set out to reorganize France's political space by replacing the provinces that had been acquired over centuries and stitched together to form the ancien régime's composite state with a neat set of *départements*, themselves divided into *communes*, that would serve as uniform legal, administrative, and fiscal units.[39] In September 1792, after a new, increasingly turbulent act of the revolutionary drama had begun, the government issued decrees that transferred the registry of births, marriages, and deaths from the Church to municipal authorities. From this moment on, the state was responsible for establishing the "civil status" and therefore the political identity of everyone who belonged to the nation.[40] Taken together, the object of these measures was to change what Sieyès called "a kingdom bristling with every kind of barrier, a chaos of local customs, regulations, and prohibitions" into a unified nation of (needless to say, *male*) citizens.[41]

From the start, the French revolutionaries feared their efforts to create a new kind of state and society would not be enough. Everywhere they looked, hostile forces were at work: aristocrats who hoped to reclaim their ancient privileges, devout Catholics who resisted the displacement of the Church, defenders of local institutions who opposed centralizing measures, and, most dangerous and insidious of all, those political actors who seemed to support the Revolution but in fact covertly undermined its true purpose. As the conflicts generated by the Revolution became more violent, the Revolution's central dilemma intensified: "We must," a radical delegate proclaimed in 1794, "re-create the people we wish to restore to freedom."[42]

The project of "re-creation" began with speeches and declarations, but soon produced cleansing acts of terror to destroy the enemies of the nation. Only then would the nation become the consensual community of equals on which the new regime's legitimacy relied. The idea that violence had a redemptive purpose that was necessary to create a new order would turn out to be one of the Revolution's most noxious legacies.

To its admirers and enemies alike, the French Revolution vividly demonstrated both the power and the perils that were inherent in a political order based on popular consent. As the French example made clear, a state that was able to draw on the voluntary support and active participation of its members could mobilize resources—economic, political, and, above all, military—that greatly exceeded the capacities of the old regime. Sooner or later every government recognized that it would need to harness these resources in order to survive. But although many people eventually came to believe that consent was necessary for modern states, they also wondered if it was sufficient. Would a consensual society of equals have enough cohesive strength to withstand the unavoidable conflicts that confronted every polity? Here too the example of revolutionary France remained imprinted on people's political imagination. Behind the democratic ideals and aspirations of the French Revolution was the specter of the mob, those irrational, destructive, and uncontrollable crowds that are pictured in the works of theorists such as Burke, historians such as Taine, and novelists such as Dickens.

For better or for worse, either as the dream of a brave new world bright with promise or as a chaotic nightmare to be avoided at all costs, the revolutionary experience fundamentally changed people's expectations about the character of the political order. Among the first Europeans to see this was Edmund Burke, who wrote in 1790, when the process had hardly begun, that "the French Revolution is the most extraordinary thing that has hitherto happened in the world."[43] A year later, Burke published his *Reflections on the Revolution in France*, which would become a key text for the Revolution's enemies. The title is significant: Burke realized that what was unfolding across the channel was not the *French* revolution, but the revolution *in* France, that is, a political and social upheaval that would not be confined to a single state.[44]

First in France and then throughout the world, the essence of the Revolution was a commitment to democracy's political and social promise. Politically, democracy meant a politics based on popular consent. Socially, democracy imagined a consensual community of people sufficiently alike that they would be willing to trust one another with political power, which ultimately means the power over one another. Consent, which we usually think of as the free act of an individual, is inseparable from the existence of a consensual community, a collective expression of individual will and collective obligation. Democracy's fundamental problem—at once political and social—is how to create and sustain a community that would be free enough to allow for individual will and cohesive enough to impose collective obligation. This has rarely been easy. Looking back on democracy's long and difficult history, the French political theorist Claude Lefort concluded that it inaugurated "the experience of an ungraspable, uncontrollable society in which the people will be said to be sovereign, of course, but whose identity will constantly be open to question."[45] As a political ideal, democracy promises to give power to the *demos*, but offers little guidance about how this *demos* is to be created or sustained.

In the modern political order, the most compelling answer to the question of the people's identity is some form of nationhood. At times, it seemed deceptively easy to conflate the two. Sieyès, for example, wrote that "all public power comes from the people, that is to say, the nation," and then added that the two "ought to be synonymous."[46] Because the nation seemed to provide historical roots and emotional intensity, nationality was the most effective source of that sense of common identity that Sieyès recognized democratic government demanded. In both theory and practice, therefore, nationhood promised to create a foundation for what every democracy needs, which is, as Craig Calhoun has written, "an autonomous political community capable of self-determination."[47]

The nation's power would come from the fact that it seems to be both an autonomous and a voluntary community, a community that exists independently of individual will but at the same time is persistently recreated by the action of those who willingly consent to the rule of people like themselves. Imagined and organized as a nation, the "people" could acquire the political and cultural cohesion necessary to carry the weight of sovereignty. But, in practice, Sieyès's apparently simple identification of "people" and "nation" turned out to be extraordinarily difficult.

"UN PLEBISCITE DE TOUS LES JOURS"

In March 1882, the popular philosopher Ernest Renan delivered a lecture at the Sorbonne entitled "What Is a Nation?" Renan began by rejecting conventional definitions of nationhood, such as by race, language, religion, and geography. Instead, he offered two answers to the problem of the nation's identity. The first was a sense of a common past, a collective awareness of the nation's victories and defeats. This common past is necessarily selective and sometimes invented; as Renan pointed out, for the creation of national histories, forgetting is no less important than remembering. Renan's second answer is especially important for our purposes because it tied national identity to democratic politics. A nation, he maintained, must rest on consent, on people's willingness to belong, the "desire to live together, the desire to continue to invest in the heritage that we have jointly received." His famous metaphor for the "clearly expressed desire to continue a common life" was the image of the nation as a "daily plebiscite" in which its citizens persistently reaffirm their commitment to the national community.[48]

Renan's essay reflected rather than resolved the central paradox of nationhood that we examined in the preceding section. His belief that the nation depended on "the heritage that we have jointly received" presupposed that there is a "we," a community with an autonomous existence, independent of individual decisions. But at the same time, like the revolutionaries of 1789, Renan realized that this "we" had to register their desire to belong to the nation not just once, but over and over again.[49]

Renan's plebiscite metaphor is often quoted in support of the nation's dependence on expressions of individual commitment. But plebiscites are always more than the sum of individual acts; they are necessarily collective practices in which an individual's action has meaning only as part of a larger community.[50] Equally important, plebiscites require rules that define who has the right to vote and also an elaborate set of institutions to conduct the process and ratify the results. In a way that Renan may not have intended, therefore, his metaphor points us toward how the nation rests on a fusion of subjective and objective elements, the expression of individual desire and the existence of a separate juridical and administrative apparatus.[51] Nationhood, therefore, illustrates Claude Lefort's insight that nothing political can exist without a form that gives it meaning ("mise en sense") and at the same time enables it to be enacted ("mise-en-scène").[52]

It is significant that Renan selected an election as his metaphor for the consensual basis of nationhood. Although plebiscites themselves are rare, elections have become the most important way that democracy takes on a form that gives a consensual polity both meaning and enactment. There were, of course, many sorts of elections in the premodern world. Some of them, like the selection of the pope or the Holy Roman emperor, were elaborate rituals conducted by a small group of privileged individuals. Others, like the village democracies so admired by Rousseau, were informal gatherings of neighbors who were bound together by proximity and mutual dependence. But once popular consent had become the foundation of legitimate authority, elections became the political order's most significant symbolic and practical act. Democracy, the political theorist Sheldon Wolin once noted, "is not about [perhaps it would be better to say, not only about] where the political is located but how it is experienced."[53] Elections are a consensual polity's most characteristic political experience. They are the way nations express, and experience, the transformation of their internal divisions into a common identity.

Differing vastly in style and substance, elections have nevertheless become an essential element in the public life of virtually every state. Like the spread of legal codes, constitutions, and other important parts of the modern political order, the evolution of electoral practices has been diverse and uneven. In Britain, they began in the old regime and were reformed very gradually in response to changes in politics and society. Sometimes, as we saw in France in 1788, they were introduced by governments to mobilize popular support for a particular policy or, as occurred throughout Europe in 1848, in response to a revolutionary crisis. By and large, in Central and Eastern Europe elections came later and had less political importance than in the West. But in most of Europe, pressures to allow voting became irresistible, even though some conservative regimes, such as Prussia's in the first half of the nineteenth century, attempted to delay the process by restricting elections to local and provincial representative bodies. In the matter of elections, as in most other aspects of the modern political order, states took different paths to the same destination: all of them eventually introduced some kind of formalized and regularly scheduled expressions of popular opinion.[54]

The major conflicts over election laws usually had to do with the size and character of the electorate. These conflicts were intense because they were not only about who could vote but also about the nature of the nation itself. In a consensual polity, membership in the political community was not just a legal status, but carried the right to actively participate in public life. This is why voting was such a significant issue, both practical and symbolic, for those groups that were categorically excluded, most obviously women, whose dependent status was reaffirmed by the fact that they could not participate directly in civic affairs, but had to be represented by men, first their fathers, then their husbands. Arguments against female suffrage, like arguments against giving the vote to unpropertied males, usually centered around the fact that they did not have the capacity to act independently and therefore could not be active members of a consensual community.[55]

Just as democracy made citizenship more significant for the life of the state, it also made ethnicity an increasingly important condition for citizenship. To be a citizen was to be a member of the nation, which meant sharing the nation's history and the marks of its core identity—usually language, often religion, sometimes race. Although many acknowledged that national identity could be acquired, it seemed more and more to be a hereditary condition. There was, therefore, a significant shift in the definition of citizenship from *jus soli*, that is, citizenship based on place of birth (soil) to *jus sanguinis*, citizenship based on descent (blood).[56]

Unevenly and sometimes with great difficulty, states gradually expanded their electorates by removing property qualifications on adult males (once common in most states and lasting into the early twentieth century in countries such as Britain); in the twentieth century, the franchise was extended to women and, in many states, the voting age was lowered.[57] This movement toward universal suffrage at once reflected and reaffirmed new expectations about the legal, political, and cultural definition of the consensual community and, therefore, of the nation itself. Legitimate authority now had to come from an inclusive community of equally empowered citizens that was cohesive enough to carry the weight of political decision-making, not just once but again and again.[58]

Electoral systems have different rules about how voting should be organized and the results counted. In general, the democratization of elections has encouraged a move away from the indirect method of voting that was common in many European states in the nineteenth century (and still retains a consequential afterlife in the U.S. Electoral College for presidential elections). Some countries have a form of proportional representation that reflects voter preferences accurately but can lead to political fragmentation. In order to prevent the proliferation of small parties, states such as Germany and Turkey set a minimum percentage that is required to elect a representative. The size of election districts varies, as does how—and by whom—district boundaries are defined and revised. Taken together, these rules shape not only how people vote but also the way political alignments are expressed. They can, therefore, have enormous influence on how a state is governed. In most states, rules on voting are very hard to change, even when (as in contemporary Israel) they make the formation of a stable government extremely difficult or (as in the United States) they produce a radically undemocratic distribution of seats in the Senate.

Equally diverse is what we might call the anthropology of elections, the rituals and symbols that surround them, their emotional tone, and the way they relate to, and can reinforce, other social relationships. In some places, elections have been rowdy, festive occasions when the machinery of democracy was lubricated with strong drink. Elsewhere they have been and are a sober civic duty, fulfilled by serious citizens in their Sunday best. Voting could celebrate a community's cohesion or spark a violent clash between opposing groups. As Tocqueville observed in his recollections of 1848, elections could reaffirm voters' deference to traditional elites. But in other parts of Europe, elections held during that same turbulent year enabled new men to find a way of influencing public affairs for the first time.[59]

More remarkable than the enormous diversity of electoral practice is the fact of its near universality. This universality underscores the way elections reflect the enduring tension in democratic politics between unity and division, the one and the many, the people as a cohesive community that can exert legitimate power over its members and the people as a collection of consenting individuals pursuing their disparate private interests and desires. In a political order based on kinship, the polity had to come to terms with the vicissitudes of biology. Democracies must come to terms with the conflicts inherent in social differences, the danger that the *demos* may not cohere, that public virtue, a sense of common purpose, and a willingness to tolerate dissent might not be sufficient to contain the disintegrating forces that can turn the sovereign people into an unruly mob.

In dynastic states, the tension between the ruler's mortal body and his or her role as the personification of the immortal state was both expressed and transcended in the political order's most important rituals, especially the coronation. In democracies, elections are the equivalent of coronations. Just as the coronation both expresses and transcends the monarch's human nature, elections express and transcend the people's divisions, simultaneously acknowledging and overcoming the political order's central tension. The coronation affirmed that one king was dead, but another lived; elections are a persistent feature of democratic political life because they are supposed to serve as an essential reminder, constantly repeated, that the many can and must be made one. This is why modern dictatorships hold elections. Even when these regimes do not allow the "many" an opportunity to express their differences, it is important for every kind of government to express the presence of the "one."

Elections are conventionally viewed from below, as expressions of people's various interests and ideological commitments. But elections are also an example of the necessary connection between the growth of national communities and the expansion of state power. The institutional infrastructure that we described in chapter 2 is as important for electoral politics as it is for the projections of state power. Elections require knowledge, rules, and agents: accurate maps that define electoral districts, census data that identify eligible voters, laws about how the voting should be conducted, and a governmental apparatus to regulate the process and validate its results. Here too we are struck by the diversity in electoral practice. In some states, officials strictly enforce the rules governing elections, honestly count the ballots, and accept the results even when they favor the opposition. But fraud and intimidation, sometimes minor, sometimes massive, have been part of electoral politics from its earliest beginnings. Powerful people frequently use their resources to bribe, threaten, or practically disenfranchise some part of electorate. No electoral system is totally free of such abuses, but few were as systematically corrupt as the American South where a combination of violence and legal chicanery managed to prevent African Americans from exercising their right to vote for a century after their formal emancipation. But however it was used, everywhere the power of the state was an essential element in every electoral system.[60]

Elections are just one of many examples of the intimate relationship between the expansion of the state's infrastructure and the growth of national communities. This relationship is not unidirectional: nations usually do not create states, as conventional nationalist narratives once claimed; nor can most states create nations, as many scholars, in reaction against these conventional accounts, now argue. It might be more helpful to think of the deep and complex historical connection between states and nations as being one of "elective affinity." The term, borrowed by Goethe from eighteenth-century chemistry and then applied to social analysis by Max Weber, suggests reciprocal encouragement and interaction rather than straightforward causality. Weber's most famous application of the term was in his analysis of the relationship between Protestantism and capitalism.[61] States and nations grew together, each shaping, and being shaped by, the other. And the relationship between states and nations was often inherently contentious.[62]

We find an elective affinity between states and nations at work in many of the modern political order's characteristic institutions. Consider, for example, the mass-conscript army. Here too the revolutionary era opened a new chapter in the history of European states and nations. When the French Revolutionary regime went to war against the Central European powers in 1792, it had access to the resources and institutions of one of the richest and best organized states in the world. But at the same time, the revolutionaries were able to mobilize the population behind the war effort. A product of both dire necessity and ideological conviction, mass mobilization for a "people's war" culminated in the famous decree of August 1793, which declared that "until the enemies have been driven from the territory of the republic, the French people are in permanent requisition for army service. The young men shall go to battle; the married men shall forge arms and transport provision; the women shall make tents and clothes, and shall serve in the hospitals; the children shall turn old linen into lint; the old men shall repair to the public places, to stimulate the courage of the warriors and preach the unity of the Republic and hatred of kings."[63] In defense of the Revolution, France's army became what François Furet called "the incarnation of the national dream."[64]

In his analysis of the Revolution's impact on warfare, Carl von Clausewitz recognized that the most significant changes were political rather than military. The Revolution, he wrote, "set in motion new means and new forces, and has thus made possible a degree of energy in war that otherwise would have been inconceivable."[65] Success on the battlefield now required the capacity to harness this energy. The problem was how to do this without unleashing the political forces that could destroy the regimes that they were mobilized to defend.

Throughout the nineteenth century, European states attempted to create armies that were both militarily effective and politically reliable. These attempts involved drafting young men to serve for a relatively brief period (usually two or three years) on active duty and then for a much longer time in a reserve unit. With the exception of Great Britain, every European state eventually possessed an army of citizen soldiers who were expected to kill and die for their fatherlands. By 1914, one out of every ten Frenchmen and one of thirteen Germans were trained for a war in which millions of them would perish.[66]

Military service also integrated a substantial portion of the *male* population into the life of nation (and, as such, was another expression of the connection between gender and citizenship). In some countries, such as Italy, the state made a conscious effort to sever recruits' connections with their region by stationing them far away from home. But everywhere, the army was regarded as "the school of the nation," the place where—to borrow the title of Eugen Weber's fine book—peasants became Frenchmen (or Germans, or, with less success, Italians and Russians). In many countries, the social bonds and political lessons of active duty were sustained by years in the reserves and also by organizations of veterans: in Imperial Germany, these veterans' associations (Kriegervereine) were especially popular.[67]

Governments hoped, and not without reason, that military service would create citizens who were aware of the nation's history, infused with its ideals, and therefore committed to its defense at home and abroad. But military service could also give men a new awareness of their place in the political and social order. For many, military service was the first time they had been away from their native village, an occasion to learn the national language and to acquire new skills, tastes, and aspirations. Friedrich Engels, Marx's collaborator, a former Prussian officer and a well-informed student of military matters, was convinced that "contrary to appearance, compulsory military service surpassed the general franchise as an agent of democracy." Conscription, therefore, expressed and expanded the power of the state, but also mobilized and engaged the population. That is why, as Dominique Schnapper pointed out, universal suffrage and conscription were both essential for "the logic and the ideal of the democratic nation."[68]

In an important essay on the "nationality question," first published in 1907, the Austrian Social Democrat Otto Bauer drew attention to the connection between education and military service: "What the school began, the army continued." Both prepared men to be citizens by bringing them out of their local communities into the larger world: "The effect initially exercised by the school on the child and by compulsory military service on the young man is fully realized by democracy in the case of the adult."[69] Once again, we find that elective affinity of state and nation, the interaction between regulation and mobilization that is characteristic of the modern political order.

At the same time that European states gave a growing number of its citizens the right to vote and conscripted them into the army, they began to require their populations to attend school. Like many other institutions, schooling in the ancien régime had been diverse and uneven, in some places virtually nonexistent, everywhere limited to a few, usually privileged groups. In different ways and with varying degrees of success, most European governments in the late eighteenth and early nineteenth centuries set about reforming and expanding their educational institutions in order to provide their inhabitants with the basic skills necessary to function in a modern society.[70] The schoolmaster, like the policeman, postal clerk, tax collector, and drill sergeant, became a prominent representative of the state's presence, the personification of the linkage between the local world in which most people still lived and an increasingly intrusive national community.

Advocates of educational reform were fully aware of the school's potential political influence. Conservatives were eager to instill traditional values, such as obedience to the state, loyalty to the monarch, and devotion to established religion. Catholics, often confronted by a hostile state, fought to keep control over instruction so that the forces of secular liberalism would not infect their communities. They had good reason to be concerned: the French politician Jules Ferry, for example, firmly believed that schools should teach religion, but for him that meant "the religion of the fatherland," a patriotism that was "at once ardent and reasoned, with which we want to penetrate the heart and mind of the child."[71] Some of the indoctrination in schools must have worked, but it is difficult to determine how much. Students, as we know, frequently find ways to resist their teachers' best efforts to impose conventional values and acceptable behavior. But as Otto Bauer pointed out, schools did loosen the restraints of the local community by providing their pupils with new skills and aspirations and at the same time connecting them to one another and to the wider community. In that sense, Dominique Schnapper is right to insist that the school eventually became "the institution par excellence of the nation."[72]

Saskia Sassen has argued that "it took work to make society national."[73] This work included classroom lessons and school excursions, military service and parades, election campaigns and voting, all of which provided the symbols and rituals that represented the nation. The influence of these practices was reinforced by the many quotidian objects and events that expressed national identity: postage stamps, banknotes, murals and maps on the walls of public buildings, the statues of national heroes in the town square, and the celebration of national holidays.[74] These things reminded people of the national community to which they belonged or, as we will see in the next section, of the community from which they were, either willingly or unwillingly, excluded.

National communities took many different forms and could grow in many different settings, from the kind of terrorist cell that inspired an assassin such as Gavrilo Princip to the highly respectable patriotic societies that sponsored festive banquets on national holidays. Our attention is drawn to the violent and exotic manifestations of nationhood, but we should not overlook how the national identity of ordinary men and women was affirmed by countless personal experiences. "The idea of one's own nation," Otto Bauer wrote, "is linked spatially and temporally with other ideas, the emotional connotation of which passes to the idea of the nation." Like Bauer, the American anthropologist Michael Herzfeld recognized that nationalism works because its "basic building blocks are already familiar." Family ties, childhood memories, classroom lessons, popular novels, and patriotic songs, all these increase people's capacity to imagine how they could be members of an extended community of strangers or, as could also happen, to make them aware of the community to which they did not belong.[75]

The nation's political significance came less from the power of its ideas (the philosophical foundation of nationhood is very thin) or from economic self-interest (which was, for most people, quite limited), but rather from how it was embedded in people's daily lives. Here is where nationhood—to quote Robert Wiebe once again—"addressed basic human needs." Weber's term *Veralltäglichung* (making something part of everyday life) nicely captures the essence of this process of incorporating national identity into people's quotidian existence and thereby making it an essential element in their expectations about the political order.[76] At moments of national crisis, this sense of identity could produce those dramatic (and extraordinary) outbursts of national enthusiasm, such as many Europeans seemed to have experienced in the summer of 1914. In ordinary times, identity with the nation helped to legitimate the increasingly intrusive presence of the state in society.

A great deal of what Sassen called the "work" of nation-making—education, military service, elections, and reading material of all sorts—has to do with language. Of course, language always had a close if complex connection to national identity. As Benedict Anderson eloquently put it, "What the eye is to the lover . . . language is to the patriot." Through language, "pasts are restored, fellowships are imagined, and futures dreamed."[77] In the eighteenth century, when both language and national identity became important subjects for study and debate, the connection between them was often emphasized. For example, J. G. Herder, one of the first and most profound students of nationhood, insisted that language was the source and substance of national identity. Like nationality, Herder believed, language was both natural and historical; we acquired it at birth as our "mother tongue" and it remained with us thereafter. Our language, a German poet wrote in 1771, "was what we were when Tacitus described us."[78] Like the nation itself, the national language had to be celebrated, but also re-created by being purged of its imperfections and alien elements. The eighteenth and early nineteenth century was the great age of grammars and dictionaries, which sought to unify linguistic practice just as maps unified space and law codes unified the rules governing social life. The reform, and in some places the recovery or even the invention, of the national language was regarded as a patriotic project, a vital contribution to the formation of a national community.[79]

The significance of language for nationhood is a good example of how the nation could be both ancient and modern. Linguistic communities have deep historical roots and are among what Clifford Geertz called the "givens" that sustain national identity. One might say that national histories began when efforts to build the Tower of Babel were frustrated by linguistic diversity.[80] In the eighteenth century, however, the political role of language fundamentally changed when national communities, like the rest of the political order, began to become legible. The emergence and expansion of a culture based on written communication gave the traditional link between language and national identity a new institutional framework and an increased political salience. In letters, books, and periodicals, written language connected people—readers and writers—across time and space. It encouraged them to experience and imagine loyalties and commitments that were no longer bounded by their immediate experience or tied to their local communities. Written material helped to create and communicate those shared sentiments, values, and experiences that Renan and many of his contemporaries believed were an essential source of nationhood. Everywhere in Europe, the modern political public was, in different ways and with different consequences, a national public.[81]

Language is an activity, not a possession; it is something that people "do" rather than something that they "have." Like social equality, political consent, and national identity, language requires a community; none of them has meaning for an isolated individual. To imagine a language, Ludwig Wittgenstein wrote, "is to imagine a form of life."[82] The same thing can be said about nationhood: to imagine a nation is to imagine a form of life, a certain way of living together. Nationhood is given form and direction by people's ideas and is persistently tested by people's experiences. Together these ideas and experiences shape, and are shaped by, expectations about the character and significance of national communities.

Language requires and makes possible Wittgenstein's "form of life." But language can divide as well as unite; this was, after all, the message of the biblical account of Babel. Legibility increases language's power to unite and divide. In an oral culture, most people lived in a single linguistic community; for most activities, the local dialect was sufficient; dialects were another marker of belonging to a particular place. Beyond the local community, people could get along with a few phrases or rely on a small group of experts—clergy, officials, merchants—who had the required linguistic skills. But when written forms of communication became an increasingly important part of social, cultural, and political life, it was necessary to have a common language, officially recognized and intelligible throughout the state's institutions. In classrooms and courthouses, in the barracks and at the polling place, those who were willing and/or able to master the official language were united to one another, while those who did not were necessarily excluded from full membership in the life of the community. Here again, in the creation of these linguistic loyalties and divisions, we find the elective affinity between state making and nationhood.[83]

Languages and national identities at once brought people together and separated them from others. Like most sources of legitimacy, nationhood was both essential for collective action and the cause of enduring conflicts. The significance of these conflicts between and within national communities is the subject of the next section.

THE NATION AS AN "ESSENTIALLY CONTESTED CONCEPT"

The elective affinity between states and nations makes national ideas, the loyalties they evoke, and the actions they inspire intensely, inevitably political. In the modern political order, therefore, nationhood is closely connected to the struggle for, and the exercise of, political power. Above all, it is this connection that separates modern expectations about nations from the way nations were experienced and imagined in the premodern world. "Ethnicity turned into nationalism," Robert Wiebe argues, "when cultural consciousness acquired a political objective."[84] It would be better to refer to "political objectives" because nationhood has always been deployed for more than one purpose. There is nothing singular about the politics of nations and nationality.

Like every other source of political legitimacy, nationhood had a distinctive set of strengths and weaknesses. In the ancien régime, the dynastic order's claims to legitimacy came from its particularity, which was represented, but also limited by, the body of the king. In the modern world, the strengths and weaknesses of the nation as a source of legitimacy come from its diversity. Because it can mean so many different things, the nation pervades the political order. But the inherent diversity of nationhood also makes its meaning the subject of persistent dispute.

The nation is, to borrow the phrase made famous by the philosopher W. B. Gallie, an "essentially contested concept," one of those terms "the proper use of which inevitably involves endless disputes" about its meaning and application.[85] Gallie is referring to contests about a concept's use in language, but actions can also be essentially contested. As the subject of both political thinking and political practice, the nation "inevitably involves endless disputes." This essential contestability shapes how we imagine nations and how we use them to act in the world.

National theory and practice are contestable because the nation is the product of political imagination; it is connected to, but also necessarily transcends, people's direct experience. There is, therefore, always a gap between imagination and experience, a gap in which a variety of competing ideas, aspirations, and desires can coexist. This space between imagination and experience exists throughout the political order, but it is particularly wide in the case of nations. As Ernest Gellner pointed out, national rhetoric is "inversely related to social reality."[86] The nation is imagined as a community with deep, ancient historical roots, whereas most nations are relatively recent constructions. Nations are thought to have an enduring character, but in fact they are constantly being made and remade. Nations are supposed to be homogeneous, but they usually are not; nations promise to provide unity, but they are full of divisions. When people imagine the nation, they often invoke its origins in the traditional world of folk customs and village communities, but national movements could not exist without modern institutions—printing presses, political parties, railroads. Nationalists imagine a community (a *Gemeinschaft*) but they live in a society (a *Gesellschaft*). Given this disconnect between imagination and reality, it is not surprising that national histories are so full of disillusion and disappointment. The reality of nationhood rarely (if ever) fulfills the hopes and dreams of those who imagine it.

Another reason for the contestability of nationhood is that national theory and practice have no defining political or social content. Nations can be monarchies or republics, small or large, expansionist or isolationist. Nor does nationhood require any specific commitment about the character and distribution of property, the single most significant issue in many modern societies. Nationhood can be invoked to defend capitalism or socialism, economic inequality or the redistribution of wealth, the preeminence of the bourgeoisie or the dictatorship of the proletariat.

This lack of an institutional anchorage means that nations are more like myths than ideologies. Ideologies provide maps of the social and political landscape; nations project highly diverse and extraordinarily malleable images of what the political community can or should be.[87] To a nineteenth-century critic of nationalism such as Lord Acton, this indeterminate quality of nationhood was the source of its subversive power: "Nationality does not aim either at liberty or prosperity, both of which it sacrifices to the imperative necessity of making the nation the mold and measure of the state."[88] This imperative was often extraordinarily difficult to put into practice.

National ideas and actions can exist all across the ideological spectrum. The first section of this chapter described how the modern concept of the nation entered the political arena from the left, when French revolutionaries tried to imagine a "people" that was cohesive enough to carry the weight of sovereign power. For a century or more, progressive Europeans assumed that the people and the nation were (or should be) one. To John Stuart Mill, for example, a people's right to have their own nation was self-evident. "One hardly knows what any division of the human race should be free to do," he wrote in 1861, "if not to determine with which of the various bodies of human beings they choose to associate themselves." And for Mill, the most important of these "various bodies" was the nation.[89]

Throughout the nineteenth and early twentieth centuries, Mill's assumptions about national self-determination remained part of the liberal agenda, both in Europe and the rest of the world. Tocqueville believed that "the interests of the human race are better served by giving every man a particular fatherland than by trying to inflame his passions for the whole of humanity." Despite a great deal of depressing evidence that "giving every man a particular fatherland" was a formidably difficult thing to do, the association of nationhood and progress has persisted and is, to some degree at least, still an important part of our political expectations. In a book first published in 1927 and then reprinted twenty years later, Ernest Barker expressed his enduring conviction that "the cause of liberty found its basis and secures its roots in the autonomy of a national group."[90]

After the middle of nineteenth century, national ideas and actions were adopted by a new generation of conservative leaders who recognized nationhood's political power and potential. Among the most significant of them was Otto von Bismarck, who became minister president of Prussia in 1862 and then the first chancellor of the German Empire in 1871. Bismarck had begun his political career as an opponent of liberal nationalism, which he viewed as a challenge to the integrity of the Prussian state and the authority of its king. In the aftermath of the failed liberal revolution of 1848, however, Bismarck realized that German nationalism was malleable enough to support both Prussia and the monarchy. There is, he wrote in 1858, "nothing more German than Prussia's special interests properly understood."[91] Considering the link between nationhood and democracy that we just examined, it is worth noting that Bismarck's opportunistic adoption of the national cause was closely tied to his calculated compromise with democratic politics. When he introduced universal manhood suffrage for the newly created German Parliament in 1867, Bismarck imagined an electorate of deferential voters, such as the peasants on his estates, men who could be marched to the polls to support king and country.[92] Not for the first time or the last, the national community did not turn out to be what its founders had imagined.

At the same time European conservatives such as Bismarck embraced nationhood, some left-wing radicals seemed to be moving in the other direction. Karl Marx viewed nationalism as a sham, yet another of those many illusions with which the established order sought to distract the proletariat from its real interest. As Marx and Engels insisted in the *Commu-*

nist Manifesto, "The working men have no country." Once the working class took power, the distinction between states would diminish, perhaps even disappear because the postrevolutionary international order would not be dominated by national elites, but by those who can speak to and for the universal interests of mankind.[93] The institutional expression of these convictions were the two international organizations of socialist parties (1864–76 and 1889–1916), which held congresses designed to coordinate political action that transcended national boundaries.[94]

In practice, the politics of the socialist movement illustrated the magnetic power of nationhood. Even when they retained a programmatic commitment to internationalism, many party leaders and their constituents were inexorably drawn into a web of national institutions. Left-wing parties such as the German Social Democrats were critical of their nations' foreign policies and hostile to the overheated patriotic rhetoric that became prevalent among certain right-wing groups, but they shared their fellow countrymen's expectations about the nation's value and significance. This would lead a majority of them to support their nation during the twentieth century's first world war. For socialists, as for conservatives and Catholics, it was international ties and loyalties, not national ones, which were, to quote Eric Hobsbawm again, "remote from real experience."[95]

The politics of nationhood, like all democratic politics, is shaped by an ongoing dialectic of inclusion and exclusion. The public life of democracies is driven by their citizens' constant efforts to acquire allies and isolate opponents. Democratic governments work best when the differences between ally and opponent are limited, fluid, and open to compromise. When this is the case, new issues can engender new alignments; yesterday's opponent can be tomorrow's ally. In the politics of nationhood, however, the dialectic of inclusion and exclusion threatens to become absolute, a matter of identity rather than choice. The division between ally and opponent tends to become fixed and impermeable. This tendency was apparent from the start. Sieyès, it will be remembered, identified the Third Estate with the nation by permanently excluding the other two estates from the national community. Bismarck was in the habit of calling his domestic opponents *Reichsfeinde* ("enemies of the Reich"), thereby suggesting that their loyalties—to the pope or the socialist international—disqualified them from being *real* Germans. For whatever reason (and there were always a great many available), to deny that one's political opponents were part of the nation was to exclude them from legitimate politics. This exclusion might begin as a rhetorical tactic but it could easily lead to the loss of civic identity, the legal protection of citizenship, and, in extreme situations, the right to life itself.[96]

The politics of nationhood was about the nation's composition and also its conduct, about what it should *be* in addition to what it should *do*. In the United States, the question of the nation's political identity was often connected to race and ethnicity. American history is full of claims that some groups—Blacks, Catholics, Hispanics, Muslims—were fundamentally and permanently "not American." Elsewhere, exclusion from the nation might be a matter of ideological commitment or religious belief. "Real" Englishmen were Protestants, "real" Frenchmen embraced the ideals of 1789, "real" Italians rejected the sovereign rights of the papacy. Those who did not fit its self-proclaimed advocates' definition of the real nation forfeited the right to be part of the consensual community on which legitimate authority depended.

Conflicts about the definition of nationhood occurred in many states, but these conflicts were especially significant when more than one national community occupied the same territory. As we saw in chapter 1, during the ancien régime, ethnic homogeneity was not an especially important consideration in the construction of composite states. "National" cohesion did not matter much for state-makers, who expected that groups with different languages, customs, and regional loyalties were united by their common ties to the monarch. These different groups did not have to live or act together. Nor did most inhabitants of these states always object to be governed by "foreigners," who were regarded as no better (or it might be more accurate to say, no worse) than other ruling elites. Expectations about the political role of nationality began to change when the nature of states was gradually transformed by the developments we described in chapter 2: the new infrastructure of governmental power—maps, censuses, law codes, and administrative organizations—led to new ways of organizing and imagining political communities. As states became legible, distinctions that had been easy to blur in the localized world of the ancien régime created new reasons to include some groups and exclude others.

A more serious and intractable challenge to multinational states, however, came from the gradual but inexorable democratization of public life. In the old regime, legitimate authority was based on differences between rulers and ruled. In a democratic order, the relationship between rulers and ruled was transformed; now people expected to be governed by those like themselves. That is why Dankwart Rustow argued that a consensus about the nation is a "background condition" for democratic politics: "The vast majority of citizens in a democracy-to-be must have no doubt or mental reservation as to which political community they belong."[97] Doubts and reservations about nationhood, however, were hard to avoid in multi-national states. Without Rustow's "background condition," would it be possible to create a democratic community from different national groups, some of them permanently estranged from their governments and, no less important, from one another?

In his discussion of nationality published in 1861, John Stuart Mill argued that the answer to this question was no. Autocracies, Mill pointed out, could tolerate, even encourage, a variety of nationalities in their realm; all of them were, after all, equally powerless. But in a state with participatory institutions, differences in language and what Mill called "fellow feeling" would prevent the creation of the "united public opinion" that was essential for representative government. Without this united opinion, anti-democratic forces would always be able to undermine attempts at political reform by manipulating national divisions. A necessary prerequisite of free institutions, he maintained, was that "the boundaries of governments should coincide in the main with those of nationalities." In multinational states, it would be "next to impossible" for freedom to flourish.[98]

Despite these misgivings, Mill remained cautiously optimistic about the future of both freedom and nationality. Multinational autocracies (the Habsburgs, for instance) would probably not survive. But many national minorities would decide that they should assimilate with the more advanced national community, just as Bretons had done in France and, he hoped, the Irish would do in Britain. In what was not one of Mill's more prescient pronouncements, he predicted that the Irish question would be solved when Irishmen finally recognized that union with England was in their own best interest. After all, "there is now next to nothing, except the memory of the past, and the difference in the predominant religion, to keep apart two races perhaps the most fitted of any two in the world to be the completing counterpart of one another."[99] As Irish history would make abundantly apparent, memories of the past and religious differences were more than enough to prevent Ireland from being part of a multi-national British state. The same was true for much of Eastern Europe, where religious differences and historical memories significantly inhibited the kind of voluntary integration that Mill expected.

Mill's confidence that both nationality and freedom could prevail was based on his assumption that the national state was the natural political unit in the modern world. When there is a strong "sentiment of nationality," Mill believed, then there is "a prima facie case for unity of all members of the nationality under the same government, and a government to themselves apart." Mill's expectation was shared by most of his liberal contemporaries. "Every nation is called and justified to form a state," wrote the Swiss liberal theorist J. C. Bluntschli in 1875. "Every nation a state, every state a national being." Max Weber, who was both a fervent German nationalist and a somewhat skeptical analyst of nationhood, described the nation as "a community of sentiment, which could find its adequate expression in state of its own, and which thus normally strives to create one." In the early twentieth century, Ernest Barker was convinced that "just as the national readily passes from the area of social expression into the political form of a state, so a state . . . must necessarily seek to make itself coextensive with a nation."[100] Most theorists of nations and nationalism continue to take the coincidence of nations and state for granted: in Ernst Gellner's influential formulation, the essence of nationalism is the conviction "that the political and the national unit should be congruent."[101]

In nineteenth-century Europe, there seemed to be good reason for Western European liberals to believe that nations and states would eventually cohere. Between 1859 and 1871, Germans and Italians created national states, ending centuries of political fragmentation. Further east, various nationalities, aided by self-interested patrons among the great powers, were able to carve sovereign states out of the multinational Ottoman Empire. Nonetheless, Europe did not become a continent of coherent nation states. If we look closely at the geopolitical map, it is hard to resist John Breuilly's conclusion that the apparent fusion of states and nations is the result of "a sleight of hand dependent on using the same term, 'nation,' in different ways."[102] Like many acts of political legerdemain, this one served particular interests: in this case, states that claimed to act for the nation and national movements that sought to press their claims for a state of their own.

We will return to the problematic relationship of nations and states in chapter 4, but for now let us conclude our account of the contested politics of nationhood by considering the Habsburg Empire, perhaps nineteenth-century Europe's most significant multinational state.[103] The monarchy played a crucial part in the creation of the European order in 1815 and in its destruction a century later. Equally important for our purposes is the fact that, from the later nineteenth century to the present, the Habsburg experience shaped the way some of nationhood's most prominent and influential analysts viewed their subject. To cite just a few examples: Otto Bauer, born in Vienna, 1881, and died in Paris, 1938; Hans Kohn, born in Prague, 1891, died in Philadelphia, 1971; Ernest Gellner, born in Paris, 1925, lived in Prague until 1939, spent most of career in Britain, and died in Prague, 1995; Eric Hobsbawm, born in Egypt, 1917, spent his childhood in Vienna and Berlin before moving to Britain, where he died in 2012.[104]

The Habsburgs ruled over a classic example of a composite state that had been assembled from territories acquired over centuries. These territories included a wide variety of linguistic, religious, and historical communities that made up what Robert Evans called "an agglutination of bewilderingly heterogeneous elements."[105] In the eighteenth century, the Habsburgs attempted to manage their heterogeneous realm by developing the kind of governmental infrastructure that was increasingly necessary for a modern state: maps, censuses, laws codes, and administrative institutions. Not without difficulty, the dynasty was able to deploy enough political and military resources to survive the revolutionary storms at the end of the eighteenth century and to emerge in 1815 as one of the five great powers that dominated the European system. State-making brought the empire's various populations together but also made them more aware of their differences, setting in motion that familiar dialectic of inclusion and exclusion, which took place on a particularly diverse ethnic and political landscape. Both dimensions of this dialectic were intensified by the fitful democratization of public life that followed the failed midcentury revolutions. In the Austrian half of the empire, as in the rest of Europe, elections became an important part of this process; here too the government eventually yielded to pressures for expanding the suffrage, first to men without property in 1897, and then in 1907 to all males. Ethnic identity may not have been the only, and perhaps not always the most important, source of political alignments, but in its final decades, the empire's national differences sharpened political and social divisions both in representative bodies and in the streets.

By the end of the nineteenth century, the alternatives facing the monarchy's different nationalities resemble Albert Hirschman's well-known trio of responses to institutional crisis: "exit, voice, and loyalty."[106] Loyalty, which Hirschman regarded as the willingness to remain within the institution, was often closely connected to what he called "voice," that is, the opportunity to influence the institution's direction. Loyalty bought with voice was the option extracted by the Hungarians in 1867 when, twenty years after their efforts to exit had been repressed following the failed revolution of 1848, they accepted a compromise arrangement that gave them control over a part of the empire (including several other nationalities) and also a veto role in determining foreign and military policy.[107] Loyalty, with or without voice, appeared to be the only option for the monarchy's smaller national groups for whom exit did not seem to be a viable alternative. The loyalty option was more difficult to accept for nationalities that felt a certain connection with national communities outside the empire: Poles, who still dreamed of a rebirth of their historic nation; Italians, who after 1866 could look to an Italian national state; and South Slavs, who were divided by religion, but might still be drawn to the kingdom of Serbia. And finally, there were the Czechs, whose historical memories of the national autonomy that had been lost in the seventeenth century were activated by contemporary struggles over language, educational institutions, and local government. The conflict between Czechs and Germans in the late nineteenth and early twentieth centuries was a classic example of how ethnic antagonisms could encourage, and be encouraged by, social, economic, and cultural differences.

Was "exit" the only alternative for the Habsburg nationalities? After the empire was defeated in 1918, it certainly seemed that its dissolution had been inevitable. Perhaps. It is nonetheless worth noting that before 1914, even when national tensions seemed to be increasing, most of the Habsburgs' subjects could not imagine a world without the empire. In states, unlike the economic institutions that Hirschman studied, the price of exit is often prohibitively high. If the empire had had the gift of time, might it have reached some kind of accommodation with its various national communities? Or was Mill right when he argued that democratization doomed multinational states? This is not the sort of question to which we can expect a definitive answer. One thing does seem certain: the timing and character of the Habsburg monarchy's dissolution were determined by disruptive forces in the international environment rather than by the irresistible power of national movements.[108]

This environment is the subject of chapter 4, in which we will see how modern states and national communities shaped, and were shaped by, a new kind of international society. It was here, in the rough and tumble world of international politics, that both the strengths and vulnerabilities of the nation state became vividly apparent.

CHAPTER FOUR

A Society of Nation States

In the modern political order, we expect domestic and foreign affairs to belong to different realms, based on different calculations, and governed by different sorts of rules. International law, for example, which attempts to regulate the relationship among states, has a radically different character from the laws that govern a state's domestic politics. Yet although there are obvious and important differences between foreign and domestic politics, people's expectations about international politics are closely connected to their expectations about the nature of states and nations. Like Janus, the modern state has two faces, one looking inward, the other outward, but both faces are part of the same body, united by similar political ideas and experiences. To paraphrase what Clausewitz once said about war, international politics has a grammar, but not a logic, of its own.[1]

People's expectations about the political order shape the principles of legitimacy that define membership in international society (states, with clearly defined boundaries, constitutions, and administrations) and how such members should behave (which increasingly involves some degree of popular consent).[2] An influential school of international relations scholars insists that such considerations about legitimacy have no place in international affairs.[3] Only "power" and "national interests" really matter. In fact, we can no more banish questions of value from politics than we can create a purely descriptive language. Words like "power" and "national interests" always carry hidden normative weight. As Isaiah Berlin reminds us, "Those who are concerned with human affairs are committed to the use of the moral categories and concepts which normal language incorporates and expresses."[4]

In relationships among states, however, even more than in domestic politics, there is a gap between legitimacy and action, principle and practice, how people ought to behave and how they do. In his important study of sovereignty, Stephen Krasner referred to this gap as "organized hypocrisy." This is a useful concept if we remember the great seventeenth-century moralist Rochefoucauld's famous definition of hypocrisy as the homage vice pays to virtue.[5] Hypocrisy requires vice *and* virtue, and nowhere is this more apparent than in the society of states, where conduct is influenced by both norms and deviancy, principles of legitimacy and imperatives of power.[6]

This chapter examines the evolution of people's expectations about the society of states from the end of the eighteenth century to the present. At the heart of our story will be two periods of international violence and domestic upheaval: the wars of the French Revolution and Napoleon from 1792 to 1815; and the era of war and revolution between 1914 and 1945. These crises accelerated and intensified structural changes in the political order, thereby transforming people's expectations about states, nations, and international society. Although the modern political order had a global dimension by the end of the eighteenth century, only in the second half of the twentieth did political institutions and expectations become, for the first time in human history, truly worldwide. With the creation of this global order, that is, the world in which we now live, the chapter will conclude.

STATES AND NATIONS IN THE LONG NINETEENTH CENTURY

In 1795, Immanuel Kant, Europe's greatest living philosopher, published an essay entitled "On Perpetual Peace." Three things about this remarkable treatise make it an appropriate place to begin our consideration of the modern society of states. First, Kant took for granted that the international order was based on states, not princes. The state, he wrote, was "a society of men, which no one other than itself can command or dispose of." Since it was not a composite of princely possessions, the state's territory could not be acquired by purchase, inheritance, or gift. Like earlier theorists, he used an organic metaphor for the state, but instead of a body that united different parts, his was a tree, a living thing with its own deep roots and distinctive identity: "To graft it on to another state as if it were a shoot is to terminate its existence as a moral personality."[7] Second, Kant recognized that domestic and international politics were inseparable. The first step toward an enduring peace was the creation of what he called "republican constitutions," polities that were based on freedom and legal equality. Finally, Kant argued that in a society of republican states, war would cease being an unavoidable evil. He predicted that in this new, peaceful world states would no longer face one another like gladiators with weapons at the ready; they would be equal and at the same time interdependent members of a new sort of international society. This dream of perpetual peace would take many different forms in the years ahead, but it would remain among the modern political order's most persistent visions of a better future, albeit a vision that coexisted with, indeed was often nourished by, an expanding arc of international violence that extended from the second half of eighteenth century into the first half of the twentieth.[8]

When Kant set forth his vision of perpetual peace, the European society of states was midway into four tumultuous decades of ruthless aggression, endemic violence, and territorial instability.[9] After a brief period of relative calm following what Winston Churchill called "the first world war" (known in Europe as the Seven Years' War; in America as the French and Indian War, 1756–63), a series of crises engulfed Europe. In 1772, for example, the three eastern monarchies—Russia, Austria, and Prussia—seized and divided territory belonging to the Polish Commonwealth; this was the first of three predatory actions that would eventually result in Poland's extinction as a state. Writing in 1862, Lord Acton claimed that the partition of Poland signaled the end of "the ancient European system" and the start of "a new world [that] was rising in its place."[10] Beginning in the 1770s, a number of other conflicts—in Britain's American colonies, the Low Countries, the Holy Roman Empire, and along the always volatile Ottoman frontier—generated a series of international crises that by 1787 threatened to plunge the European powers into a new "world war."[11]

After 1789, these crises were absorbed into the revolutionary maelstrom in France that helped to transform Europeans' expectations about the political order. From April 1792, when France declared war on Austria, until Napoleon's final defeat at Waterloo in June 1815, the European states were, with a few scattered intermissions, continually at war with one another. These were not "tournament wars" fought by dynastic states for honor, glory, or territorial expansion, but a new kind of war that required the mobilization of men, materials, and national engagement far beyond the capacities of states in the ancien régime.[12]

Both the revolutionaries and their antagonists saw that revolution and war, that is, violent struggles against enemies at home and abroad, were inseparable. Revolution, Robespierre declared in 1793, "is the war waged by liberty against its enemies."[13] The purpose of war, the revolutionaries believed, was the defense of liberty at home and the spread of liberty abroad. General Bonaparte, at the start of his extraordinary career as a revolutionary warlord, told the Italian people in April 1796 that "the French army comes to break your chains. . . . We are waging war as generous enemies, and we wish only to crush the tyrants who enslave you."[14]

From the other end of the political spectrum, Edmund Burke agreed that war and revolution had become part of the same historical process. That was why, as Burke wrote in 1796, the struggle against revolutionary France was "a war of a peculiar nature. It is not with an ordinary community, which is hostile or friendly as passion or as interest may veer about; not with a State which makes war through wantonness and abandons it through lassitude." This enemy was an "armed doctrine" that might at the moment be based in France but had disciples and therefore potential allies everywhere. With such an enemy, Burke insisted, negotiations were useless because true peace was impossible. The only option was to destroy this radically new kind of regime, one that "has never been hitherto seen, or even imagined, in Europe."[15] In Burke's somewhat overheated prose we find what would become an all too familiar call for war against an ideology—an "armed doctrine"—rather than against a state. In the twentieth century, when it would be greatly amplified by technological progress and ideological commitment, the destructive power of this kind of war would surpass anything Robespierre or Burke could have imagined.

Although it took them longer than one might have expected, the leaders of the states allied against revolutionary France and its successor, Napoleon, eventually realized that the link between war and revolution had transformed not only the scale but also the stakes of battle. They saw ancient polities such as the Holy Roman Empire vanish, vast territories change hands, the social order itself put at risk. Domestic upheavals, which had once been regarded as episodes in the life of a particular state, were now a permanent part of the historical process. To survive the perils of the revolutionary age, statesmen recognized that it would be necessary to avoid the kind of conflict that had disrupted European political life for the past quarter century. They did not, of course, embrace Kant's vision of perpetual peace; war remained a possibility for which they had to be prepared. But going to war against one another was no longer an ordinary part of the life of European states; armed conflict among states was always possible, but it was something to be avoided or contained.

These new attitudes about war produced a combination of ideas and institutions that transformed the European society of states.[16] The nature of this transformation was foreshadowed in the peace treaty that was signed by Napoleon's victorious opponents after his first defeat and exile in 1814. Here the allies promised to "make every effort to preserve, not only among themselves, but also, as far as it depends on them, among all the states of Europe, the good harmony and understanding that is so necessary for its repose."[17] Harmony and understanding were not always easy to achieve when the great powers (Britain, Russia, Austria, and Prussia, eventually joined by France) met in Vienna a few months later. Indeed, there were moments when it appeared that the allies, having finally defeated Napoleon, would turn against one another. But in the end they were able to establish some measure of order for a continent that had endured a quarter century of unprecedented social, political, and international upheaval.[18]

In 1815, most statesmen assumed that the international order would depend on these five great powers. Their distinctive status had been tentatively defined in the last third of the eighteenth century and would remain a feature of the European system until the second decade of the twentieth. The emergence and, even more importantly, the longevity of this international hierarchy was the result of those new ways of imagining and organizing states that we examined in chapter 2. To qualify as a Great Power, it was necessary to have a sufficiently large resource base (wealth, territory, population) and a sufficiently efficient infrastructure with which to create and sustain a modern military establishment. States without these qualifications were permanently consigned to a secondary rank, even if—as was the case with Spain, the Netherlands, and the Ottoman Empire—they had once been major players on the international stage. At the end of the century, two additional states, the United States and Japan, had the potential to be great powers, but neither was part of the European society of states, which before 1914 remained where the global hierarchy was defined and had to be sustained.[19]

After Napoleon's defeat, some statesmen hoped that, by acting in concert, the Great Powers could impose an enduring stability on international society. In 1818, for example, Lord Castlereagh spoke of having a "concert" that would give "to the Great Powers an efficiency and almost simplicity of a single state."[20] Needless to say, this did not happen. After a promising beginning, the concert was undermined by changing governments, competing interests, and external pressures. Yet at critical moments in the decades after 1815, the powers managed to get European states to cooperate either by using the mechanisms of everyday diplomacy or, on special occasions, by summoning congresses (for example, in Paris in 1856 at the end of the Crimean War; in Berlin in 1878 following the Russo-Turkish War) or conferences (Berlin in 1884–85 on Africa; London in 1912–13 after the Balkan Wars) to manage conflicts or impose settlements.[21] In history, as in nature, our eye is attracted to motion, but it is also important to note those many occasions when something did *not* happen: sparks that did not ignite, potential turning points at which the course of events did not turn.[22]

With all its flaws and inconsistencies, the order created in 1814–15 worked remarkably well, at least for European states, even as the rest of the world remained a very violent place. Between 1815 and 1914, Europe did not experience the kind of global conflict that had twice before (1756–63 and 1792–1815) engaged all the major powers. Although every Great Power did go to war in the 1850s and 1860s, only once (in the rather odd conflict fought in the Crimea) were more than two involved. Overall, significantly fewer Europeans died in battle in the nineteenth century than they had in the eighteenth century or would in the twentieth.[23]

Despite what is sometimes argued, the purpose of statecraft in 1815 was not a "restoration" of the old regime. Some dynasties—most importantly, the Bourbons in France—were restored, but most of the regimes swept away by the revolutionary tsunami were not. A majority of former rulers who showed up in Vienna with the hope of getting back what they had lost left the city disappointed. The goal of the peacemakers was not restoration but stability, a stability that would rest on a set of ideas and institutions flexible enough to limit, absorb, or at least contain the conflicts that might, if allowed free rein, once again threaten the political and social order.

Perhaps the best example of Great Powers' approach to international politics in 1815 was their answer to the German question, which was then, as it would be in 1918 and 1945, a key to a European peace. No effort was made to restore either the Holy Roman Empire or the scores of sovereign and semisovereign principalities that it had once sustained. Many of the territorial changes that had been imposed by Napoleon survived, as did most of the middle-sized states he had constructed as a buffer along France's eastern frontier. The Congress created a Confederation of German States that was supposed to balance the influence of Austria and Prussia, the two major German powers, with the interests of their weaker neighbors. Although it was guaranteed by the Great Powers, the Confederation depended on the willingness of Prussia and Austria to cooperate. It lasted as long as they worked together; it collapsed in 1866, when Prussia decided to go its own way.[24]

As in every political order, the stability of the nineteenth-century society of states required a shared sense of legitimacy. In one important respect, the post-1815 order did resemble the ancien régime: in both, dynastic ties were essential for legitimizing power. Except for a few cities (and that perennial exception, Switzerland), most European states were monarchies. In 1815, this included all five of the Great Powers; France became a republic in 1871, but the others remained dynastic states until the end of the First World War. An even more striking indication of the longevity of monarchical institutions was the fact that every one of the new states created in Europe during the long nineteenth century acquired a monarch, usually selected from one of the smaller German dynasties that had dominated the export market for kings and consorts since the eighteenth century.[25]

In both domestic and international politics, heredity may have been necessary for legitimacy, but by the nineteenth century it was no longer sufficient. As we have seen, a legitimate state also had to be legible, with clearly defined borders, published laws, and effective administrative institutions. The society of European states was no longer a collection of monarchs, but became—in Hedley Bull's concise formulation—"a body of independent political communities linked by common rules and institutions as well as by contact and interaction."[26] Legitimate membership was determined by legal status and effective control over territory, not divine sanctions or a hereditary title. Legitimacy came neither from God nor from nature; it was what the society of states—and this often meant the five Great Powers—determined it to be.[27]

Although the nineteenth-century society of states was dominated by the Great Powers, in other ways membership tended to become more formally equal, at least for those entities that qualified as sovereign states, which meant European states, former European colonies in North and South America, and a few other non-European states that had managed to preserve their autonomy.[28] There was, of course, no international representative institution such as the League of Nations, but individual states did join an expanding network of organizations that tried to regulate aspects of international life, such as with maritime law, postal regulations, and time zones. In 1899 and 1907, states also participated as equals in two conferences at The Hague devoted to establishing rules for the prevention and limitation of international violence. By 1909, there were 37 intergovernmental and 176 nongovernmental international organizations, numbers that would dramatically increase in the decades to follow.[29]

Since sovereignty was now based on bounded territoriality and expressed in laws and political institutions, the geopolitical configuration of international society tended to become *relatively* more stable. Within Europe (but not, of course, in the rest of the world) when territorial alterations occurred, they were regarded as extraordinary events that needed to be justified and explained, not as an inevitable component of international life. One reason why Lord Acton found the partition of Poland in the eighteenth century so shocking was because he saw it through the lens of nineteenth-century expectations that Europe should be composed of a relatively stable collection of sovereign states.[30]

After 1815, popular consent, which was becoming the foundation for legitimate authority within states, also had a powerful impact on the international order. Increasingly, territorial alterations within Europe had to be justified by claims to national self-determination. Coming to terms with these claims, which meant trying to reconcile them with the territorial sovereignty of states, was, and still is, the most enduring source of conflict within the modern society of states.[31]

In the nineteenth century, among the first and most celebrated examples of a nationally motivated challenge to the established order was the Greek war for independence from the Ottoman Empire. Every nation is

the imagined projection of a community. In the Greek case, the act of national imagination was particularly challenging since the Greek population,
which had been scattered throughout the eastern Mediterranean for more
than two thousand years, shared very little. Throughout their long and
painful struggle for national independence, the leaders of the Greek revolt
remained deeply divided by social, regional, and personal differences. And
even after finally achieving nationhood, the Greeks had to decide which
of several versions of their language should be the official one. Their sense
of ethnic identity was religious, the status that made them a separate
community—sometimes privileged, sometimes discriminated against—
within the multinational Ottoman realm.[32]

In 1821, when some Greeks revolted against Ottoman rule, the Sultan's government responded violently, which set in motion what would
become a familiar cycle of reciprocally reinforcing rebellion and repression. In part because of European elites' reverence for the cultural heritage
of classical Greece (with which most modern Greeks had little connection), in part because of Europeans' sympathy for their fellow Christians,
the Greek rebellion found widespread public support in many states. In
1824, Lord Byron, who would personify the philhellenic movement among
European intellectuals, died while aiding the rebels in Missolonghi; that
same year, Delacroix's great painting *Massacre at Chios* was displayed in
the Paris Salon.[33] The enthusiasm of people such as Byron and Delacroix
had some influence on policymakers in the Great Powers, but their most
important reason for eventually (and for some of them, reluctantly) intervening in the Greek revolt was the fear that it would destabilize the eastern Mediterranean.

In May 1832, the powers recognized the independence of a Greek state
in a treaty that begins with the following lines: "The Courts of Great
Britain, France, and Russia, exercising the power conveyed to them by the
Greek Nation, to make choice of a Sovereign for Greece, raised to the rank
of an Independent State . . . have resolved to offer the Crown of the new
Greek State to the Prince Frederick Otto of Bavaria."[34] Here we see the
tangled threads from which nineteenth-century expectations about international legitimacy were woven: the alleged authority of the "Greek Nation," the distinctive responsibility of the Great Powers, the importance of
creating an "independent state" (a provision not without irony considering
that the powers imposed a ruler on the Greek nation), and, finally, the

legitimacy provided by a monarch, who was supposed to establish both political stability and a link to the larger society of states.

Behind these carefully chosen phrases was the Great Powers' primary goal, which was to create stability and avoid conflict, a goal that they accomplished, as so often happened, at the expense of a weaker state, in this case the Ottoman Empire. In the decades that followed, the Greek pattern would be repeated with several other nationalities within the Ottomans' European territories. Each had its own, often painful, history of rebellion, repression, and Great Power intervention.[35]

Like Greece, an independent Belgium was also the result of internal revolt and international engagement. In 1830, fifteen years after it had been created in Vienna, the Kingdom of the Low Countries (including what is now the Netherlands and Belgium) came apart. After a year of unrest and uncertainty, the representatives of the Great Powers met in London and, "taking into account the events in the Low Countries since September 1830 [when the revolt began] and seeking to avoid having these events disrupt the general peace," signed a treaty that created an independent and perpetually neutral Belgian kingdom. Included in the treaty was a provision that allowed people to move between Belgium and the Netherlands without legal or economic sanctions. This implicit acknowledgment that some degree of ethnic cohesion was important for political order was a benign form of the population transfers that would often be part of nation-building in the modern world.[36]

In 1848, the European order was challenged by an epidemic of popular uprisings that began in the Kingdom of Naples and eventually spread throughout the European continent. From the English Channel to the Russian border, a diverse collection of popular movements demanded political reforms that, in the German and Italian lands and also in the Habsburg Empire, included the creation of new national states. Within a few months, these revolutionary energies began to dissipate; within a year they were defeated, in part because of the divisions among the revolutionaries themselves, in part because the forces of order recovered the ability and will to react.[37]

Although the revolutionaries did not achieve their aspirations for radical change, these midcentury upheavals did intensify the developments we described in chapters 2 and 3: throughout Europe, states built stronger infrastructures in the 1850s, and, after a brief period of repression, national movements became more active.[38] At the same time, a new generation of leaders came to power who were prepared to take risks that Metternich and his contemporaries had done their best to avoid. The result was a series of wars: France, Britain, and the Ottoman Empire against Russia in 1854–56; Savoy (allied with France) against Austria in 1859; Austria and Prussia against Denmark in 1864; Prussia against Austria in 1866; and a Prussian-led alliance of German states against France in 1870–71. From these wars, two new nation-states emerged, the Kingdom of Italy and the German Empire. Both were created at the initiative of states—Savoy in the Italian case, Prussia in the German—that claimed to be acting in the name of national self-determination.[39]

Did these developments, and especially the creation of a unified German nation-state, fundamentally change people's expectations about the European order? Many have thought so, both at the time and later. Benjamin Disraeli, for example, told the House of Commons in February 1871 that "the German Revolution" was a "greater political event than the French Revolution of the last century," adding that "there is not a diplomatic tradition which has not been swept away. You have a new world, new influences at work, new and unknown objects and dangers with which to cope."[40]

Given what we know is coming, it is difficult not to be impressed by Disraeli's prophetic powers. There is no doubt that the creation of a united Germany introduced a new, often destabilizing element into the society of European states. Nevertheless, it is important not to lose sight of the lines of continuity that run from 1815 through 1871 into the following decades. Most obviously, the five Great Powers all survived: their relative weight may have changed, but their special status did not. Moreover, the interstate violence of the 1850s and 1860s did not lead to a return of the endemic dynastic conflicts of the ancien régime or to the ideologically charged wars of the revolutionary era. Because the leaders of the major states continued to recognize that a European war would have unpredictable and potentially devastating consequences, they still believed that an important goal of international politics was to avoid armed conflicts among themselves. The eventual failure of their efforts should not obscure the fact that the powers managed to avoid a major European war for more than four decades after 1871.[41]

Until the European order collapsed in the summer of 1914, statesmen were usually able to fulfill what George Kennan once described as the purpose of diplomacy, which was not "to inhibit [the] process of change by imposing a legal straitjacket on it, but rather to facilitate it, to ease its transitions, to temper the asperities to which it often leads, to isolate and moderate the conflicts to which it gives rise, and to see that these conflicts do not assume forms too unsettling for international life in general."[42] In order to understand why the European society of states found this goal increasingly difficult—and eventually impossible—to achieve, we must turn our attention away from Europe and consider the changing relationship of Europeans to the rest of the world.

Throughout the nineteenth century, Europeans controlled a disproportionate share of the world's natural resources, productive capacity, and—perhaps most important—effective military power. In some places, they had used these advantages to conquer territories and exploit them directly; elsewhere their influence was more selective and indirect, involving the control of seaports, the imposition of favorable commercial arrangements, or the exercise of extraterritorial rights. The result of this complex process was one of world history's most significant developments: the gradual, uneven, but irresistible creation of a global system that was inherently unequal and intermittently violent. We should not underestimate the ability of the world's peoples to resist or adapt to this process, but the process itself was driven by—and largely operated for the benefit of—Europeans. By the eve of the Great War, 42 percent of the world's land and 32 percent of its population were ruled by a colonial power. Imperial rule was often violent, but it was not just a matter of military conquest; it also included a combination of political, economic, and cultural penetration and appropriation. "Empire building," A. G. Hopkins pointed out, "was an exercise in compulsory globalization."[43]

Europeans legitimized their conquest of the world with a widely accepted distinction between "civilized" and "uncivilized" states. Among civilized states, sovereignty and consent mattered; different rules applied to the rest of the world. It was a grave error, John Stuart Mill wrote in 1859, "to suppose that the same international customs, and the same rules of international morality, can obtain . . . between civilized nations and barbarians." In dealing with one another, Mill goes on, civilized nations have "sacred duties" that require a mutual recognition of "independence and nationality."

These duties do not apply to barbarians who "have no rights as a nation." To this Mill added a qualification, "except a right to such treatment as may, at the earliest possible period, fit them for becoming one." The historical record suggests that this qualification did not play a major part in Europeans' relationships with the non-European world.[44]

In practice, the distinction between civilized and barbarian nations was not sharply defined, but rather ranged along a spectrum. At one end were established states such as the Ottoman Empire, which had been included in the society of states in the Treaty of Paris that ended the Crimean War in 1856. The Ottomans, however, were hardly equal members of the international community since they had been forced to accept limitations on their sovereignty (including management of the public debt and a special legal status for foreigners) that no European state would have been expected to tolerate. In addition to the Ottomans, there were many other states (including 550 princely states in British India) that retained some measure of sovereign independence in return for varying degrees of accommodation to European control. At the other end of the spectrum were the inhabitants of tribal areas—the American west, the Russian steppes, the Pacific islands, much of Africa—whose lands could be taken, often by violence that was sometimes masked with token payments or unequal treaties.[45] Some referred to these parts of the world as "terra nullius," land that belonged to no one; more often they were regarded as what the international lawyer Sir Mark Lindley called "backward territory," that is, "territory inhabited by natives as low on the scale of civilization as those of Central Africa."[46] The lower on the "scale of civilization" a land was thought to be, the more readily it could be seized, exchanged, bought, and sold. In the case of the Belgian Congo, it was still possible to think of this territory (and its inhabitants) as the private property of an individual who could exercise the power of both proprietor and sovereign.[47]

Imperial ambitions had always been the source of some deep rivalries among colonial powers. Until the end of the eighteenth century, competition for overseas territory had led to violent conflicts between European states, as can be seen, for example, in the long Anglo-French struggle for North America. After 1815, colonial rivalries continued and on occasion might bring the powers close to war. Nevertheless, although European states were more than willing to use violence to conquer or control their overseas territories or to force non-European states to comply with their demands, they were not prepared to engage in a European war for an additional piece of Africa or Asia. In the end, therefore, participants in colonial disputes always backed down, sometimes with reluctance, usually with relief. One of the reasons why the nineteenth-century system lasted for so long was the European states' ability to separate these overseas rivalries from their core relationships.

By the end of the century, however, European statesmen found it increasingly difficult to insulate their core relationships from colonial conflicts. In the first place, the competition for colonies had intensified. In part this was because three new players—Japan, the United States, and the German Empire—had come on the scene. All three had fought civil wars during the 1860s, consolidated their domestic regimes in the 1870s, and then built blue-water navies and began to acquire overseas possessions in the 1880s and 1890s. At the same time the number of imperial powers grew, the territory available for colonization shrank. Between 1876 and 1915, one-fourth of the earth had been distributed or redistributed among the Great Powers. Africa was now almost completely under European domination. Europeans, together with the United States and Japan, had increased their holdings in the Pacific by seizing formerly independent islands (Hawaii, for example, became a U.S. territory in 1898) and expanding at the expense of the Chinese Empire (Germany acquired a base on Kiautschou Bay, Japan occupied Korea and Formosa).[48]

As these colonial empires grew, many contemporaries realized that because the world's frontiers were closing, opportunities for further expansion were disappearing. Lord Rosebery, for example, told the Royal Colonial Institute in 1893 that the British Empire had to keep expanding while it still had the chance. Because land on earth was limited, Rosebery argued, "we are engaged at the present moment, in the language of mining, in 'pegging our claims' for the future."[49] Shortly before his death in 1902, that quintessential imperialist Cecil Rhodes lamented that "the world is nearly parceled out, and what there is left is being divided up, conquered, and colonized."[50] International politics now took place on a global stage where the struggle for power became a zero-sum game and every local conflict might have repercussions throughout the system.

Among those who saw the global significance of this closing of geopolitical space was the British geographer Halford Mackinder. "From the present time forth," he wrote in 1904, "we shall again have to deal with a closed political system, and none the less that it will be one of worldwide scope. Every explosion of social force . . . will be sharply re-echoed from the far side of the globe and weak elements in the political and economic organism of the world will be shattered in consequence." Especially vulnerable to an "explosion of social forces" were those traditional states that occupied what the historian John Darwin called "the vast uneasy borderland of Europe's global colonialism."[51] Until the end of the nineteenth century, many of these states had managed to survive the expansion of European power but now their sovereign status was coming under vastly increased pressure. Some of them—Burma and Hawaii, for example—were taken over by imperial predators. In three others—the Persian, Chinese, and Ottoman Empires—there were revolutions whose leaders wanted to introduce changes at home to help them defend or regain the nation's independence.

We are still dealing with the consequences of these three revolutions, but in the early twentieth century, the most significant was the so-called Young Turk revolution of 1908. Instead of the era of reform and regeneration for which its leaders aimed, the revolution of 1908 was followed by a period of instability that whetted the appetites of potential predators. In 1911, Italy launched an unprovoked attack on the Ottomans in an attempt to conquer the North African province of Libya. Eventually, the European powers managed to impose a settlement that stopped the war, but not before the Balkan states, encouraged by Russia, formed an alliance against the Ottomans. Two wars followed, both marked by extraordinary brutality among soldiers and civilians. Once again, the powers intervened—it was the European concert's final attempt to restore some measure of stability in an increasingly volatile region. The big winner of the Balkan Wars was the Kingdom of Serbia, a client of Russia and an active rival of the Habsburg monarchy.[52]

The nineteenth-century international system ended where it began, in Vienna. In 1815, Metternich had worked to create a set of institutions that he hoped would provide the kind of order and stability that Europe, and especially the Habsburgs' multinational realm, needed to survive.[53] In the following decades, the price of survival increased, while the monarchy's capacity to pay steadily declined.

The weakest and most vulnerable of the great powers, the Habsburg monarchy became, both geographically and institutionally, the link between the core of the European system and the embattled empires throughout the non-European world. Since the middle of the nineteenth century, the monarchy had survived, and thus had contributed to the survival of the European system, by making a series of painful concessions: accepting defeat on the Italian peninsula and in the German Confederation, yielding to Hungarian demands for semiautonomy, and trying to placate other dissent groups throughout the empire.[54]

By the time Archduke Franz Ferdinand, the heir to the Habsburg throne, was assassinated by a Serbian-sponsored terrorist in June 1914, many decision-makers in Vienna had concluded that there was no more room for retreat. Instead, they decided to do what other states (Japan against China, the United States against Spain, Britain against the Boer Republic, and, most recently, Italy against the Ottoman Empire) had done with increasing frequency around the turn of the century: impose their will on a weaker rival with the threat or deployment of violence. To the war party in Vienna, this meant using Franz Ferdinand's murder as an excuse to restore the monarchy's authority along its southern flank by disciplining Serbia and thereby consolidating the monarchy's hold over its own South Slav population. This decision began the chain of events that produced what statesmen since 1815 had most wanted to avoid: a war among all of Europe's Great Powers.

A WORLD MADE BY WAR, 1914–1945

Like many events that fundamentally change the direction of history, the outbreak of war in 1914 came as a surprise when it happened, and then, after the fact, seemed inevitable. Both reactions tell us something important about the war's origins and character. Contemporaries were right to be surprised: a European war need not have happened, at least not in the summer of 1914 and perhaps not at all; how, why, when, and where the war began were the results of a series of decisions, many of them mistakes and miscalculations that could have been avoided. Although statesmen's individual decisions led to war in the summer of 1914, the international conflicts that created the context for their actions had been around for decades.[55] Moreover, the war that their decisions produced was shaped by deeply rooted attitudes and institutions. Without the governmental infrastructure and national communities that had been created over the previous two centuries, European governments could not have fought a war that transformed millions of people's expectations about states, nations, and the society of nation states.[56]

When European states made a new kind of war in 1914, that war helped to make a new kind of European state. It did not take long for statesmen to realize that the war they had started would be bigger, last longer, and cause more destruction than anyone had imagined. (If they had known what was coming, would any decision-maker have acted as they did in the summer of 1914?) As the fighting dragged on, sustaining the war required that states vastly increase their capacity to mobilize their population, extract resources, and regulate social life. Armies of unprecedented size had to be raised, trained, deployed, and supplied; casualties had to be treated, fatalities identified, their families notified, their place in the ranks filled with new recruits. To do these things, states had to know more about their population, expand their ability to communicate, and, when necessary, strengthen their powers of enforcement. Every belligerent had to find ways of harnessing its economy to the war effort. That meant imposing controls on the production and distribution of material directly connected to the war and eventually on practically everything else. Because total war required a total commitment of resources, governments issued a dense web of rules on work and leisure, including what factories could produce and how long pubs could serve alcohol. The war did not create the modern state, but it did accelerate its growth and magnify people's expectations about what their governments could and should be able to do.

The war also intensified the interaction between the expansion of state power and the growth of national consciousness. At first, most national communities supported their governments. We should not overestimate the breadth of popular enthusiasm for the war, even in its earliest stages, but there is no doubt that a widespread sense of national cohesion enabled the belligerents to mobilize their armed forces and, at least for a while, to justify the massive costs in blood and treasure that the war imposed. This was true in Britain, which expanded its professional army with a flood of volunteers, and also in the Habsburg monarchy, where every nationality filled its enlistment quotas and seemed willing to fight and die for the fatherland.

As the pressures of war intensified, the interplay between inclusion and exclusion that had always been part of national politics became charged with wartime passions and infected by the willingness to employ violence that had begun to seep into public life. Proclamations of national solidarity, therefore, were soon accompanied by expressions of national hatred directed not just against foreign enemies, but also against those domestic opponents regarded as insufficiently patriotic: pacifists who opposed the war, "defeatists" who, as the war ground on, began to urge a negotiated peace, and a variety of alleged shirkers, profiteers, and enemy sympathizers. At the same time, a minority on the left came to the conviction that the war would never end without a domestic revolution that would drive the warmongers from power. The most dangerous enemy, some people began to recognize, was at home.

Every multinational state felt the tension between inclusion and exclusion: in 1916, for example, a small minority of Irish nationalists seized Dublin's main post office, thereby provoking a violent response from the authorities. This triggered a rampage of terror and counterterror that would eventually lead to civil war and political partition. National minorities were especially vulnerable to charges of disloyalty. Jews, who had often been scapegoats during times of crisis, once again became the targets of popular animosity. This newly energized and widespread anti-Semitism would become the most lethal of the many toxins that the war injected into European politics. During the war itself, the most vicious expression of exclusionary nationalism occurred in the Ottoman Empire, where the government used the war as an occasion to wage a genocidal campaign against Armenians and other Christian minorities.[57]

The war transformed people's expectations not only about states and nationhood but also about the society of states. In the 1790s, it had taken most statesmen years to realize that they were engaged in a new kind of war; in 1914, the values and assumptions that had sustained the nineteenth-century system seemed to evaporate in a few weeks. On September 22, 1914, Walter Hines Page, the U.S. ambassador in London, observed that "the whole world is bound to change as result of this war." Page, who was deeply hostile to Germany, believed that the German monarchy should be destroyed. He worried—as Burke had in 1796—that peace might come before the essential transformation of the enemy's domestic order had been accomplished.[58] Once the participants' war aims included the transformation of their enemy's domestic institutions, the chances for a negotiated peace significantly narrowed. Rather than just territorial advantage or national prestige, states now fought for their own survival, which increasingly seemed to require the destruction of their opponents.

About the same time that Page noted the end of the existing international order, Germany's chancellor, Theobald von Bethmann Hollweg, instructed his secretary to prepare a memorandum on the postwar world. The result, which Bethmann Hollweg announced to selected groups in September, called for a radical transformation of Europe under German leadership, including the imposition of a crippling postwar indemnity on France, significant territorial adjustments, a Central European economic community led by Germany, and the eventual redistribution of France's and Britain's African colonies. Historians have often overstated the significance of this document (misleadingly called the "September Program"). It was not a blueprint for German policy, but there is no doubt that the memorandum represented Bethmann Hollweg's realization that the old international system was obsolete.[59] This view was shared by policymakers in every belligerent state. In 1915, for example, Britain and France signed a secret treaty with Italy that called for a radical geopolitical reorganization of the eastern Mediterranean. In 1918, Germany and its allies imposed a peace treaty on the embattled Bolshevik regime that remade the political geography of Eastern Europe with a massive transfer of populations, territory, and resources.[60]

We have seen how nineteenth-century European states had tried, usually with some success, to settle disagreements among themselves at the expense of weaker states and colonized territories. After 1914, they turned against one another, seeking security by transforming the distribution of power within Europe itself. No European policymaker expected that after the war the society of states would be governed by the search for a collective stability that was based on balance and restraint. In the twentieth century's first half, the predatory appetites that Europeans had exported throughout the world came home.

By 1917, national minorities that had originally supported their governments became increasingly receptive to demands for political autonomy. In an effort to weaken their opponents, every belligerent supported these demands (for example, the Germans in Ireland, the British in the Ottoman Empire's Arab provinces). Especially in Eastern Europe, where the states' infrastructure buckled under the weight of the war effort, more and more national groups began to believe that they needed a state of their own to defend their community's identity and interests. The most vulnerable target of these movements was the Habsburg monarchy. The steady erosion of the Habsburg state's effectiveness during the war combined with the trauma of military defeat to create a situation in which, for the first time, self-appointed leaders of the monarchy's nationalities imagined a postimperial world.[61] Exiting the empire, which had once been unthinkable, now seemed unavoidable. As a result, the Habsburgs' realm, which had survived so many storms, eventually collapsed. It was the only one of the five great powers of 1815 to disappear completely from the global scene.

As one empire departed, two new ones arrived: Bolshevik Russia, still the embattled product of a revolutionary coup, and the United States, an established state that had only recently (and with some ambivalence) become a major actor on the world stage. Both countries were led by extraordinary men: V. I. Lenin and Woodrow Wilson, who brought into the war's last turbulent months radically new expectations about the international order. Lenin was convinced that a lasting peace required a global social revolution that would end, once and for all, the hegemony of imperialist capitalism. For Wilson, peace demanded the application of liberal institutions to the relationship among states: commercial freedom, open diplomacy, and an international representative institution. Together these reforms would create a society of states that reflected and reinforced democratic principles and practices.[62]

So different in background, experience, and political position, Lenin and Wilson nonetheless shared the conviction that self-determination was the essential source of legitimacy, both at home and abroad. Neither was consistent about what this meant in theory or practice. For Lenin, self-determination in international affairs was a way of undermining the existing order and opening the road to revolution. For Wilson, self-determination meant not revolution but a durable international order based on what he believed were the inherently peaceful instincts of people everywhere.

In part because it could mean so many different things, the ideal of self-determination had a global appeal, both to national minorities within Europe and to the inhabitants of European colonies, some of whom had been drawn into the war effort as workers, soldiers, or engaged observers.[63] In the winter of 1918–19, during the hopeful weeks following Germany's surrender, there were many who shared a Japanese statesman's conviction that a "politics based on the people, reflecting the will of the people, namely democracy, has, like a race to heaven, conquered the thought of the entire world."[64]

This seemed to be, to cite the title of Erez Manela's influential book, "the Wilsonian moment," when the U.S. president's eloquent if easily misinterpreted call for a democratic world order found eager audiences in Asia, Africa, and the Middle East.[65] In the second half of the twentieth century, some version of the Wilsonian vision would prevail in many parts of the world, as self-determination became the basis for global expectations about international legitimacy. But in 1919, as the hard-edged realities of the postwar world began to intrude, the difficulty of applying Wilsonian ideals became increasingly apparent. In the colonial realm, as in most of Central and Eastern Europe, the ideal of self-determination created expectations about the political order that could not be fulfilled. Almost everywhere, the immediate future was decided not by the energy and resolve of popular movements, but by those who controlled the instruments of effective force.[66]

Throughout the non-European world, popular movements were defeated and imperial authority was reasserted. In fact, after the war, the British Empire reached its peak, including 12.2 million square miles (just under a quarter of the earth's landmass), with 502 million inhabitants.[67] This expansion of European rule was not, however, simply a new chapter in the old story of nineteenth-century imperialism. Although temporarily repressed, independence movements remained, some of them now supported by the new regime in the Soviet Russia. The right of "civilized" states to rule "barbarians," which liberals such as John Stuart Mill had accepted without question, was still espoused by many Europeans, but a significant minority had begun to question the imperial project's justice and utility. To Paul Valéry, for example, the war revealed both the moral and material weakness of European civilization. We now know, he wrote in 1919, that we are mortal: "Will Europe now become what it is in reality—that is, a little promontory on the continent of Asia?"[68]

One sign of a growing uncertainty about the imperial project was the fact that the colonial territories lost by Germany and the Ottoman Empire were not simply taken by the winners, but rather had to be administered as "mandates" that were supposed to be governed in trust for their populations. On the one hand, mandates were merely a new way of exerting imperial power.[69] On the other hand, however, the mandate system acknowledged that the possession of colonial territories was subject to legal restrictions and mutual obligations. In that way, mandates foreshadowed those changes in global expectations that, a few decades later, would bring the age of imperialism to an end. In the years between the wars, however, mandates were part of rich diversity of power arrangements in what one contemporary called "a tropical luxuriance of political and legal organization, competence, and status."[70] After 1919, as in the nineteenth century, the society of independent states shared the world with colonial empires, protectorates, and a variety of other entities with highly qualified or ambiguous sovereignties.

Once the fog of postwar euphoria had lifted, it became apparent that neither Lenin nor Wilson had been able to remake the political order. Lenin's Bolsheviks survived to become the history's first—and for a quarter century, unique—socialist state, but only where the Red Army prevailed over local forces—for example, in Georgia, Armenia, and Ukraine—was a communist regime installed.[71] Elsewhere, there were Communist parties and underground organizations that could be irritating and disruptive, but never came close to taking power, either by electoral victories or successful subversion. Lenin's dream of a global revolution was deferred until after the century's second great war, when it was realized, incompletely and under very different conditions.[72]

Wilson, who for a few months had been the most popular statesman in the history of the world, could not impose his ideal of a liberal democratic peace, either at home, where the Senate rejected the peace treaty, or abroad, where his vision was contested by former friends and new enemies. Some elements of the Wilsonian moment did survive. For a decade or more, the League of Nations—without U.S. participation—kept alive many people's hope that states could find a way of settling their differences peacefully. In some parts of Europe, plebiscites were held to legitimate territorial transfers. And several of the states created in the aftermath of the war were compelled to sign treaties that guaranteed the rights of their minority populations. None of these innovations worked as the Wilsonians had hoped. All of them ultimately failed to protect minorities in the new states or to avoid another catastrophic international conflict.

The postwar political order did not conform to Lenin's hopes for a global proletarian revolution or Wilson's vision of liberal democracy, but they—and the movements they personified—did reflect a fundamental shift in how millions of people thought about states and nations. This shift involved, above all, a growing commitment to political democracy as the basis for legitimacy in both domestic institutions and the society of states.

In 1921, Lord Bryce began his survey of modern democracy by noting its extraordinary progress over the preceding century. Democracy, which Bryce defined as "the rule of the whole people expressing their sovereign will by their votes," had once been hated and feared, its practice limited to local governments and a few exceptional states like Switzerland. Now, he maintained, there was a "universal acceptance of democracy as the normal and natural form of government."[73] The Great War, Bryce was convinced, marked a significant milestone in the eventual triumph of democracy as the basis for legitimacy in the modern political order.

We can find expressions of this growing acceptance of democratic ideas everywhere we look in the years right after the war: in the expansion of suffrage (including giving women the right to vote and hold elected office); in the growth of participatory organizations of every sort; in the waning influence of dynastic institutions (none of the new states created after the war had monarchs); and, most significantly, in the national movements that proliferated across the continent, from the Atlantic to the Urals.[74] The expansion of participatory politics seemed to offer men and women a chance to shape their political destinies. At the same time, however, it was accompanied by political unrest, social conflict, economic dislocation, and national antagonism. In the impoverished and turbulent world created by the war, people's aspirations and frustrations made the establishment of effective democratic institutions all the more necessary and all the more difficult. Necessity and difficulty flowed from the same source: the need to create a *demos* strong and united enough to bear the weight of sovereignty. By 1918, more and more people agreed about the value of self-determination. They did not agree about who constituted this collective "self," that is, the political community, and how it should be defined and organized.[75]

Most of the states of western and northern Europe were able to respond to the challenges of democratic politics with some degree of success. They certainly did not accomplish this easily, as the troubled history of interwar democracy clearly demonstrates. Nevertheless, the governments of Britain, France, Belgium, and also the smaller states that had stayed out of the war, were strong enough to avoid being overwhelmed by the new political currents that swirled around them. With few exceptions (Ireland, Italy, and Spain, for example), western and northern Europe's geopolitical and institutional configurations proved remarkably resilient; in fact, they are much the same in the third decade of the twenty-first century as they were at the beginning of the twentieth. In Eastern Europe, the geopolitical landscape was (and in some places still is) much less stable. Here newly created or enlarged states had weaker infrastructures, fewer resources, and, most importantly, faced conflicts over both the legitimacy of their governments and the identity of their nations. Under the weight of these conflicts, all of these states (except Czechoslovakia) eventually succumbed to some form of authoritarian rule.[76] Germany, in this regard as in many others, occupied an intermediate position between East and West. Its democratic regime, created in 1919 in the midst of military defeat and social revolution, survived a series of crises that culminated in 1923, and thereafter was able to achieve a measure of stability. In the face of a new round of challenges generated by the worldwide depression of 1929, however, German democracy finally collapsed in 1933.

European politics between the wars is often seen as an epic contest between dictatorship and democracy. It seems to me that it is better understood as an endemic and multifaceted crisis of democracy, a crisis from which several different kinds of dictatorship emerged. Nowhere was this crisis more apparent than in the era's two totalitarian regimes, Soviet Communism and German National Socialism, which were both shaped by their relationship to democracy.[77] Of course, these regimes were tyrannies that celebrated the cult of a charismatic leader, repressed dissent, and enforced conformity. But unlike traditional dictatorships, there was a democratic element in both of them. Nazism and Communism demanded more than passive compliance; they needed enthusiastic supporters, not merely obedient subjects. That was why they created mass parties, organized their citizens in a variety of participatory institutions, and sought to mold their people's values and opinions through education, cultural activities, and propaganda. Both promised to create a "new man," and thus a new kind of community that would transcend social divisions, by destroying either alien races or class enemies.

Nazism and Bolshevism were necessarily, essentially modern, not simply because they could not have functioned without modern technology, but also because their tyrannical and democratic dimensions were intensified—if perverted—expressions of the governmental infrastructure and communitarian nationalism that characterized the modern political order. Although the Nazi and Soviet regimes seized and remained in power by means of lies, intrigue, and state-sponsored terror, they managed to acquire a broad basis of support in their own populations and to exert a sinister fascination for discontented people in other countries throughout the world. We recognize them, quite accurately, as the evil manifestations of modernity's deepest problems. To many contemporaries, however, these regimes appeared to be compelling answers to modernity's discontents. This "totalitarian temptation" remains the most disturbing example of what can happen when the political order fails to meet people's expectations.[78]

It is important not to overlook the significant differences between National Socialism and Soviet Communism. These differences were rooted in the social and economic institutions that the term *totalitarianism*—which is largely a political and psychological category—tends to ignore. In 1933, Hitler swiftly took control of Europe's richest and best-organized society. To be sure, Germany had been temporarily debilitated by economic depression and social unrest, but its potential power was still intact. The Bolsheviks, on the other hand, after seizing power in 1917, had to fight a bitter civil war in order to consolidate their rule over an economically underdeveloped society that had been devastated by almost a decade of foreign and internal strife. Nazism was grafted on to a modern social and economic system; Soviet Communism had to carry out a rapid modernizing revolution. Stalin was forced to create the kind of a society that Hitler had simply inherited.

The socioeconomic differences between the two totalitarian regimes had profound consequences for their leaders' view of the international system. Whatever Stalin's long-term goals might have been, his short-term foreign policy was based on his awareness of the Soviet Union's vulnerability, which led him to try to avoid international conflicts if at all possible. In the 1930s, therefore, he responded cautiously when confronted by two aggressively anticommunist powers, Germany in the west, Japan in the east. He recognized the threat these powers posed, but he was equally afraid that the capitalist states in the West (which he regarded as his implacable long-term antagonists) would draw him into conflicts with Germany and Japan, and then watch from the sidelines as they destroyed one another. Eventually, Stalin made agreements with both Japan and Germany: the former lasted from April 1941 until the final week of the war in 1945; the latter, signed in the summer of 1939, ended when Hitler invaded his still-compliant ally in June 1941.[79]

To protect his revolutionary regime, Stalin needed peace, at least in the short run; Hitler needed war to transform Germany's domestic institutions and international position. As soon as he had established control over Germany's well-organized state and highly developed economy, therefore, he embarked on a series of increasingly bold diplomatic moves and at the same time rebuilt a powerful military machine. For Hitler, war was necessary to achieve both territorial expansion and racial revolution, the inseparable goals that he had pursued since the beginning of his political career.[80]

The postwar society of states was singularly ill-equipped to respond to the challenges of a resurgent Germany. Of the Great Powers that had tried to establish a new order in 1815, one (the Habsburg monarchy) was gone, another (Russia) was isolated, and two others (Britain and France) had to confront an expanding set of global challenges with a steadily contracting supply of material resources. While the number of Great Powers shrank, the number of small, fragile states grew, most of them recently assembled from the wreckage of Europe's multinational empires. In 1914, there had been six small states in Eastern Europe; in 1920, there were thirteen, stretching from the Baltic to the Balkans; by 1923, 80 million (out of a total of 104 million) people in Eastern Europe lived in a new state.[81] Almost all of these states were weakened by unresolved foreign conflicts and deeply rooted social and ethnic divisions. Nevertheless, despite these inherent tensions at home and abroad, most Europeans were eager to avoid another devastating war. In 1938, when Neville Chamberlain seemed to have secured peace by appeasing Hitler at Munich, his efforts were greeted with widespread popular enthusiasm throughout Europe (including Germany).[82]

For most participants, the Second World War was a war of necessity, not choice.[83] In 1939, Hitler imposed war on his antagonists and then continued to impose it on a series of reluctant allies and unwilling victims. In the Great War it had been possible for most states (Serbia and Belgium were the exceptions) to opt out of the fighting; those that entered after the summer of 1914 chose to do so because they believed (in every case, wrongly) that it was in their interest. After 1939, neutrality was a luxury enjoyed only (with the exception of the Swiss) by those on the geopolitical periphery (Spain, the Irish Free State, Sweden, Turkey).

There was another, much more significant difference between the twentieth century's two world wars. The first had been fought in Europe with some overseas episodes; the second was truly global, with major battles on both of the earth's great oceans and across the Eurasian land mass. The second war was globally extended, but it was fought separately in the East and the West. Had the Axis powers been able to coordinate their strategies (which they never seriously considered doing), the outcome might have been different. Instead, after December 1941 the most powerful element uniting the fighting in Europe and Asia was the United States, which, safe from attack behind its two-ocean glacis, provided some of the manpower and, more importantly, many of the material resources that eventually defeated Germany and Japan.[84]

Although the European and Asian wars were fought separately, they had a strikingly similar dynamic. In the opening stage of both campaigns, Japan and Germany won a series of impressive victories that enabled them to occupy large stretches of territory. In neither theater, however, were these victories decisive: in Asia, Chinese forces suffered enormous losses but did not quit; in Europe, Hitler dominated the continent after 1940 but was unable to force Britain out of the war. Both Germany and Japan responded to these strategic frustrations by widening the war: in June 1941, Germany invaded the Soviet Union; six months later, Japan attacked the U.S. fleet at Pearl Harbor.

Considering the enormous disparity in their size and material resources, Japan's attack on the United States was incredibly reckless. It had been undertaken with great reluctance because Japanese policymakers believed that, given Japan's need for resources (especially oil), it was their only option. Hitler's decision to abandon his alliance with Stalin was somewhat more reasonable considering the apparent superiority of the German military. But the invasion of Russia, like the bombing of Pearl Harbor, turned out to be a monumental blunder. By the end of 1942, the war that Japan and Germany had wanted to fight and expected to win was over. Instead, the two confronted long, bloody wars of attrition in which they could not prevail. Although many political and military leaders recognized that victory was beyond their grasp, the regimes in Tokyo and Berlin did not abandon the war, even as their losses in battle mounted and Allied bombers unleashed a campaign of death and destruction against their civilian populations. Hitler kept the war going until Soviet troops were at the door of his underground hideout. In Japan, two atomic bombs ultimately persuaded the emperor that the only available alternatives were surrender or total annihilation. Not without some hesitation he finally ordered his military commanders to give up.

The European and Asian wars had a similar dynamic, but vastly different consequences. In Europe, the power vacuum left by the collapse of Nazi Germany and its various allies was quickly filled, in the east by the Soviet army and in the west by the United States, Great Britain, and the restored regimes in France and the Low Countries. When relations between the Soviet Union and the West deteriorated, Europe was divided between, and dominated by, the two superpowers. This ended Europe's global hegemony, but at the same time encouraged the emergence of radically new expectations about European states, nations, and the society of states.

The consequences of Japan's defeat were very different. Japan was occupied by the United States, which presided over constitutional reform and enforced demilitarization. On the Asian mainland, however, the geopolitical space once dominated by the Japanese Empire remained open. Neither of the superpowers was willing or able to impose on Asia the kind of order that created a new Europe.

In Asia, a number of different competitors struggled to resolve two outstanding questions. First, who would rule China? Chiang Kai-shek's Nationalist regime had contributed significantly to the Japanese defeat, but in the process had suffered enormous losses. Unlike the Soviet Union in Europe, it did not emerge strong enough to end the prolonged internal struggles that had engulfed China since the fall of the imperial regime in 1911. Weakened by the war against Japan, undermined by its own inefficiencies and corruption, and insufficiently assisted by the United States, the Nationalist regime finally lost out to the Chinese Communists in 1949. From the perspective of the twenty-first century, this may have been the world war's most important consequence.

The second question left unresolved in 1945 concerned the future of Europe's East Asian possessions—French Indochina, the Dutch East Indies, British Malaysia and Hong Kong. Could the colonial powers reassert the authority that had been swept away by the Japanese? Or would movements for national self-determination, now greatly strengthened by wartime experiences, succeed in creating independent nation-states? Like China's future, the fate of European colonies was decided by force. This took a long time. In some ways, the world war in Asia, which had begun with the Japanese invasion of Manchuria in 1931, did not finally end until the United States withdrew from Indochina in 1975.

For four decades after 1945, the world's society of states would be shaped by two developments: the military, political, and cultural rivalry of the superpowers, and the dissolution of Europe's formal empires. Both developments were complex, taking different forms at different times and in different places. Both were products of the wars that dominated global history between 1914 and 1945, but had deep historical roots in the nineteenth century. The next section will examine how superpower conflicts and the struggles against colonial rule combined to produce a radically new international order.

TOWARD A GLOBAL POLITICAL ORDER

In August 1941, Winston Churchill boarded the battleship H.M.S. *Prince of Wales* to journey to Placentia Bay, Newfoundland, to spend three days with the president of the United States, Franklin D. Roosevelt. Embarking on a long and perilous voyage when the very existence of his nation was still in doubt was a bold, even reckless move, motivated by the prime minister's conviction that without the full support of the United States, a British victory in the war against Nazi Germany would be impossible. Churchill was absolutely right. His presence on the Canadian coast that summer was also a dramatic expression of one of the most important developments in the second half of the twentieth century: the shift of geopolitical power away from Europe and to the United States. Can one imagine the prime minister of Great Britain (not to mention the premier of France) crossing the Atlantic in 1917 to solicit Woodrow Wilson's support? Just a quarter of a century later, it seemed like the only thing to do. The era of European hegemony was drawing to an end.[85]

An important product of the meeting between Churchill and Roosevelt was a joint statement that become known as "The Atlantic Charter." At the core of this brief document was the two leaders' commitment to a new version of Wilsonian self-determination, expressed by their promise to "respect the right of all peoples to choose the form of government under which they will live."[86] The Atlantic Charter had no legal status. Moreover, Churchill swiftly modified his support for self-determination so that it did not seem to undermine the legitimacy of the British Empire. Nevertheless, in the course of the war the allies frequently invoked the Charter to explain what they were fighting for. In February 1945, for example, when Churchill, Roosevelt, and Stalin met at Yalta, they solemnly affirmed their faith in the Charter's principles. War could no longer be justified by the right of conquest (the Charter had explicitly renounced territorial gains) or even self-defense; war now had to be fought in the name of what Edmund Burke had called "an armed doctrine." In the 1940s, as in the era of the French Revolution, that doctrine was some form of democracy. The Allies, of course, were far more powerfully armed advocates of democratic doctrine than the French revolutionaries. Nevertheless, it would soon become clear that in the middle of the twentieth century, as in the final decade of the eighteenth, democratic ideals were far easier to proclaim than to put into practice.[87]

The final declaration of the Yalta Conference also announced the three Allies' support for the creation of an international organization that could provide the institutional foundation for the postwar society of states. From April to June 1945, representatives of fifty governments met in San Francisco to establish the United Nations, the twentieth century's second attempt to form a representative body that would enable states to resolve their differences with consultation and compromise rather than violence. Like the League of Nations, the UN was created by the winners, but this time, as underscored by the location of the body's first meeting and of its permanent headquarters, the United States was the prime mover.

The UN, like the League of Nations, represented a society of sovereign states. For a state, membership in these international organizations was a source of political legitimacy, the legal recognition of its sovereignty and its right to be a fully qualified member of the international community.[88] But the founding documents of the two organizations revealed a subtle yet significant shift in people's expectations about the international order. According to the first words of its Covenant, the League of Nations was created by the "High Contracting Parties," that is, the leaders of the founding states. The source of the UN, on the other hand, was "the peoples of the United Nations," which was a further indication of democracy's significance as a source of legitimacy in both foreign and domestic politics.[89]

As always in democratic theory and practice, the key issue is how to define the *demos*: Who were "the peoples" in whose name the UN was founded? And what was their relationship to the organization's member states, a relationship apparently established by the deceptively simple phrase "of the United Nations"? The relationship between peoples and states would be an enduring source of tension within the international order that began to take shape in 1945, a tension expressed but not resolved in the organization of the UN.

Although the UN, like the League, affirmed the legal equality of its member states, its organization more clearly reflected the hierarchical structure of international society. In the League, important decisions had required unanimity, whereas in the UN, only the five permanent members of the Security Council—the United States, the Soviet Union, France, Britain, and China—had the ability to veto unacceptable resolutions. The distinctive role of these five powers created a persistent tension between the Security Council and the democratically organized General Assembly. Since 1945, the Council's original permanent members have managed to hold onto their special status (even after two of them, China and the Soviet Union, experienced radical regime changes), whereas the General Assembly's expanding size and composition reflect the transformation of the global society of states to which the rest of this chapter is devoted.[90]

The League of Nations had been humiliated and ultimately paralyzed by its failure to prevent blatant acts of aggression, first by Japan, then Italy, and finally Germany. No wonder that the League was an uncomfortable memory at the UN's foundation in San Francisco, where the League's few remaining employees were largely ignored. Unlike its predecessor, the UN has survived and has sometimes played an important role in international life. Over the years, its peacekeeping missions have helped to contain and occasionally to resolve local conflicts. The UN sponsors organizations, especially the High Commission for Refugees, that work to ease the sufferings of millions of the world's most unfortunate peoples. And although global society is surely better off with the UN than it would be without it, even the organization's most enthusiastic supporters could not argue that it has fulfilled the purpose stated in Article One:

> To maintain international peace and security, and to that end: to take effective collective measures for the prevention and removal of threats to the peace, and for the suppression of acts of aggression or other breaches of the peace, and to bring about by peaceful means, and in conformity with the principles of justice and international law, adjustment or settlement of international disputes or situations which might lead to a breach of the peace.[91]

The limitations on the UN's ability "to maintain international peace and security" were clearly revealed by its failure to mediate what was for forty years the world's most dangerous postwar conflict, the so-called Cold War between the United States and the Soviet Union. The obvious reason for this failure was the fact that since both antagonists had veto power in the Security Council, each could effectively block any collective action that was not in its interests.[92] Instead of using the UN as a means of settling their differences, the two states used it as a platform from which to condemn one another. International crises—Berlin, Cuba, the Middle East—were addressed elsewhere. Neither at the beginning of the Cold War nor at its end did the UN play an important role.

A great deal of scholarly energy has been expended to explain the Cold War's origins.[93] In fact, given their deep ideological and geopolitical differences, it is hardly surprising that the two most powerful states to emerge from the Second World War would become rivals. But the origins and character of their rivalry came from the superpowers' similarities as well as their differences. The United States, like the Soviet Union, regarded itself as the true representative of global democracy, the defender of the armed doctrine that dominated the twentieth century's political order. Each state believed that its version of democracy had universal validity and that its eventual triumph was the only satisfactory destination for human history.

Given this interplay of differences and similarities, it is not remarkable that there was a global contest between the two superpowers; it is more remarkable that during the Cold War's four long and sometimes crisis-filled decades, the two rivals did not actually fight one another. The most important reason for this, of course, was the existence of nuclear weapons whose use would have threatened the existence of both states (and much of the world). The most powerful weapons in human history, nuclear armaments were also oddly impotent, since they could not be used to do what weapons had always done, defeat the enemy in battle. From a nuclear battlefield, no one would emerge victorious.[94]

The Western view of the Cold War is shaped by events in Europe. It was in Europe that the superpowers' rivalry first emerged. For both of them, controlling Europe was vital: only here could the global balance of power have been fundamentally altered, which is what finally happened when the Soviets' European empire collapsed after 1989 (another of those events that came as a surprise but retrospectively seemed inevitable). Europe was the only place in the world where Soviet and U.S. forces directly faced one another, deployed along the border between the two postwar German states and armed with the greatest concentration of destructive power in history. More than anything else, the fear of unleashing this destructive power kept the Cold War in Europe cold.

An important consequence of the superpowers' geopolitical stalemate was that, for the first time in Europe's long and bloodstained history, the possibility of war among the states of Western Europe gradually faded. War was always a driving force in the process of European state-making. Now the long European peace made a new kind of state possible, a state in which military institutions were pushed to the margins and, in their place, civilian values and goals dominated public policy.[95] These states, first in the West and then, after 1989, in parts of the East, created what would become the European Union, a new sort of multinational organization to which members surrendered parts of their sovereign authority. Some commentators compared this organization to the Holy Roman Empire, but in fact nothing like it had ever existed.

During the Cold War, Europe, a source and site of global violence for centuries, became relatively peaceful. But in much of the world, the antagonism between the superpowers was not "cold." Outside of Europe, both the Soviets and the Americans encouraged, aided, and in some places instigated internal and external wars that were fought by a diverse array of allies, clients, and surrogates. Until the 1970s, Asia was the epicenter of this inter- and intrastate violence; between 1946 and 1979, the region accounted for 80 percent of the world's deaths in battle.[96] But proxy wars also occurred throughout the world: in Africa, the Middle East, and Latin America.[97]

The origins and character of these proxy wars were closely connected to what was perhaps the single most important development in the second half of the twentieth century, the struggle of the world's subject peoples against their colonial masters. As self-proclaimed advocates of democratic rule, both superpowers should have been on the anticolonial side. In practice, however, the superpowers' relationship to the global struggles against imperialism was complex and inconsistent. One thing was clear: the United States and the Soviet Union could influence but could not dominate these struggles. Neither could control would-be allies, who were usually motivated by local rather than global interests and ideologies. Moreover, neither

the model of communist revolution nor of capitalist modernization captured the kinetic complexities of decolonization. The record of superpower
involvement, therefore, was full of frustrations, miscalculations, and unintended consequences. It was usually the superpowers' local allies and
enemies—in Indochina, for example, or Afghanistan—who paid the price
for their frequently misguided interventions.[98]

A sign of the limitations on the superpowers' global influence was
the popularity of the concept of a "third world" of states that could claim
not to be aligned with either the United States or the Soviet Union. The
phrase was coined by a French writer in 1952, who associated the "tiers
monde" with the universalist aspirations of the "tiers état" in 1789. The
self-proclaimed representatives of the "third world" drew on elements from
liberal democracy (self-determination) and communism (the need for
revolutionary change) but added to them an emphasis on the importance
of race, both for the imposition and rejection of imperial rule. For its pro-
ponents, therefore, the emancipation of the Third World required not only
a struggle of the colonized against the colonizer and of the poor against the
rich, but also—and perhaps more significantly—of colored peoples against
the political and cultural oppression of their white masters.[99] The emphasis
on race had considerable appeal throughout the non-Western world and
among European and American intellectuals, but the advocates of a Third
World were not able to dominate the complex process of decolonization.
Like appeals to class conflict or economic development, the appeal to racial identity could not contain the diverse and often competing elements
in the global revolt against colonial rule.[100]

The collapse of colonial regimes was part of the massive shift in geopolitical power away from Europe that had begun in 1914. After 1945, this
was in part a shift to the superpowers, especially the United States. But the
decline of Europe was also connected to the ebbing of Europeans' political
control over formerly dependent or semidependent entities throughout the
non-Western world. Imperialism was a compulsory, often violent form of
globalization. Decolonization was also a form of global transformation.
At its core was the struggle for political autonomy, but ending colonial rule
also involved changes in economic, social, and cultural life, both in Europe
and the rest of the world.[101]

Colonization took centuries; decolonization took decades. It began in
1945, picked up speed in the 1960s (in 1960 alone, seventeen new African

states joined the UN), and was largely finished by the mid-1970s, when Portugal (originally among the first and eventually the last of the colonial powers) finally abandoned the costly effort to retain its African possessions. Willingly or unwillingly, peacefully or after a long and often vicious conflict, every European state surrendered its overseas empire. In part this was because Europeans no longer had a monopoly of the relatively inexpensive (for the colonizers, that is) instruments of violence that had enabled them to project their power throughout the world. But even when it might have still been possible to do so, defending their imperial rule eventually cost more in blood and treasure than most of the European public was willing to pay. It is not an accident that the longest campaign to hold on to a colonial empire was conducted in Angola from 1951 to 1975 by Portugal, the least democratic of the imperial powers.[102]

The universality of decolonization was not merely—and I think not primarily—a matter of military power. The use of violence was a necessary but not sufficient explanation for why European colonialism ended when and how it did. Sooner or later, Europeans gave up their empires because they no longer believed that it was either just or profitable to keep them. One reason for this was the collapse of the distinction between civilized and barbarian states that had sustained nineteenth-century imperialism. Without this distinction, expectations about self-determination became global. Moreover, postwar European publics calculated their private and political interests differently than they had before 1945: wealth and power were no longer identified with the direct control of territory beyond the borders of the nation; maintaining economic growth and providing social welfare were now the primary goals of European states. By the 1960s, therefore, the ability to dominate lands and peoples far from home ceased to be an essential part of most Europeans' expectations about the political order. Behind the great diversity of decolonization as a historical process, it was this swift and widespread shift in expectations about what states should do that may have mattered most.[103]

The dramatic growth in the number of sovereign states in the world is the clearest measure of decolonization's impact on the international system. In 1945, the UN had fifty founding states. A few years later, when plans were being made for the organization's new buildings, the architects calculated that they should allocate space for about twenty new members of the General Assembly. This turned out to be a substantial underestimation:

between 1940 and 1980, eighty-one former colonies and four quasi-colonies became independent. In 1989, the disintegration of the Soviets' European empire began a smaller but still substantial round of state formations. At the end of the Cold War in 1990, there were eight states in Eastern and Central Europe; two decades later there are twenty-six.[104] At present, the UN has 193 members. Around a dozen other polities have more or less plausible claims to sovereignty.[105]

Figure 6 represents a world of states, the product of what David Armitage has called "the great political fact of the last five hundred years," one that more than any other "fundamentally defines the political universe we all inhabit."[106] As we saw in chapters 1 and 2, maps reflect and reaffirm expectations about how political space is organized and imagined. This modern map displays a world almost entirely divided into sovereign units, each defined by clearly marked boundaries. We expect these units, having different sizes and shapes, to be formally equal; all have sovereign power and a legal status affirmed by their membership in the UN.[107]

It is easy to take for granted the remarkable situation that this map represents, a situation that has no precedent in world history. For the first time, the "tropical luxuriance of political and legal organization, competence, and status" that once characterized the world's political space has been replaced by uniformity and equality. People may not like their state, but most of the world's population live in one. "The sovereign states system," Robert Jackson wrote, "is the only global system of authority that has ever existed."[108]

The world's states all express their sovereign status with similar symbols and ceremonies: flags, postage stamps, military parades, and official holidays. Except for a few ceremonial units, their armies have similar organizations and uniforms. Like armies, school systems throughout the world vary enormously in quality, but here too most states make some effort to educate their populations. Every state has attempted to create the same kind of governmental institutions: maps, censuses, constitutions, legal codes, and administrative agencies. Despite the powerful influence of local traditions, interests, and resources, almost all modern states have adapted the infrastructure that we described in chapter 2. To paraphrase the statement by Marx and Engels about the bourgeoisie, the European state seems to have compelled the rest of the world to accept its expectations about political symbols and institutions: it has, in other words, created a world after its own image.[109]

We know, of course, that behind the uniformity represented on our maps there are anomalies: large ones, such as Antarctica, which is governed by an international condominium; small ones, such as the Channel Islands, whose ambiguous international status is the residue of another era. Contested territories often must adopt alternatives to the normative language of sovereignty: the Palestinian government is an "Authority," not at state; during the Cold War, when the two Germanies established diplomatic relations without fully recognizing each other's sovereignty, they exchanged "permanent representatives," not ambassadors. There are also a score of microstates, such as the Vatican and Monaco, and fifty-odd dependent territories, some of them uninhabited, almost all of them small, like the seventeen nonsovereign islands in the Caribbean. These are the exceptions that test, but do not fundamentally challenge, the norm of universal sovereignty.

We also know that the formal equality of states coexists with enormous and often debilitating differences in wealth and power that limit states' capacity to enforce their claims to sovereign status. Some states, such as Somalia since the early 1990s, are unable to press their claims to sovereignty, largely because they do not have a monopoly of legitimate violence. But the very notion of a "failed state" assumes that we have a clear expectation about what a successful state would be.[110] Robert Jackson may have been right when he wrote in 1990 that "never have the disparities between the outward forms and inward substance of sovereign states been any greater than they are today." But in the international society of states, as in a domestic society of individuals, it is the principle of formal equality that makes us acutely aware of endemic economic and political inequalities.[111]

An awareness of the anomalies and inequalities in the global order prompted Clifford Geertz to argue that the mental image of the world that is produced by "the pictorial conventions of our political atlases" is just "an illusion."[112] An illusion perhaps, but not *just* an illusion: the map's conventions may distort and oversimplify the world, but they are not merely projections of an imaginary order. These conventions reflect and reinforce our expectations about the way the political order is and should be. As I have argued in these pages more than once, these expectations—sometimes inaccurate, often misguided, and always insufficient—shape the way we think about and administer political space. They are indispensable: they can and often do mislead us, but we could not get along without them.

Figure 6. Political Map of the World (Central Intelligence Agency)

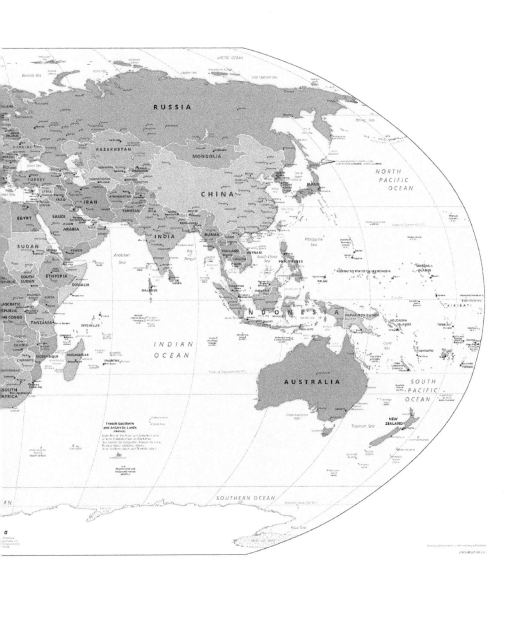

The states that emerged from the global revolt against colonial rule derived their legitimacy from the principle of self-determination.[113] Again and again in the decades after the publication of the Atlantic Charter, the right of peoples to choose their own form of government was proclaimed, most often in connection with the struggles against imperialism. In October 1970, for example, the twenty-fifth annual meeting of the UN General Assembly adopted an elaborate "Declaration on Principles of International Law concerning Friendly Relations and Co-operation among States in Accordance with the Charter of the United Nations." Here the world's states reaffirmed that they had the duty "to bring a speedy end to colonialism, having due regard to the freely expressed will of the peoples concerned." The document went on to make clear that "the peoples concerned" were those who suffered from the "alien subjugation, domination, and exploitation" that violated both human rights and the principles of the UN Charter.

That self-determination applied to the struggle of former colonies for independence was clear enough, but what about "the freely expressed will" of other peoples to have a state of their own? Here the prevailing expectations within the society of states were more ambiguous. The same Declaration of 1970 that legitimized, indeed encouraged, people's rejection of "alien subjugation" also restated the UN's commitment to "the territorial integrity and political independence" of states. Rejecting colonialism was not supposed to authorize or encourage "any action which would dismember or impair, totally or in part, the territorial integrity or political unity" of states that accepted the principle of self-determination and had a "government representing the whole people belonging to the territory without distinction as to race, creed, or color."[114] After the self-determination card has been played and a new state emerges, it is not easy to use it again. Most states, for example, supported the Congo's independence from Belgium, but very few were in favor of the separatist movements within the new Congolese state. Self-determination, therefore, is an even better example than sovereignty of what Stephen Krasner called the "organized hypocrisy" that animates the international order.

It is not surprising that the international community's commitment to territorial integrity and political unity is relatively robust and consistent. After all, the community is dominated by states who recognize that it is in their mutual interest to sustain sovereign claims. Of course, some states violate another's sovereign rights, but they usually do so in alliance with domestic allies or in the name of some higher principle or humanitarian cause. Our expectation is that such violations of sovereignty, though occasionally necessary, are extraordinary actions that need to be explained and justified. Hypocrisy requires both virtue and vice, a belief in norms and a willingness to violate them.

In the modern society of states, territory is still sometimes taken by force, as happened in 2014 when the Russian Federation seized Crimea from Ukraine (and, as I write these lines in April 2022, is now happening throughout the Ukrainian state). And there remain a number of territorial disputes between states, especially in Asia and the Middle East. Some of these—for example, Turkey and Greece in the eastern Mediterranean; India and Pakistan in Kashmir; India and China in Aksai Chin and Arunachal; Armenia and Azerbaijan in Nagorno-Karabakh; Israel and Syria in the Golan Heights; and, especially, the People's Republic of China and Taiwan—produce episodic outbreaks of violence and have the potential to spark larger conflicts.[115] But in comparison to the endemic conflicts over territory during the ancien régime and the imperial conquests of the nineteenth century, most of these disputes are limited in both quantity and intensity. They capture our attention not simply because of their threat to the global order, but because we no longer assume that territorial conflicts are an inevitable part of international politics.

The issue of territorial conflicts in the modern society of states is closely related to the complex problem of war's changing role in the international system. In a much-discussed book published in 2011, the American psychologist Steven Pinker argued that violence of every sort has significantly decreased relative to the size of the population.[116] There is plenty of evidence to show that major wars between states *have* become less frequent and less destructive than in the first half of the twentieth century. In some parts of the world, Western Europe and the Americas, for example, international war has disappeared and seems unlikely to return.[117] The incidence of political violence, however, including internal wars, insurrections, and organized crime, remains widespread and is much more difficult to calculate than interstate conflicts.[118] Nevertheless, it seems clear that our expectations about political violence have changed. We may or may not believe in Kant's precocious vision of perpetual peace, but we do not assume that violence is an intrinsic, if perhaps regrettable, element in the lives of states. Violence has come to be seen as pathological, a violation of our expectations about how the international order should work.

In fact, compared to any other period in human history, the territorial composition of modern states has become relatively stable. Because we expect that stability is the norm, we are fascinated and often disconcerted by those moments of political upheaval—1918, 1945, 1989—when old states died and new ones were born. But it is our pervasive assumption of territorial stability and not these occasional incidents of radical change that makes the present society of states unique. The death of states, which was a constant feature of the ancien régime, has not stopped happening, but it is no longer part of most people's expectations about international affairs.[119] In 1992, for example, the National Geographic Society noted with some alarm that in the past year it had had to revise its map of the world six times. Two centuries earlier, such a calculation would have been impossible, not only because more political entities were created and destroyed than anyone could count but also because an accurate map of the world's fragmented and constantly changing political landscape did not exist.

The durability of sovereignty is also revealed by the reluctance of states to give up their sovereign claims. An apparent exception to this is the EU, which was the product of the peaceful European environment created after 1945 by the Cold War. Here, in fact, states have voluntarily surrendered powers—over their borders, currencies, and economic regulations—that would not have seemed possible before 1945. Throughout the postwar era, some Europeans believed that ultimately the states themselves would disappear. And although the EU has created an elaborate apparatus of common institutions and laws, it has not developed into the federal superstate for which some of its founders yearned. The EU's foreign policy has not been very influential; its efforts to create common military institutions have remained fruitless. Indeed, as the twenty-first century's third decade begins, there are a number of signs that the centrifugal pull of sovereign independence within the EU is increasing.[120]

The experience of other multinational organizations in the postwar period provides vivid illustrations of how difficult it is to transcend sovereign autonomy. Consider, for example, the attempt by Syria and Egypt to form a United Arab Republic in 1958, which ended with Syria's secession three years later. Similarly, the Cooperation Council for the Arab States of the Gulf, founded in 1981, has not been able to create cohesive institutions despite an unusually high degree of political and cultural communality among its members. With few exceptions, the most durable international organizations are those, such the UN or NATO, which take the sovereign autonomy of their members for granted.

Hedley Bull defined the foundation of international society as the "general acceptance of the principle that men and territory are divided into states, each with its own proper sphere of authority, but linked together by a common set of rules."[121] As frequently happens, the most semantically complex word here is the simplest, the deceptively straightforward conjunction in the phrase, "men *and* territory." This obscures what we have seen as the fundamental tension in the modern political order: the tension between political geography and political community, between the ways in which territory and people (Bull's "men") are imagined and organized. This is the tension between what Geertz called "country" and "nation," the former, a "political arena," the latter, a "political force."[122]

Our expectations tend to downplay this tension; we assume that political communities and territorial units should go together, each reciprocally reinforcing the other. Our political vocabulary blurs the distinction between states and nations, often combining the two terms or using them interchangeably.[123] In practice, however, the clearly defined "political arena" of states and the "political force" of nations are frequently in conflict. Sometimes the two are fundamentally opposed to one another; more often, they coexist without quite coinciding.[124] "Matching state and nation," Nicholas Onuf has written, "is one of the great projects of the modern age. Notwithstanding the resources devoted to it, this project has succeeded only some of the time, and only then at great cost."[125] A brief look at the histories of Ireland, the former Yugoslavia, or Rwanda reveals just how great these costs can be.

Because communities of "men"—to repeat Bull's term—are much more difficult to define and divide than "territory," we should not be surprised that states and nations often do not cohere. In fact, a majority of states contain two or more ethnic groups defined by different languages, religions, or traditional cultures.[126] These differences can be, and often are, mobilized for political purposes, which can then set off the dialectic of inclusion and exclusion, which we examined in chapter 3. Within the confines of a sovereign state, this dialectic can have powerful and potentially deadly implications. By the end of the twentieth century, in a world of sovereign states, these implications had become globally extended and remain the primary source of political violence.

One of the reasons why postwar Europe has been relatively free of the political violence that had been so much a part of its history is that a number of its most pressing nationality problems were "solved," first by the disappearance of several multinational states after the First World War, then by the forcible removal of minority populations during and after the Second World War. But the potential for bloody national conflicts has by no means disappeared from Europe, as the Yugoslav wars of secession in the 1990s and current war in Ukraine have clearly demonstrated. Communal tensions remain even in well-established multinational states, such as Spain, the UK, and Belgium, and also in the newly created states that emerged from the collapse of the Soviet Union. Moreover, the growing number of immigrants from outside of Europe has created new sources of conflict.

The tension between nations and states continues in Europe, where most states have infrastructures that are strong enough to limit conflict and impose cohesion on their national community (or communities), but that tension is much more disruptive in the scores of nation states that were created after 1945. The boundaries of these states were usually imposed by colonial powers as the result of military conflicts, diplomatic negotiations, or historical accidents. Within these boundaries, a variety of groups, often with little in common, found themselves contained in the same political space. These ethnic, linguistic, and religious differences were frequently muted during the struggle for independence when, as Jawaharlal Nehru proclaimed in 1947, "the soul of a nation, long suppressed, finds utterance."[127] Unfortunately, as was the case with Nehru's India, once independence had been won, the nation's soul often spoke with many voices, some of them full of anger and appeals to violence.

Self-determination and sovereignty, the two key elements in our expectations about the modern society of states, were easy enough to express in the same declaration of principles, but often difficult to reconcile in practice. Most states are able to manage, more or less successfully, the inherent tension between sovereignty and self-determination. Their success depends on the effectiveness of their institutions, the relative weakness of the contesting communities, and the habit of compromising with, and accommodating to, national differences. As with most things having to do with states, geographical location is frequently an important cause of success or failure. A multinational state such as Belgium that is surrounded by relatively stable and prosperous neighbors has a much better chance of living peacefully (if not gracefully) with its diversity than states such as Georgia or Syria that must struggle to survive in much more dangerous neighborhoods. The most perilous location for a multinational state is one where neighboring states are tempted to intervene on behalf of an embattled minority; here the distinction between domestic and international politics disappears, often causing endemic violence.

The state's management of national differences can be messy and imperfect, but it is usually preferable to the alternatives. If the tension between the central government and national communities is not managed, it can erupt into communal violence that, within the territorial confines of a state, swiftly takes on a life of its own.[128] Government repression and popular resistance reinforce one another; divisions between communities increase as the voices of moderation are silenced. More and more people are compelled to choose sides, increasingly empowering those with a stake in keeping the conflict going. In some cases, outside forces intervene, because it seems to be in their interest to do so or because they have (or claim to have) some ethnic or religious connection to one of the contesting parties. This produces that interplay of interstate and intrastate conflict that can be seen in the unhappy recent histories of Bosnia, Libya, Syria, and Yemen.

With or without the intervention of outsiders, the onset of violence in communal conflicts significantly narrows the list of possible outcomes, none of which are appealing. There is compelling historical evidence to confirm Hannah Arendt's judgment that the "most probable result of violence is to produce a more violent world."[129] Sometimes, the dominant community—that is, the one in control of the state—can prevail, but often at great cost, such as in the bloody civil war in Sri Lanka that eventually defeated the Tamils' struggle for autonomy. Sometimes, however, the rebels prevail and are, for better or worse, able to create their own state. But whatever the outcome, the chances of building an effective consensual community in the aftermath of civil war are slim.

Secession movements are the clearest expression of the inherent tension between self-determination and sovereignty. Ryan Griffiths, who conducted a systematic study of the phenomenon, estimates that since 1945 there have been more than fifty secession movements a year, many of them secessions from colonial empires. The number has not significantly declined since the end of decolonization. In 2011, for instance, Griffiths found

fifty-five active secessionist groups. Many of these were small, with relatively little chance of success, but all of them point to enduring conflicts
over a state's legitimacy.[130] On rare occasions, such as the split between
Norway and Sweden in 1905 or between the Czech Republic and Slovakia
in 1993, secession can be peaceful. More often it is attended by a significant
amount of violence, both during and after the seceding state is formed.[131]

Since secession is difficult and painful, many violent struggles between national communities end in stalemate; sometimes—as in Bosnia,
for example—the stalemate is imposed by outside forces. This kind of solution usually involves some sort of territorial partition in which a national
minority achieves security and semiautonomy but not the legal status of a
sovereign state. The Kurds in Iraq, the Serbs in Bosnia, the Turks in Cy-
prus are examples of such a situation, one in which the principles of sovereignty and self-determination are simultaneously acknowledged and
compromised. The result is almost always awkward, volatile, and inherently
unsatisfactory. But since the alternative to partition is continued violence,
it is the lesser of two evils. Bosnia may be a mess, but it is better off than
it was before an imperfect order was imposed.[132]

"The relation of borders to people," Ryan Irwin wrote, is a "quintessen-
tially postcolonial problem."[133] In fact, it is a—perhaps *the*—quintessential
problem of the global society of nation states. The problematic relationship of borders to people can take many forms, from the peaceful if sometimes difficult accommodations in states such as Belgium and Canada,
to the debilitating civil wars in Ethiopia or Sudan. A particularly painful expression of the problem is the condition of statelessness, in which
people, often members of a national minority, lack the legal identity that
only states can provide.[134] Closely related to statelessness is the problem of
international migration by those millions of the world's citizens who move
across state borders in search of security or opportunity. The movement
of populations has always been part of human history, but the division of
the world into sovereign states has given this expression of the problematic "relation of borders to people" a distinctively modern and often deeply
tragic character.[135]

In the last decade of the twentieth century, some observers believed
that the significance of state borders was ebbing, while the power of people
to determine their own destinies was on the rise.[136] Globalization, driven
by a cluster of new technologies, seemed to have created a social and eco-

nomic world connected by computers, multinational corporations, and container ships, a "flat" world in which borders would eventually become irrelevant. As a result, some optimists argued, people would no longer be contained by territorial limits, national identities would wane, human rights would be universally acknowledged. In the third decade of the twenty-first century, these hopeful visions of the future seem less plausible than they did twenty years ago. Borders, both territorial and institutional, have not gone away; indeed in some places they have become less porous and more heavily defended. In most of the world, the sort of boundaries that were mapped and measured by the Cassinis and their counterparts in the eighteenth century remain the conventional means of defining political space. Groups that must exist without secure boundaries of their own—the Kurds or the Palestinians, for example—deeply resent their absence.

As we know from the history of states, the creation of bounded political territories has often been—and in many places, still is—a cruel and bloody business. And yet history also suggests that only within the boundaries of a state do individual freedom and the rule of law have some chance to prevail. States are still the essential source of what Arendt called "the right to have rights." This means that the vexed relationship between borders and people, sovereignty and self-determination, states and nations will remain the dominant characteristic of the modern political order. There is, I believe, no sign that it will disappear any time soon.

Conclusion

Beyond the Horizon

In order to survive, every political order must be able to live with internal tensions and contradictions. Consider, for example, the dynastic order portrayed in Shakespeare's plays. Shakespeare describes in harrowing detail virtually every imaginable misfortune that could befall a monarchical state: evil, incompetent, unlucky rulers; unreliable councilors and rebellious subjects; moral, physical, or psychological collapse. In some of the plays, such as *Macbeth*, order is restored by the arrival of a legitimate monarch. More often, and especially in the History Plays, the contradictions of dynastic rule are displayed but not resolved. But even when the reign of individual rulers ends badly, leaving behind a stage littered with corpses, the dynastic order itself goes on. Within Shakespeare's horizon of expectations, the deficiencies of the existing order are apparent, an alternative source of order is not. Only after another source of order arrives will the system he describes fade away. And that, as we know but he did not, will take another two centuries or more.

Challenges to a political order come from many different directions. Some come from the outside, invading armies, devastating epidemics, natural disasters; others come from within, corrupt leaders, social dislocation, spiritual crises. Even when these challenges are manageable, few political orders meet people's expectations. There is usually a gap between aspirations and accomplishments, between what people think ought to happen and what actually does occur. Dissatisfaction, distrust, and disappointment are part of most people's political experience. That is why every important thinker about politics has viewed the world with a certain amount (and sometimes a great deal) of anxiety.

At the beginning of the twenty-first century's third decade, it is not difficult to find good reasons for dissatisfaction with the present and anxiety about the future. There is nothing new about this. Like its predecessors, the contemporary political order provides many things to be discontented about: corruption, dictatorship, endemic violence, rampant inequality, institutional paralysis—the list goes on and on. And yet these problems, though surely worrisome and, in some places, cruel and debilitating, should not distract us from the underlying strengths that sustain our political institutions.

In the contemporary world, for example, the infrastructure of most states is more robust than ever before in human history. Governments have an unprecedented capacity to define their territory, count and classify their populations, formulate and enforce laws, and provide services to their citizens. Of course, even relatively successful states can and do fail to meet our expectations. States are rarely as fair, efficient, and competent as we wish them to be; most stimulate more demands for services than they can provide; few fulfill their own promise to create a just order. Despite—or, as some think, because of—the state's enormous resources, many people still suffer from the misfortunes that have always been part of the human condition.

Just as states have greater capacity than ever before, in the twenty-first century more people have a greater say in how they are governed. There is no more pervasive and powerful element in our expectations about the political order than the conviction that legitimate authority rests on popular consent. Needless to say, tyranny has not disappeared from the earth. There are plenty of states where consent is a sham, evoked by the more or less overt exercise of corruption and coercion. It is nonetheless significant that even dictatorships feel obliged to call themselves democracies.[1] In functioning democracies, where governments must make some effort to respond to the popular will, there are always disenchanted citizens who believe that the voice of the "people" is not being heard by those in power. States create an appetite for order and justice they usually cannot fulfill; democracies promise a consensual politics that they can rarely deliver.

The faith that legitimate power rests with the people, usually defined as a nation, is sometimes hard to sustain. The history of nationhood was—and is—full of disillusionment because we often do not get the nation we want. Nonetheless, we still expect the world to be divided into national communities for which some people are willing to die (and to kill). Nations, like states, are firmly embedded in our political expectations. Inhabitants of an established nation can take its existence for granted; those who live in a nation at risk or yearn for a nation of their own can become obsessed by the distance between their national aspirations and reality.

One of the characteristics of the modern political order is that, from its origins in the eighteenth century to the present, some have imagined permanent solutions to its drawbacks and deficiencies. These millenarian visions have taken many different forms. Some have indulged in what Francis Fukuyama called "the myth of statelessness" that imagines a world in which the state would wither away. More often these utopias imagine a new kind of community in which what Kant saw as humanity's "unsocial sociability" would disappear and it would no longer be necessary to contend with the strain created by our "tendency to come together in society, coupled, however, with a continual resistance which constantly threatens to break this society up."[2] The many would be made one, once and for all.

Utopian visions of the future exist at every point on the ideological spectrum. What they all have in common is a willingness to imagine a world without politics. This would be a world in which the bitter conflicts and messy compromises of public life would be transcended, for example, by the embrace of a shared religious faith, or the universal solidarity of the working class, or the autonomous efficiency of the market. These are fantasies and, as history shows us, often dangerous ones. Without politics, communities in the modern world cannot manage the enduring tension between individual desires and collective obligations and thus sustain the "standing miracle" of organized society.[3]

Because it so often engenders expectations that are not, perhaps cannot, be met, the modern political order seems to vacillate between overconfidence and excessive despair. Living with modernity demands that we recognize both its promise and its imperfections. The fact that most of our problems must be managed rather than solved is not a reason to abandon hope but to accept the limitations of our efforts. To act politically, as Michael Oakeshott reminded us, is "to sail on a boundless and bottomless sea; there is neither harbor for shelter nor floor for anchorage, neither starting place nor appointed destination."[4] But precisely because there is no safe harbor, political action is unavoidable, a voyage on which we must embark. The quest for order is never finished.

Will the modern order that I have described in this book eventually give way to a different set of expectations about space, community, and power, new ways of organizing and imagining what generations of German political thinkers called *Land*, *Volk*, and *Macht*? Probably. But if the past is any guide to this process, people will recognize the new order only after they are within a new horizon of expectations. "On waxen tablets," Francis Bacon wrote four centuries ago, "you cannot write anything new until you rub out the old. With the mind it is not so, there you cannot rub out the old until you have written in the new."[5]

When—or if—this new order arrives, those experiencing it will be surprised, as were those who lived in 1789, and then in retrospect they will come to regard the collapse of the ancien régime as inevitable. The inhabitants of the new order will know both more and less than we do about the world in which we now live. They will know, as we do not, how and when it ended, but they will never fully understand what it was like for us to live without that knowledge. And, like us, they will not be able to see what lies on the other side of the horizon that sets the limits of their expectations about the world.

What of hegemonic aspirations today?

The American presence & its challenges?

BRICS?

Globalization : esp. digital, & Anglophone.

NOTES

Introduction

1. Whitehead, *Symbolism*, 71, 73. Walzer, "On the Role of Symbolism."

2. On the concept of order, see Shils, "Charisma, Order, and Status," in *Constitution of Society*, esp. 125–26.

3. Toulmin, *Cosmopolis*, 1–2.

4. Merriam, *Systematic Politics*, v. Pierre Manent called this experience the "primordial, prescientific knowledge of the political regime in which we live, a kind of knowledge that we gather by observation, experience, and immersion as members of society and citizens" (Manent, "Modern Democracy," 114).

5. Dunn, *Breaking Democracy's Spell*, 29.

6. Morgan, *Inventing the People*, 13. For a similar view, see the essays in Shils, *Constitution of Society*.

7. Taylor, *Modern Social Imaginaries*, 25.

8. Cf. ibid., 23.

9. Plato, *Laws*, bk. 7, 817b, in *The Collected Dialogues*, 1387.

10. Quoted in Wight, *Systems of States*, 112.

11. "The aspects of things that are most important for us are hidden because of their simplicity and familiarity" (Wittgenstein, *Philosophical Investigations*, sec. 129). Taylor, *Modern Social Imaginaries*, 2, makes much the same point.

12. There is a thoughtful analysis of Europe's place in global history in Darwin, *After Tamerlane*, especially his introductory chapter, "Orientations."

13. Quoted in Wolin, *Tocqueville between Two Worlds*, 307.

14. Ryan, *On Politics*, 958.

CHAPTER ONE. The Ancien Régime

1. Lefort, *Democracy and Political Theory*, 2.

2. "One of the difficulties of the history of ideas is that names are more permanent than things. Institutions change, but the terms used to describe them remain the same" (Cobban, *Nation State*, 23).

3. Weber, as quoted in Reinhard, *Geschichte der Staatsgewalt*, 305.

4. See Welu, "The Map," on the map. On the painting, see Asemissen, *Vermeer*.

5. For example, Price, *The Dutch Republic*, chap. 1.

6. Gotthard, *In der Ferne*, 83. There is a good summary of the Prussian case in Clark, *Iron Kingdom*.

7. On the Duchy of Prussia, see Davies, *Vanished Kingdoms*, 325–93.

8. Koenigsberger, *Monarchies*; Elliott, "A Europe of Composite Monarchies." There is a fine collection of essays edited by Greengrass, *Conquest and Coalescence*.

9. Scott, *City-State*, 211. On Venice, see Landwehr, *Erschaffung Venedigs*.

10. Benton, *Search for Sovereignty*, 2.

11. Erbe, *Revolutionäre Erschütterung*, 152–53. To complicate matters further, the state's ruler was also a general in the Prussian army, who commanded the invading forces at Valmy in 1792 and was killed at Jena fourteen years later.

12. On the fall of Rome and its aftermath, see the excellent account in Scheidel, *Escape from Rome*. For Europe's regional variety, see Szücs, "Regions," esp. 139–40.

13. See Sahlins, "Natural Frontiers Revisited."

14. Oakeshott, *On Human Conduct*, 188. "No dynasty set out to build a nation state" (Kiernan, "State and Nation in Western Europe," 35).

15. Hobbes, *Leviathan* (1997), 55–56.

16. The best elaboration of Tilly's position is in Tilly, *Coercion, Capital, and European States*. For a critique, see Taylor and Botea, "Tilly Tally."

17. Quoted in Robertson, "Empire and Union," 11.

18. Koenigsberger, *Monarchies*, 11.

19. Giddens, *The Nation-State*, 10, makes the useful distinction between the "scope" and "intensity" of state power. In the ancien régime, rulers often aspired to a broad range of powers, but lacked the capacity to impose them.

20. On the importance of geography for state-making, see Fox, *History in Geographic Perspective*; Febvre, *Geographical Introduction to History*; and Gottmann, *Significance of Territory*. On transportation, see Vance, *Capturing the Horizon*. There are some useful examples of the advantage of water transport in Scott, *How the Old World Ended*, 6.

21. Fukuyama, *Origins of Political Order*; Møller, "Ecclesiastical Roots," emphasizes the importance of representative institutions in Western Europe, which he contrasts to Russia.

22. On "management" as a way of thinking about political action, see Darwin, *Empire Project*, 13.

23. Machiavelli, *Prince*, 14–15.

24. Among the most influential participants in this debate are Giddens, *The Nation-State*; Abrams, "Notes on the Difficulty of Studying the State";

Ertman, *Birth of the Leviathan*; Skinner, "From the State of Princes"; Mager, *Entstehung des modernen Staatsbegriffs*; Bourdieu, *On the State*; Osiander, "Before Sovereignty," is especially useful.

25. See Mansfield, "On the Impersonality of the Modern State."

26. Bodin, *Six Books of the Commonwealth*, 1.

27. Machiavelli, *Prince*, 4.

28. Montesquieu, *The Spirit of the Laws*, 124.

29. For a stimulating comparison, see Schieder, "Shakespeare und Machiavelli." Roman Polanski's great cinematic version of *Macbeth* ends with a hint that the cycle of violence unleashed by the king's murder did not end with the restoration of a new monarch. Machiavelli might have appreciated (but not applauded) this modern addition, but it goes against Shakespeare's convictions about the dynastic foundations of a legitimate political order. On the context for Shakespeare's concern for dynastic legitimacy, see Axton, *Queen's Two Bodies*. On Shakespeare's politics, see the excellent analysis in Lake, *How Shakespeare Put Politics on the Stage*.

30. See Oakley, *Kingship*, and Duindam, *Dynasties*, a useful survey.

31. Hendrik Spruyt, *The Sovereign State and Its Competitors*, has some useful material on this process.

32. Quoted in Baker, *Inventing the French Revolution*, 224.

33. Bredekamp, *Leviathan*.

34. For the symbolic importance of kingship, see Koschorke et al., *Der Fiktive Staat*.

35. Koenigsberger, *Monarchies*, 168.

36. The classic account of the court's significance is Elias, *Civilizing Process*. For a modern synthesis, see Duindam, *Myths of Power*.

37. Blanning, *Frederick the Great*, 5.

38. The holdings of the Metternich family, for example, stretched across Central Europe from the Rhineland to Bohemia; see Siemann, *Metternich*, 181–82.

39. On this, see Otto Brunner, *Land and Lordship*. Although women could occupy positions of authority, the term *Herrschaft* illustrates how assumptions about gender were hardwired into the political order during the ancien régime and, as we know, for a long time thereafter.

40. Bodin, *Six Books on the Commonwealth*, 6.

41. Bagehot, *The English Constitution*, chap. 3.

42. Bourdieu, *On the State*, 290. Bourdieu compared marriage strategies among French peasants to dynastic calculations (see 236).

43. *Richard II*, 3.3.54–57. The tension between Richard's sacred status and his human frailty is at the heart of Shakespeare's play.

44. Hocart, *Kings and Councillors*, 213. For a stimulating analysis of the relationship between power and the sacred, see Joas, *Power of the Sacred*, 250–72.

45. Nisbet, "Leadership," 711.

46. Kantorowicz, *King's Two Bodies*. For some wide-ranging reflections on the two-body metaphor, see Reed, *Power in Modernity*, and Santner, *Royal Remains*.

47. Bertelli, *King's Body*; Hocart, *Kingship*.

48. Schoch, *Herrscherbild*.

49. This shift in the nature of community is at the core of most theories of modernization. Its classic expression was Ferdinand Tönnies's account of the transition from *Gemeinschaft* (community) to *Gesellschaft* (society). With slightly different emphasis, the same process is described by Henry Maine (from status to contract), Herbert Spencer, and many others.

50. The phrase is from Peter Laslett, "Face to Face Society." For a brilliant account of the primacy of local institutions in the German lands, see Walker, *German Home Towns*.

51. Vargas Llosa, "A Novel for the Twenty-First Century," 131, used the phrase to describe the image of Spain that emerges from *Don Quixote*.

52. Scribner, "Symbolizing Boundaries." On Mantua, see Maczak, *Travel in Early Modern Europe*, 119. On the importance of gates, see Jütte, "Entering a City," and Jütte, *The Strait Gate*, chap. 5. On city walls, see Mintzker, *Defortification*. On movement in the Holy Roman Empire, that classic example of an ancien régime state, see Luca Scholz, *Borders and Freedom of Movement*.

53. Thompson, *Making of the English Working Class*, 9–10.

54. On the concept of imagination, see Warnock, *Imagination*.

55. Anderson, *Imagined Communities*. It is important not to confuse *imagined* with *imaginary*, which is, I suspect, a not uncommon misreading of Anderson. *Imaginary* has to with the ontological status of an object or experience; *imagined* described an epistemological process.

56. A good introduction is Bossy, *Christianity in the West*.

57. Smith, *Lectures on the Religion of the Semites*, 29–30. Duffy, *Voices of Morebath*, which is based on the records of a Devonshire parish in the sixteenth century, is a marvelous case study of the interpenetration of religious and secular life.

58. Duffy, *Voices of Morebath*, shows the Reformation's impact on a community.

59. On Jews, see Vital, *People Apart*. I am grateful to John Connelly for pointing out the variety of Jewish experience and the differences between East and West.

60. Quoted in Osiander, *Before the State*, 223.

61. There is a deeply researched account of this process in one German village in Sabean, *Property, Production, and Family*; on the Prussian province of Brandenburg, see Hagen, *Ordinary Prussians*. For a useful survey, see Blum, "The Internal Structure and Polity of the European Village."

62. For a good introduction to the rituals of power, see Stollberg-Rilinger, *Emperor's Old Clothes*.

63. Smith, *Antiquity of Nations*; Geary, *Myth of Nations*. For a forceful, but in my opinion not entirely convincing statement of the "perennialist" view, see Gat, *Nations*. A recent survey of the literature on nationalism is Storm, "A New Dawn in Nationalism Studies?"

64. Connor, *National Question*, xiv

65. Shakespeare, *The Merchant of Venice*, 1.2.36–91.

66. Maczak, *Travel in Early Modern Europe*, 110.

67. Shakespeare, *Henry V*, 3.1.33–35. For more on this, see Lake, *How Shakespeare Put Politics on the Stage*.

68. Erasmus, *Education of a Christian Prince*, 107–8.

69. Osiander, *States System of Europe*, is an excellent introduction to these issues.

70. Greengrass, *Christendom Destroyed*, 262.

71. Lazzarini, *Communication and Conflict*, 28.

72. Rowe, *From Reich to State*, 15.

73. Pounds, *Historical Geography*, 142.

74. Sorel, *Europe under the Old Regime*, 33–34.

75. Clark, *Seventeenth Century*, 144.

76. Greengrass, *Christendom Destroyed*, 262.

77. The great nineteenth-century legal historian F. W. Maitland wrote that our understanding of the premodern world will certainly "go astray . . . unless we can suffer communities to acquire and lose the character of states somewhat easily, somewhat insensibly" (quoted in the introduction to Gierke, *Political Theories*, ix).

78. Alberoni, quoted in Rowen, *The King's State*, 108. See also Whitman, *Verdict of Battle*.

79. Machiavelli, *Prince*, 10. Around 1300, there were more than eighty city-states in Italy, a century later, fewer than fifteen (Somaini, "Collapse of City States," 241).

80. Quoted in Sorel, *Europe under the Old Regime*, 11.

81. Hoffman, *Why Did Europe Conquer the World?*, 22. The endemic violence of the old regime is a central theme in Sorel, *Europe under the Old Regime*. See also Whitman, *Verdict of Battle*.

82. Machiavelli, *Prince*, 40; Bodin, *Six Books of the Commonwealth*, 19.

83. Dandelet, *Renaissance of Empire*.

84. Gibbon, *Decline and Fall*, 3:879. On why the empire was never re-created, see Scheidel, *Escape from Rome*.

85. Quoted in Burrow, *History of Histories*, 326.

86. Guizot, "Civilization," in *Historical Essays*, 166.

87. See the classic Mattingly, *Renaissance Diplomacy*, and Lazzarini, *Communication and Conflict*.

88. Bodin, *Six Books of the Commonwealth*, 22.

89. See the useful edition of de Callières, *Art of Diplomacy*, ed. H. M. A. Keens-Soper and Karl Schweitzer.

90. Quoted in Bukovansky, *Legitimacy and Power Politics*, 83.

91. Spawforth, *Versailles*, 85–86.

92. For some examples, see Lesaffer, *Peace Treaties*.

93. Tischer, *Kriegsbegründungen*.

94. Wight, *Systems of States*, 153. See also Bibó, *Paralysis of International Institutions*; Clark, *Legitimacy*; and Ferrero, *Principles of Power*.

95. Fichtner, "Dynastic Marriage."

96. Schilling, *Konfessionalisierung und Staatsinteressen*, is a good survey of this process.

97. On this, see Gregory, *Salvation at Stake*.

98. Quoted in Wight, *Power Politics*, 87. See Nexon, *Struggle for Power*.

99. Bodin, *Six Books of the Commonwealth*, 176.

100. Hobbes, *Leviathan* (n.d.), 306.

101. See Nexon, *Struggle for Power*; Croxton, *Westphalia*; Teschke, *Myth of 1648*; Glanville, "Myth of 'Traditional Sovereignty'"; and esp. Osiander, *States System of Europe*.

CHAPTER TWO.   Making States Modern

1. Febvre quoted in Gottmann, *Geography of Europe*, 52.

2. For a good introduction to these issues, see the essays in Bonney, *Rise of the Fiscal State*. On the evolution of European military institutions, the place to begin is Howard, *War in European History*. In her recent book on constitutions, Linda Colley emphasizes the central importance of war for state-making; see Colley, *The Gun, the Ship, and the Pen*.

3. The questions of why and how are, of course, inseparable. As John Thompson recently argued, in trying to explain a historical phenomenon, "examining *how* it came about is usually the best way to find out *why*" (Thompson, *Sense of Power*, 22).

4. Mann, "The Autonomous Power of the State." See also Axtmann, "The Formation of the Modern State."

5. These tasks made up what the political scientist Alexander Wendt called state-making's "ongoing accomplishment of practice" (Wendt, "Anarchy Is What States Makes of It," 413).

6. This point is nicely made with regard to England by Braddick, *State Formation*, 88. See also Bourdieu, *On the State*.

7. Weber, *Economy and Society*, 225. See also Patrick Joyce, *State of Freedom*. The close connection between knowledge and power is, of course, a central theme in the work of Michel Foucault, whose concept of "governmentality" has inspired a good deal of recent scholarship. For some recent reflections on these issues, see Maier, "Leviathan," 155–72; Higgs, "Rise of the Information State," provides an empirically grounded critique of the conventional identification of information and social control.

8. Machiavelli, *Prince*; Erasmus, *Education of a Christian Prince*, 65.

9. Leibniz, *Schriften*, 4th series, 3:340.

10. For a general introduction to the issues, see Branch, "Mapping the Sovereign State," and Branch, *The Cartographic State*, Biggs, "Putting the State on the Map," 374–405, and Dunlop, *Cartophilia*. Of particular interest is the stimulating discussion in Schlögel, *Im Raume lesen wir die Zeit*.

11. The best study of the Cassini family is Pelletier, *Les Cartes des Cassini*. See also Konvitz, *Cartography in France*, Branch, *The Cartographic State*, chap. 7, and Sahlins, *Boundaries*.

12. Kivelson, *Cartographies of Tsardom*; King, *Ghost of Freedom*, 143, on the Caucasus.

13. Vann, "Mapping under the Austrian Habsburgs."

14. On Britain, see Hewitt, *Map of a Nation*.

15. Quoted in Nobles, "Straight Lines and Stability," 22.

16. Harley, "Maps, Knowledge, and Power," 79. See also the essays in Hooson, *Geography and National Identity*.

17. Seegel, *Mapping Europe's Borderlands*. Carroll, *Science, Culture, and Modern State Formation*, argues that in the nineteenth century, Ireland was the best-mapped region in Europe. On colonial cartography, see the influential work on India by Matthew Edney, *Mapping an Empire*.

18. Quoted in Kertzer and Arel, *Census and Identity*, 6.

19. Among these innovations was the introduction of house numbers by several eighteenth-century governments, which created the legible urban space that we now take for granted. See Tantner, "Addressing the House."

20. That is why according to the census results in one French village during the 1870s, only females seem to have born—demographically improbable but perfectly understandable if we remember the reluctance of peasants to send their sons to the army. See Weber, *Peasants into Frenchmen*, 296.

21. Quoted by Faure, in Koren, *History of Statistics*, 258–59.

22. Levitan, *Cultural History of the British Census*, 16.

23. Quoted in Levitan, *Cultural History of the British Census*, 15.

24. There is a great deal of useful information on statistical projects in the various chapters in Koren, *History of Statistics*. For a brief introduction, see Stuart Woolf, "Statistics and the Modern State"; Headrick, *When Information Came of Age*; Randeraad, *States and Statistics*; and Tooze, *Statistics and the German State*.

25. Jensen, in Koren, *History of Statistics*.

26. See Faure in Koren, *History of Statistics*; Rusnock, "Quantification"; and Le Bras, "Statistique."

27. Cohn, "Census, Social Structure and Objectification."

28. The foundational work on these issues remains Brix, *Umgangssprachen in Altösterreich*.

29. See Immerwahr, *To Hide an Empire*, 78–79.

30. A. L. Schlözer as quoted in Hans Erich Bödeker, "Origins of the Statistical Gaze," 169.

31. Woolf, "Statistics and the Modern State," 593.

32. Porter, *Rise of Statistical Thinking*, 11.

33. Randeraad, *States and Statistics*, 55.

34. See Klueting, *Lehre von der Macht der Staaten*, and the essays in Collin and Horstmann, *Wissen des Staates*. Achim Landwehr points to the importance of knowledge for what he calls a "cultural history of the political" (see Landwehr, "Diskurs"). See also Dudley, *Word and the Sword*.

35. For more on taxation, conscription, elections, see the third section of this chapter and the second section of chapter 3.

36. See Kafka, *Office Writings*.

37. Quoted in Schmidt, *Statistik und Staatlichkeit*, 85.

38. Scott, *Seeing Like a State*.

39. There are some useful reflections on the materiality of state-making in Joyce, *State of Freedom*. See also volume 9 (1997) of the *Jahrbuch für europäische Verwaltungsgeschichte*, ed. Heyen, which is devoted to "Informations- und Kommunikationstechniken der öffentlichen Verwaltung." On these issues, historians of state-making can learn a lot from students of business enterprises: see, for example, the exemplary study by Yates, *Control through Communication*.

40. Branch, *The Cartographic State*, is especially useful on this point.

41. Godlewska, *Geography Unbound*, 21. On the definition of territory, see Agnew and Crobridge, *Mastering Space*; Elden, *The Birth of Territory*; Maier, *Once within Borders*; and Sack, *Territoriality*.

42. Quoted in Hewitt, *Map of a Nation*, 106–7.

43. Quoted in Finer, *History of Government*, 157–58.

44. The shift from community to state as a source of civic identity is one of the central themes in Walker, *German Home Towns*.

45. The definition of citizenship posed a particular set of problems for multinational states.

46. See Siegelberg, *Statelessness*.

47. On surveying private land, which parallels the division of political space, see Linklater, *Owning the Earth*, 200–211.

48. Kenneth Burke called this process "metaphorical extension" through which words that once referred to concrete and specific things were applied to

those in what he calls the "incorporeal" realm. Eventually "the original corporeal reference is forgotten, and the incorporeal, metaphorical extension survives"; quoted in Koschorke et al., *Der Fiktive Staat*, 64n14.

49. Febvre, *Geographical Introduction to History*, 311.

50. On this process, see Alliès, *L'invention du territoire*, and the discussion of the French Revolution in chapter 3.

51. On standardization, see Alder, "Making Things the Same," a brilliant article. On measurement, see Kula, *Measures and Men*.

52. Ritvo, *Platypus and the Mermaid*.

53. Classification, as Bowker and Star have pointed out, "is of its nature infrastructural" (Bowker and Star, *Sorting Things Out*, 320).

54. Barker, *Principles of Social and Political Theory*, 89.

55. On the rise of print culture, see Ong, *Presence of the Word*, Ong, *Interfaces of the Word*, and Ong, *Orality and Literacy*; Goody and Watt, "Consequences of Literacy."

56. On the French case and for some stimulating comments on the larger issue of "paperwork," see Kafka, *Demon of Writing*. For more on the importance of print, see Vernon, *Distant Strangers*, 78.

57. Mill, who was replying to a parliamentary inquiry, quoted in Joyce, *State of Freedom*, 147–48, Ludwig von Jagermann is quoted on 191. Needless to say, not everything in the documents is, or ever was, "in the world."

58. Quoted in Kunisch, *Staatsverfassung und Mächtepolitik*, 37. Kunisch provides an excellent analysis of these laws and their significance. Note how the monarch's personal property is considered in the same way as the territories of his realm, further evidence of the proprietary character of dynastic states.

59. Robertson, "Empire and Union." On the influence of the Union on constitutional developments, especially in the United States, see Scott, *How the Old World Ended*, 242–45.

60. Sellin, *Gewalt und Legitimität*, 46.

61. Quoted in Herzog, *Short History of European Law*, 252n. On the variety of law and institutions in France, see also Henshall, *Myth of Absolutism*.

62. Bell, *Lawyers and Citizens*, 22.

63. A useful summary can be found in Jenks, "The European Codes."

64. Strakosch, *State Absolutism and the Rule of Law*.

65. Prussia, *Allgemeines Landrecht für die Preußischen Staaten von 1794*. On the Landrecht, see Koselleck, *Preussen zwischen Reform und Revolution*. For a comparison of the German and Russian experiences, see Raeff, *The Well-Ordered Police State*.

66. On the codes, see Giovanni Tarello, *Storia della cultura giuridica moderna*, 485–557.

67. See Amos, "Code"; Fisher, "Codes"; and Herzog, *Short History of European Law*, chap. 12.

68. Cairns, "Blackstone." Herzog, *Short History of European Law*, chap. 13.

69. Bellomo, *Common Legal Past of Europe*, 10–11.

70. Constant, *Political Writings*, 73.

71. Tocqueville, *Democracy in America*, 2:645; Rosanvallon, *Demands of Liberty*, 57.

72. For a stimulating discussion of these issues, see Longo, *Politics of Borders*, esp. chap. 1.

73. Burgdorf, "Proto-constitutionalism." See also Stourzh, "Constitution."

74. Michael Stolleis, "Verfassungsideale," 17. Stolleis's generalization even applies to Great Britain, the one important European state that has never had a written constitution. For a stimulating account of constitutions and their global significance, see Colley, *The Gun, the Ship, and the Pen*.

75. Wheare, *Constitutions*, 8–9.

76. On the dual meaning of the word, see Hanna Pitkin, "Idea of a Constitution," a brief but stimulating essay.

77. Carrington, "Constitution," quote from 482. See also Colley, *The Gun, the Ship, and the Pen*, 17–25.

78. For a comparison of the French and U.S. Constitutions, see Casper, "Changing Concepts of Constitutionalism," 317. On the French Constitution, see Baker, *Inventing the French Revolution*.

79. Furet, *Revolutionary France*, is a convenient guide to these documents and their political context.

80. Hegel, *Political Writings*, 144, 179. See Stollberg-Rilinger, *Emperor's Old Clothes*, 281.

81. Huber, *Dokumente*, 1:78. We will return to this in chapter 4.

82. These constitutions are reprinted in Huber, *Dokumente*, vol. 1. For a brief analysis, see Sheehan, *German History*.

83. Rotteck, quoted in Prutsch, *Making Sense of Constitutional Monarchism*, 69.

84. Pölitz (1772–1838) was a historian at the University of Leipzig. His *Verfassungen* appeared in four volumes between 1817 and 1825 and in a second edition a decade later. On the significance of published constitutions, see Colley, *The Gun, the Ship, and the Pen*, chap. 3.

85. As Colley points out, the spread of constitutional government reaffirmed the gendered character of the political order: "The new constitutions put into unyielding words on paper, into print and into law the harsh fact that the machinery and political life of states were overwhelmingly masculine preserves" (Colley, *The Gun, the Ship, and the Pen*, 269).

86. See Grimmer-Solem, *Learning Empire*, 98–106, and Colley, *The Gun, the Ship, and the Pen*, chap. 8.

87. Osterhammel, *Transformation of the World*, 558–71.

88. Elkins, Ginsburg, and Melton, *Endurance of National Constitutions*, 2, 6.

89. According to one estimate, the word count in Germany's laws was 60 percent higher in 2021 than it had been in the mid-1990s (see *The Economist*, November 20, 2021, 23).

90. On citizenship, see Fahrmeir, "Citizenships," and Fahrmeir, *Citizenship*, Gosewinkel, *Schutz und Freiheit?*, and esp. Sahlins, *Unnaturally French*.

91. Geuss, *History and Illusion*, 21, makes a useful distinction between violence and coercion.

92. "Rule by sheer violence comes into play where power is being lost" (Arendt, *On Violence*, 53).

93. MacIver, *Modern State*, 223, 230. For an excellent introduction to these issues, see Dieter Grimm, *Recht und Staat*. Law is the substance of governmental power in the modern political order; its source is the consent of the governed.

94. Constitution of the Commonwealth of Massachusetts, I, art. 30, Wikisource, https://en.wikisource.org/wiki/Constitution_of_the_Commonwealth_of_Massachusetts_(1780).

95. Law, as Noah Feldman pointed out, "can operate only through the regular, repetitive conduct of people acting in concert" (Feldman, *Fall and Rise of the Islamic State*, 10).

96. Tilly, *Coercion, Capital, and European States*, 190.

97. For an excellent comparison of Germany and England, see Hennock, *Origin of the Welfare State*. On the English case, see Aylmer, "Peculiarities of the English State."

98. On the conflict between church and state, see the essays collected in Clark and Kaiser, *Culture Wars*; there is a concise summary of France in Furet, *Revolutionary France*, 516. On Germany, see Anderson, "Kulturkampf and the Course of German History."

99. For an introduction to the problem, see the classic Hintze, "Wesen und Wandlung des modernen Staates." Also of value are Breuer, *Der Staat*; the essays in Hall, *States in History*; Poggi, *State*; Reinhard, *Geschichte der Staatsgewalt*; Stolleis, "Entstehung des Interventionsstaates"; and Van Creveld, *Rise and Decline of the State*.

100. Chapman, *Profession of Government*, 43.

101. H. Finer, *Theory and Practice of Modern Government*, 710; see also Rose, *Public Employment*. The expansion of the state's apparatus has, with very few exceptions, continued, as has the state's share of the GNP. See the brief summary in *The Economist*, November 20, 2021, 23–25, and the useful analysis in Baldwin, "Beyond Weak and Strong."

102. Wagner's original formulation was in his monograph on the Austrian budget; see Wagner, *Die Ordnung des österreichischen Staatshaushaltes* (1863).

103. Some useful surveys of the rise of bureaucracy: Barker, *Development of Public Services*; Chapman, *Profession of Government*; Finer, *History of Government*; Morstein Marx, *Administrative State*; White et al., *Service Abroad*. For an excellent collection on the evolution of administrative institutions in Britain, see Stansky, *Victorian Revolution*, and the case studies in MacLeod, *Government and Expertise*.

104. Lind, "Great Friends and Small Friends."

105. Church, *Revolution and Red Tape*, 312; Proudhon quoted in Finer, *History of Government*, 3:1610–11.

106. Koselleck, *Preussen zwischen Reform und Revolution*, chap. 2.

107. Cited in Chapman, *Profession of Government*, 36.

108. Weber discusses the problem of bureaucracy in several of his major works. For a summary, see Weber, *Economy and Society*, vol. 2, chap. 11. Gouldner, "Metaphysical Pathos," has some astute comments on Weber's theories. My thanks to Rod Aya for bringing this neglected essay to my attention.

109. Weber, *Economy and Society*, 1:54.

110. Hintze, "Staatsverfassung," 53.

111. The close connection between war and state-making is a central theme in Colley, *The Gun, the Ship, and the Pen*.

112. McNeill, *Pursuit of Power*, 257 and 287.

113. The exceptions to this, as John Connelly reminded me, were those multinational states where the army was regarded as a foreign presence and in some cases even as an occupying force.

114. Thomson, *Mercenaries*. The practice of hiring mercenaries declined but did not disappear (and currently seems to be having a revival). As usual, the Belgian Congo provides a particularly vicious example. Held as Leopold's personal property until 1908, the Congo's notorious *Force publique* was essentially his private army.

115. We will see in chapter 3 how conscription helped build national communities.

116. Leonhard, *Pandora's Box*, 129.

117. On conscription, see chapter 3, section 2.

118. The best introduction to the history of policing is the work of Clive Emsley: see esp. Emsley, *Gendarmes*, and his recent synthesis, Emsley, *Short History of Police*.

119. Chapman, *Profession of Government*, 62.

120. Raphael, *Recht und Ordnung*, 138–39.

121. For an example of the weakness of local authorities in the ancien régime, recall the motley posse mobilized against the pirates as described in R. L. Stevenson's *Treasure Island* (published in 1883, but set in the mid-eighteenth century).

122. Ladd, *Streets of Europe*.

123. Porter, *Health, Civilization and the State*; for a good example of the problem, see Evans, *Death in Hamburg*, on cholera in nineteenth-century Hamburg.

124. On the growth of the welfare state, see Conrad, "Wohlfahrtsstaat"; Ritter, *Sozialstaat*; Hennock, *Origin of the Welfare State*.

125. Kafka, *Office Writings*, has an excellent introduction to Kafka's working life and a number of primary sources.

126. Finer, "State-Building," 98.

127. On communication, see Headrick, *Tools of Empire*, part III, and Maier, *Once within Borders*, chap. 5; on the larger issue of the "transaction costs" of government, see Allen, *Institutional Revolution*.

128. Reinhard, *Geschichte der Staatsgewalt*, 307.

129. Schremmer, *Steuern und Staatsfinanzen*, 46–47.

130. Ullmann, *Steuerstaat*, is an excellent introduction to the German case. See also Petersen, "From Domain State to Tax State"; Reinhard, *Geschichte der Staatsgewalt*; Raphael, *Recht und Ordnung*; and, for the eighteenth century, the essays in Bonney, *Rise of the Fiscal State*.

131. Huber, *Dokumente*, 1:66–67.

132. On the changing role of the monarchy in the nineteenth century, see the summary in Langewiesche, *Monarchie*.

133. Anderson, *Rise of Modern Diplomacy*, 73–96, on the foreign office.

134. There is an excellent analysis of the influence of monarchs on foreign policy in Clark, *Sleepwalkers*, 170–85.

135. On William II, see the balanced account in Clark, *Kaiser Wilhelm II*.

136. Deak, *Forging a Multinational State*, 1.

137. On Weber's use of the term and an analysis of its meaning and limitations, see Joas, *Power of the Sacred*, 111–33.

138. For a vivid illustration of the changing character of the monarchy, see the excellent analysis in Schoch, *Herrscherbild*.

139. The decline of European monarchies reminds us of how one of Ernest Hemingway's characters described going bankrupt: "Gradually, then suddenly."

140. Leonhard, *Überforderte Frieden*, 466–67.

141. Nicholas II of Russia lost his crown swiftly and without violence in March 1917, but was murdered by the Bolsheviks fifteen months later. The other deposed monarchs died a natural death.

142. Douglass North called this the "natural state." See North, Wallis, and Weingast, *Violence and Social Orders*, 63.

143. On the depersonalization of sovereignty, see Eulau, "Depersonalization of the Concept of Sovereignty," and Kiernan, "State and Nation in Western Europe."

144. Scott, *Seeing Like a State*.

145. Kostof, *History of Architecture*, 3.

146. Patrick Joyce called these rituals "the repetitive enactment of everyday practices" (see Joyce, *State of Freedom*, 27). See also Sharma and Gupta, *Anthropology of the State*, 11–12; Bourdieu, *On the State*, 269–70; Herzfeld, *Social Production of Indifference*, 37; and Frank, *Democratic Sublime*, esp. 73.

147. Constant, *Political Writings*, 104.

148. See Koschorke et al., *Der Fiktive Staat.*

149. The Bavarian Constitution is quoted in Maier, *Once within Borders*, 102; Runciman, "Concept," 35.

150. Bourdieu, *On the State*, 10. See also Kharkhordin, "What Is the State?"

151. Gauchet, *Disenchantment of the World*, 95. Hegel quoted in Lefort, *Democracy and Political Theory*, 214. Kantorowicz, *King's Two Bodies*, 3. For the relevance of Kantorowicz's thesis for the modern political order, see Santner, *Royal Remains*, esp. chap. 4.

152. Quoted in Seligman, *Modernity's Wager*, 117.

CHAPTER THREE.   Nations

1. Anderson, *Imagined Communities*, 3.

2. Bagehot, *Physics and Politics*, 61.

3. Anderson, *Imagined Communities*, 4. The title of Isaacs, *Idols of the Tribe*, suggests that nationhood resembled one of those "idols" that Francis Bacon regarded as a source of human delusion.

4. Bagehot, *Physics and Politics*, 30; Hobsbawm, *Nations and Nationalism*, 46.

5. Wiebe, *Who We Are*, 11.

6. Bagehot, *Physics and Politics*, 28.

7. Aron quoted in Schnapper, *Community of Citizens*, 3.

8. Nodia, "Nationalism," 7. There is a good statement of this connection in Yack, "Sovereignty." Canovan, *People*, is a fine introduction to the subject of this chapter.

9. Durkheim, *Elementary Forms of Religious Life* (1912), quoted in Gordon, *Citizens without Sovereignty*, 242. Durkheim goes on to explain that in the social order, the idea of an ideal society is inseparable from social practice; each requires the other.

10. Manent, "Modern Democracy," 115–16.

11. The belief that consent is a source of legitimacy is almost universal, but its practical application varies widely. A great many contemporary debates are about when it is necessary (to be vaccinated, for example), how it should be expressed (in erotic encounters, for example), or whether it is valid (in election results).

12. Stasavage, *Decline and Rise of Democracy*, argues that what he calls "early democracy" was present in many parts of the world before it was, gradually and unevenly, replaced by modern democratic institutions.

13. Cicero quoted in Huntington, *Political Order*, 10.

14. Møller, "Roots." I am grateful to John Connelly for bringing Møller's work to my attention. It deserves much more extensive consideration that I have been able to give it here.

15. Blackstone in Skinner, "State," 409. For more on the historical role of consent, see Bendix, *Kings or People*.

16. Van Zanden et al., "Rise and Decline," attempt to provide a quantitative analysis of European representative institutions. Møller, "The Ecclesiastical Roots of Representation," emphasizes the significance of these institutions for Western European democratic traditions. See also Stasavage, "Representation," and Stasavage, *Decline and Rise of Democracy*.

17. *Federalist*, no. 22, quoted in Wolin, *Fugitive Democracy*, 383.

18. Collingwood, *Autobiography*, 62.

19. Plamenatz, *Consent*, is still very much worth reading for the problems that arise when consent becomes the basis for the political order. On democracy as "the historical society par excellence," see Lefort, *Democracy and Political Theory*, 16.

20. Hobbes, *Leviathan* (1997), 95–96.

21. Rousseau quoted in Bendix, *Kings or People*, 366.

22. Rousseau, *Social Contract*, 184, 192. For a stimulating recent analysis of Rousseau's views of democracy, see Frank, *Democratic Sublime*. I am grateful to Avshalom Schwartz for bringing Frank's book to my attention.

23. Rousseau, *Social Contract*, 273.

24. Lake, *How Shakespeare Put Politics on the Stage*, 45. See also the useful remarks on the relationship between the theory of popular sovereignty and what he calls "social imaginary," in Taylor, *Modern Social Imaginaries*, chap. 8.

25. The classic study of the eighteenth-century public is Habermas, *Structural Transformation of the Public Sphere*. For a good synthesis, see Melton, *Rise of the Public*.

26. See Armitage, *Declaration of Independence*. The best scholarly edition of these documents is Rakove, *Constitution*.

27. Middlekauff, *Glorious Cause*, esp. 561–69; Morgan, *Inventing the People*.

28. Quoted from the lectures that Ranke delivered to the king of Bavaria in 1854, in Nippel, *Ancient and Modern Democracy*, 281.

29. Keane, *Life and Death of Democracy*, 281–83.

30. There is a concise summary of the Revolution's global reach in Burbank and Cooper, *Empires*, chap. 8. See the famous declaration in Furet, *Interpreting the French Revolution*, part 1. For an admirably concise and acute analysis of the revolution, see the conclusion to Sewell, *Capitalism and the Emergence of Civil Equality*.

31. Baecque, *Body Politic*, 15–16.

32. Sewell, *Rhetoric of Bourgeois Revolution*, and Sewell, *Capitalism and the Emergence of Civil Equality*, provide a fine analysis that uncovers the document's complexity and contradictions. Sieyès, *Political Writings*, is a convenient collection with a useful introduction by M. Sonenscher. See also Tuck, *Sleeping Sovereign*.

33. Sieyès quoted in Rosanvallon, *Society of Equals*, 35.

34. There are some interesting reflections on the aesthetic aspects of this in Philip Rieff, "Aesthetic Functions in Modern Politics."

35. Sewell, *Rhetoric of Bourgeois Revolution*, 46.

36. Sewell, "Revolution," 95. Isser Woloch called the product of these efforts a new "civic order." See his important book, Woloch, *New Regime*.

37. Text in Stewart, *Documentary Survey of the French Revolution*, 113–15. An excellent account is Popkin, *New World Begins*, 157–69. The Declaration of Rights is also an expression of revolutionaries' assumptions about gender: men, that is, males, had rights and obligations that women did not. On this issue, see the useful introduction in Offen, *The Woman Question in France*, and the literature cited there.

38. The most important decrees are in Stewart, *Documentary Survey of the French Revolution*, 106–10.

39. Ibid., 137–41. There is a concise summary of these various measures in Sewell, "Revolution."

40. On the significance of this, see Popkin, *New World Begins*, chap. 13. Text in Stewart, *Documentary Survey of the French Revolution*, 322–33.

41. Quoted in Hont, *Jealousy of Trade*, 484.

42. Quoted in Lefort, *Democracy and Political Theory*, 79. In his plan for a Corsican constitution, published in 1768, Rousseau wrote that the difficulty was not "to form a government for the nation," but rather to "form the nation for the government"; quoted in Frank, *The Democratic Sublime*, 53.

43. Quoted in Malia, *History's Locomotives*, 179.

44. Burke, *Reflections on the Revolution in France*. Like many other influential theorists, Burke anticipated rather than described the Revolution's character.

45. Lefort, *Political Forms*, 303–4.

46. Quoted in Hont, *Jealousy of Trade*, 481.

47. Calhoun, *Nations*, 78. Bernard Yack argues that "wherever popular sovereignty leads, nationalism seems to follow" (Yack, "Sovereignty," 517). See also Schöpflin, *Nations*, esp. 40.

48. Renan, "What Is a Nation?" The most recent English edition (2018) has a useful introduction by M. F. N. Giglioli.

49. See the interesting comments on Renan in Laitin, *Nations*, 29–30, and Yack, *Nationalism*, chap. 1. For a powerful critique of the nation as a purely subjective category, see Hroch, *Social Preconditions of National Revival*.

50. On the history of plebiscites, see Wambaugh, *Monograph on Plebiscites*.

51. For this distinction, see Potter, "Historians," 64, and Rosanvallon, *Democracy*, 49.

52. Lefort, *Democracy and Political Theory*, 11.

53. Wolin, *Fugitive Democracy*, 107.

54. There is an excellent account of modern electoral history in Richter, *Moderne Wahlen*, chap. 1. Also of value is Nolte, *Demokratie*, 129–35. On the German case, see Anderson, *Practicing Democracy*.

55. See De Dijn, *Freedom*, 225–27.

56. Gosewinkel, *Schutz und Freiheit?*, is an excellent introduction to the problem of citizenship in Europe. On France, see Noiriel, *French Melting Pot*.

57. There are some stimulating insights into the evolution of suffrage in Daniel, *Demokratiegeschichte*.

58. The democratic vote, Dominique Schnapper has written, is "the symbol of the new sacred . . . which affirms social ties and traces the destiny of the collectivity" (Schnapper, *Community of Citizens*, 77).

59. Tocqueville, *Recollections*.

60. Richter, *Moderne Wahlen*, has a comparison of the Prussian and American cases.

61. See the useful summary in Howe, "Weber's Elective Affinities." Weber's own formulation is in Weber, *Protestant Ethic*, 36.

62. David Stasavage has recently argued that democracy benefits from "weak states," which are more in need of popular consent. This may be plausible in the global context that he considers, but it does not seem to work very well within Europe. See Stasavage, *Decline and Rise of Democracy*.

63. Text in Stewart, *Documentary Survey of the French Revolution*, 472–74.

64. Furet, *Revolutionary France*, 251.

65. Clausewitz, *On War*, 610.

66. On conscription, see Janowitz, "Institutions." For a brief summary, see Sheehan, *Where Have All the Soldiers Gone?*, and, for a global survey of the contemporary scene, see Sheehan, "Future of Conscription." There is an excellent account of the German case in Frevert, *Nation*.

67. Weber, *Peasants into Frenchmen*.

68. Engels, quoted in Janowitz, "Institutions," 186; Schnapper, *Community of Citizens*, 35.

69. Bauer, *Question of Nationalities*, 84. In multinational states, the nation-building role of education produced conflicts rather than cohesion.

70. As with many other aspects of state-making, Britain was the major exception.

71. Ferry quoted in Brubaker, *Ethnicity without Groups*, 107.

72. Schnapper, *Community of Citizens*, 108.

73. Sassen, *Territory*, 18.

74. For some examples of what has been called "banal nationalism," see Pointon, "Money and Nationalism."

75. Bauer, *Question of Nationalities*, 123. Herzfeld, *Social Production of Indifference*, 74. There are some useful comments on these issues in Brubaker, *Ethnicity without Groups*.

76. Three different ways to understand this process: Bentley, "Ethnicity," who deploys Bourdieu's notion of habitus; Gellner, "Scale and Nation"; and Herzfeld, *Cultural Intimacy*.

77. Anderson, *Imagined Communities*, 154.

78. See Sheehan, *German History*, 160–74 and 371–85, for some German examples.

79. For an excellent case study of language and nation-building, see Mackridge, *Language and National Identity*, on Greece.

80. Geertz, "Revolution," 259, defines "the givens of social existence" as "the sense of being born with some powerful marker of identity." On the history of attitudes about language and community, see the truly monumental work of Borst, *Turmbau*.

81. See Herzfeld, *Social Production of Indifference*, 110–12.

82. Wittgenstein, *Philosophical Investigations*, para. 19. Much more could be said about the political implications of Wittgenstein's view of language: see, for example, the work of Stanley Cavell, esp. Cavell, *Claim of Reason*.

83. For a concise statement of this, see Horowitz, *Ethnic Groups in Conflict*, 222. On the role of language in multinational states, see Evans, "Language," and Calic, *The Great Cauldron*, esp. 257ff.

84. Wiebe, *Who We Are*, 15. For a sustained and convincing argument that "nationalism is a form of politics," see Breuilly, *Nationalism*.

85. Gallie, "Concepts," 169.

86. Gellner, *Conditions of Liberty*, 107.

87. The idea of ideologies as maps comes from Geertz, "Ideology," 220.

88. Acton, "Nationality," in *Essays*, 159.

89. Mill, *Essays*, 381.

90. Tocqueville quoted in Wiebe, *Who We Are*, 44. Barker, *National Character*, 248–49.

91. Quoted in Pflanze, *Bismarck*, 124.

92. For the context and consequences of this, see Anderson, *Practicing Democracy*.

93. On Marx and nationalism, see Connor, *National Question*. The quotation from the *Manifesto* is at 7.

94. Joll, *Second International*.

95. Hobsbawm, *Nations and Nationalism*, 46.

96. On this, see the aptly titled Mann, *The Dark Side of Democracy*.

97. Rustow, "Transitions," 350.

98. Mill, *Essays*, 382.

99. Ibid., 387.

100. Bluntschli quoted in Fisch, *Right of Self-Determination*, 120; Weber quoted in Stargardt, "Idea," 22; Barker quoted in Cobban, *Nation State*, 110.

101. Gellner, *Nations and Nationalism*, 1.

102. Breuilly, *Nationalism*, 62.

103. Among the important new works on the Habsburgs, the following are of particular value: Judson, *Habsburg Empire*; Deak, *Forging a Multinational State*; and Connelly, *Peoples into Nations*. Körner, "Nation," surveys the recent scholarship.

104. Equally important, of course, was the experience of emigration. This is also a common feature among students of nationalism, including Benedict Anderson (an Irishman, born in India, active in the United States), George Mosse (born in Berlin, educated in Britain, lived in the United States), Elie Kedourie (born in Iraq, worked in Britain, died in the United States), and many more.

105. Quoted in Hochedlinger, "Monarchy," 54.

106. Hirschman, *Exit*.

107. Connelly, *Peoples into Nations*, argues that the compromise of 1867 was "a reform that made the monarchy unreformable." Significantly, Judson and Deak, who both argue that the empire might have survived, emphasize the monarchy's Austrian and not its Hungarian institutions.

108. The classic work that emphasizes the strength of national movements is Jaszi, *Dissolution of the Habsburg Monarchy*; Judson and Zahra, "Introduction," argue for what they call "national indifference." For a critique of their perspective, see Miller, "National Indifference," and Connelly, *Peoples into Nations*.

CHAPTER FOUR.   A Society of Nation States

1. The image is from Bobbio, *Democracy and Dictatorship*, 97. Clausewitz, *On War*, 87–89.

2. There is a fine brief account of legitimacy in Wight, "Legitimacy"; see also Bull, *Anarchical Society*, and Clark, *Legitimacy*.

3. The most vigorous and consistent advocate of realism is John Mearsheimer: see, for example, Mearsheimer, *The Great Delusion*. For a historically informed critique of realism, see Schroeder, *Systems, Stability, and Statecraft*.

4. Berlin, "Inevitability,", 163–64. William James makes a similar point about experience and emotion: see Joas, *Power of the Sacred*, 138–39.

5. Krasner, *Sovereignty*. Cf. Reinhold Niebuhr's remark that "perhaps the most significant moral characteristic of a nation is its hypocrisy" (Niebuhr, *Man*, 95).

6. Ian Clark captured this combination of vice and virtue when he wrote that in the society of states the concept of legitimacy "is both poacher and gamekeeper" (Clark, *Legitimacy*, 21).

7. Kant, "Perpetual Peace" (1795), in *Political Writings*, 94, 99. On the context of Kant's ideas, see Ghervas, *Conquering Peace*, 71–81.

8. Howard, *Invention of Peace*. For an expansive history of the theory and practice of peace making, see Ghervas, *Conquering Peace*.

9. The immediate occasion for Kant's essay was probably the Peace of Basel, signed a few weeks earlier. This turned out to be no more than a temporary break in hostilities.

10. Acton, "Nationality," in *Essays*, 136. On the partitions, see Hagen, "Partitions," and Schroeder, *Transformation of European Politics*, 19.

11. Schroeder, *Transformation of European Politics*.

12. For a good introduction to the period, see Howard, *War in European History*, chap. 5; Bell, *First Total War*; Blanning, *French Revolutionary Wars*; Engberg-Pedersen, *Empire of Chance*; and Kolla, *Sovereignty, International Law, and the French Revolution*.

13. Quoted in Popkin, *A New World Begins*, 381.

14. Stewart, *A Documentary Survey of the French Revolution*, 673.

15. Burke, "First Letter Concerning a Regicide Peace," in *Revolutionary Writings*, 266 and 307.

16. Schroeder, *Transformation of European Politics*.

17. Paris treaty quoted in Osiander, *States System of Europe*, 237.

18. On Vienna, see the recent work by Jarrett, *Congress of Vienna*, and Vick, *Congress of Vienna*.

19. Scott, *Birth of a Great Power System*.

20. Quoted in Simpson, *Great Powers and Outlaw States*, 114.

21. On diplomatic practice, see Anderson, *Rise of Modern Diplomacy*. There is a list of international conferences and congresses in the *American Journal of International Law* 1, no. 3 (1907): 808–29.

22. On this issue, see the excellent collection of essays edited by Dülffer, Jost, and Kröger et al., *Vermiedene Kriege*.

23. Osterhammel, *Transformation of the World*, 483–93.

24. In addition to Schroeder, *Transformation of European Politics*, and Erbe, *Revolutionäre Erschütterung*, Enno Kraehe, *Metternich's German Policy*, is still worth reading on the German question in 1815. In a stimulating if perhaps somewhat overstated analysis, Simms, *Europe*, puts the German question at the center of European international relations throughout the modern period.

25. On nineteenth-century monarchy, see Paulmann, *Pomp und Politik*.

26. Bull, *Anarchical Society*, 202.

27. Clark, *Legitimacy*, 97.

28. See Klein, *Sovereign Equality*.

29. By 1984, there were 365 governmental and 4,615 nongovernmental organizations in the world; see Held, *Political Theory and the Modern State*, 232. On international organizations, see Anderson, *Rise of Modern Diplomacy*, and Osterhammel, *Transformation of the World*, 493–99.

30. There is a useful survey of territorial changes in Cruttwell, *History of Peaceful Change*.

31. See the concise statement of this problem in Soutou, "Ordre," 301–2. On self-determination, see Fisch, *Right of Self-Determination*. For an example of the establishment position in the first half of the century, see Metternich's remarks about Italy in 1819, quoted in Siemann, *Metternich*, 521–22.

32. On Greek nationhood, see Kitromilides, "Communities," and Jusdanis, *Necessary Nation*, chap. 4.

33. On the Greek revolt, see Mazower, *Greek Revolution*, and Weitz, *World Divided*, chap. 1.

34. Oxford Historical Treaties, 388; cited and discussed by Wight, "Legitimacy," 6, and Albrecht Carré, *Concert of Europe*, 115. Three months later after this treaty was signed, the powers drew the new state's boundaries in the Treaty of Constantinople.

35. Krasner, *Sovereignty*, chap. 6.

36. Oxford Historical Treaties, 256–63. Fabry, *Recognizing States*, 79. Albrecht-Carrié, *Concert of Europe*.

37. Sperber, *Revolutions*, is a good introduction to 1848.

38. For Europe in the 1850s, see Clark, "After 1848." On the German case, Ross, *Beyond the Barricades*.

39. Although outdated in some ways, Binkley, *Realism and Nationalism*, is still worth reading.

40. Disraeli, "Speech of 9 February 1871," available online: German Historical Institute, *German History in Documents and Images*, vol. 4, *Forging an Empire*, https://germanhistorydocs.ghi-dc.org/Index.cfm?language=english.

41. For some convincing examples of the system in operation, see the essays in Dülffer, Jost, and Kröger et al., *Vermiedene Kriege*.

42. Kennan, *Diplomacy*, 98.

43. Hopkins, *American Empire*, 241. Abernethy, *Dynamics of Global Dominance*, is an excellent introduction to European imperialism.

44. Mill, "A Few Words," 377–78. Mill's views were widely shared. On the historical origins and context of these attitudes, see Pitts, *Boundaries of the International*.

45. For a good example of the variety of imperial domination, see Hopkins, *Ruling the Savage Periphery*.

46. Lindley, *Acquisition and Government of Backward Territory*, v.

47. On purchasing territory, see Press, *Rogue Empires*.

48. For a good introduction to this process, see Osterhammel, *Transformation of the World*, chaps. 7 and 8.

49. Quoted by Langewiesche, "Jahrhundert," 43–44.

50. Stead, *Last Will and Testament of Cecil John Rhodes*, 190.

51. Mackinder, "Geographical Pivot," 422; Darwin, *After Tamerlane*, 364.

52. Reynolds, *Shattering Empires*. On the Balkan Wars, see the essays in Boeckh and Rutar, *The Balkan Wars*, and Geppert, Mulligan, and Rose, *The Wars before the Great War*.

53. See Siemann, *Metternich*, esp. 433.

54. On Habsburg effort to reform, see Deak, *Forging a Multinational State*, and Connelly, *Peoples into Nations*.

55. On the war's origins, see Clark, *Sleepwalkers*. For a guide to the literature on the war, see Winter and Prost, *Great War in History*.

56. An excellent synthesis of the war's history is Leonhard, *Pandora's Box*. See, for more details, the essays in Winter, *Cambridge History of the First World War*. From June 2014 to December 2018, the *Journal of Modern History* published a series of articles on the experience of war in different parts of the world (86, no. 2; 87, no. 3; 88, nos. 2 and 4; 89 no. 4; 90, nos. 2 and 4). All of them are worth reading and have references to the most recent scholarly literature.

57. On national antagonisms in the war, see Winter, *Cambridge History of the First World War*, vol. 3, part 3; Roshwald, *Ethnic Nationalism*; the essays in Bartov and Weitz, *Shatterzone*; and Engelstein, *Russia in Flames*.

58. Hendrick, *Life and Letters of Walter H. Page*, 1:334.

59. The September Memorandum was important for Fritz Fischer's critical account of German war aims. It is reproduced on the German Historical Institute's website. On Bethmann Hollweg's views, see Jarausch, *Enigmatic Chancellor*.

60. Stevenson, *First World War and International Politics*, is a good introduction to wartime diplomacy.

61. Prott, *Politics of Self-Determination*. For a firsthand account by a key player, see Masaryk, *Making of a State*. As Larry Wolff has recently emphasized, Masaryk had a powerful influence on Wilson (Wolff, *Wilson*, 131–34). On the significance of the war for the Habsburgs' collapse, see Boyer, "Silent War," and Deak, "The Great War and the Forgotten Realm."

62. Mayer, *Political Origins of the New Diplomacy*, remains a stimulating comparison of Lenin and Wilson. For the postwar period, see the fine synthesis in Leonhard, *Der Überforderte Frieden*.

63. An excellent summary in Tooze and Fertik, "World."

64. Quoted in Tooze, *Deluge*, 8.

65. Manela, *Wilsonian Moment*; Wolff, *Wilson*; Weitz, "Self-Determination"; Fisch, *Right of Self-Determination*.

66. For some examples, see Gallagher, "Nationalisms and the Crisis of Empire."

67. Fieldhouse, *Colonial Empires*, 242.

68. Valéry, "Letters."

69. Sharon Korman called mandates "a kind of surrogate for the right of conquest" (Korman, *Right of Conquest*, 143). The most recent study of mandates is Pedersen, *Guardians*.

70. Wright, *Mandates*, 276.

71. There is an excellent account of this process in Engelstein, *Russia in Flames*.

72. McAdams, *Vanguard of the Revolution*, analyzes Communist parties in and out of power.

73. Bryce, *Modern Democracies*, 1:viii and 4.

74. Two general histories of democracy: Keane, *Life and Death of Democracy*, and Nolte, *Demokratie*.

75. Fisch, *Right of Self-Determination*.

76. There is an excellent summary of Eastern European states in Connelly, *Peoples into Nations*, see esp. 364. Also worth reading is Seton-Watson, *Eastern Europe*. For a particularly vivid example of the problems of applying self-determination, see the brilliant chapters on Ukraine in Engelstein, *Russia in Flames*, and Wolff, *Wilson*, chap. 4.

77. Lefort, *Democracy and Political Theory*, 301.

78. Revel, *Totalitarian Temptation*. The classic comparison of the two regimes is Arendt, *Origins of Totalitarianism*. See also Malia, *Russia under Western Eyes*, 335–39.

79. For a detailed analysis of Stalin's calculations, see Kotkin, *Stalin*, chaps. 10–14.

80. On the early development of Hitler's views, see Weber, *Becoming Hitler*.

81. Connelly, *Peoples into Nations*, and Stokes, *Three Eras of Political Change*.

82. The definitive accounts of international relations between the wars are Steiner, *Light That Failed*, and Steiner, *Triumph of the Dark*.

83. Overy, *Blood and Ruins*, is now the best one-volume history of the war and its global significance.

84. As Craig Symonds makes clear in his excellent book, the key to the U.S. contribution was naval power (see Symonds, *World War II at Sea*).

85. It was by no means self-evident that when Europe's global power ebbed, the United States would take its place. For a compelling analysis of how and why this happened, see Thompson, *Sense of Power*.

86. The text of the Charter is available online from the Avalon Project, https://avalon.law.yale.edu. On its historical setting, see Kennedy, *Freedom from Fear*, chap. 15.

87. The Yalta Declaration is in Avalon Project. On the conference, see Harbutt, *Yalta 1945*. For its place in the evolution of the international order, see Soutou, "Ordre."

88. John Meyer wrote that the UN "symbolizes the rules of a political system in which nation states are constitutive citizens" (Meyer, "World Polity," 117).

89. Relevant texts in the Avalon Project; Claude, "Legitimization," on the UN and legitimacy. For a fresh account of the UN's founding, see Betts, *Ruin and Renewal*, 17–22.

90. Jackson and O'Malley, *Institution of International Order*, is a recent collection of essays comparing the League and the UN. See also Mazower, *Governing the World*.

91. There is a balanced account of the UN's first sixteen years in Hoffmann, "Evaluation."

92. The exception was the war in Korea that was fought under UN auspices because the Soviet Union had temporarily boycotted Security Council meetings. This did not happen again.

93. Soutou, *Guerre de Cinquante Ans*, is a splendid introduction to the Cold War.

94. The classic analysis of nuclear weapons appeared at the very beginning of the Atomic Age; see Brodie and Dunn et al., *The Absolute Weapon*. On history of nuclear strategy, see Freedman, *Evolution of Nuclear Strategy*.

95. I develop this argument in more detail in Sheehan, *Where Have All the Soldiers Gone?* See also Ghervas, *Conquering Peace*.

96. Grosser, *L'histoire du monde se fait en Asie*, 513. Grosser's book is a powerful analysis of Asia's significance for twentieth-century history.

97. On the Cold War's global dimensions, see Lüthi, *Cold Wars*, and Westad, *The Cold War: A World History*.

98. Westad, *The Global Cold War*.

99. For a firsthand account of the movement, see Wright, *Color Curtain*.

100. Getachew, *Worldmaking*.

101. Abernethy, *Dynamics of Global Dominance*, and Darwin, *After Tamerlane*, chap. 8. There is an excellent brief account of the end of empire in Overy, *Blood and Ruins*, which relates the process to the Second World War.

102. W. Roger Louis is the world's leading historian of decolonization, especially in the Middle East. See Louis and Robinson, "Imperialism of Decolonization," for a brilliant synthesis.

103. Betts, *Ruin and Renewal*; Crawford, *Argument and Change in World Politics*, chap. 7.

104. On Eastern and Central Europe, see Wirsching, *Preis der Freiheit*, 404.

105. There are, it should be pointed out, other ways of computing the number of states in the world: if we add the UN's two "observer states" (the

Holy See and Palestine), we get 195; 206 states send a team to the Olympics; 211 are eligible to compete for the World Cup. Around a dozen states that do not have a representative at the UN claim sovereign status, half of them recognized by at least one other state. See Østerud, "The Narrow Gate," on how states enter the "club."

106. Armitage, "Contagion of Sovereignty."

107. Branch, *The Cartographic State*; Goettlich, "Rise of Linear Borders."

108. Jackson, *Quasi-States*, x. See also Mayall, *Nationalism*. For a graphic representation of this process, see Wimmer, *Waves of War*, 2, fig. 1. Two stimulating efforts to understand this global order: Meyer, "World Polity," and Giddens, *The Nation-State*.

109. Badie, *The Imported State*; Vries, "States"; Wimmer, "Rise of the Nation-State"; and the essays in Reinhard, *Verstaatlichung der Welt?*

110. For a critical analysis of the concept, see Hampel, "Dark(er) Side of 'State Failure.'"

111. Jackson, *Quasi-States*, 24–25.

112. Geertz, "World," 229. For some stimulating recent attempts to reconsider the conventional view of cartographical space, see the essays in Billé, ed., *Voluminous States*.

113. See the essays in Fisch, *Verteilung der Welt*.

114. U.N. General Assembly—Twenty-fifth Session, Resolution 2625, October 24, 1970. See Fabry, *Recognizing States*.

115. As I write this in the spring of 2022, the Russian Federation is waging war in Ukraine in the name of that state's Russian population. The parallel with the People's Republic of China's claim to Taiwan is clear and terrifying. Among the most significant questions facing the international order in 2022 is how long the island's ambiguous sovereign status can last.

116. Pinker, *Better Angels*. For a critique of Pinker, see Braumoeller, *Only the Dead*.

117. Rupert Smith begins his useful book on the uses of force with the lapidary assessment that "war no longer exists" (Smith, *Utility of Force*, 3). For a new statistical analysis, see Reiter, Stam, and Horowitz, "Revised Look at Interstate Wars." The incidence of war turns out to be much harder to calculate than it might seem. As usual, the problem is knowing what to count. That major wars have declined seems to me to be clear enough.

118. Smith calls this a new kind of war, not between armies, but "amongst peoples." See Smith, *Utility of Force*.

119. Fazal, *State Death*, esp. chap. 4, on the post-1945 period. For a provocative analysis that emphasizes the role of the Kellogg–Briand Pact of 1928 in stabilizing the international order, see Hathaway and Shapiro, *The Internationalists*.

120. The best introductions to the history of the EU are Van Middelaaar, *Passage to Europe*, and Patel, *Project Europe*.

121. Bull, *Anarchical Society*, 140.

122. Geertz, "World," 237. Geertz, "State," adds more examples. For a similar view, see Yack, *Nationalism*, 240.

123. A good example of this terminological slippage can be found in Tilly, *Formation of National States*, a widely cited collection.

124. A good summary in Parker, *Geopolitics*. See also Nootens, "Liberal Nationalism."

125. Onuf, "World-Making, State-Building," 28.

126. Toft, *Geography of Ethnic Violence*, 149–55.

127. Quoted in Hopkins, *American Empire*, 142.

128. Horowitz, *Ethnic Groups in Conflict*; Laitin, *Nations*. For an excellent case study, see Glassman's account of Zanzibar, *War of Words, War of Stones*.

129. Arendt, *On Violence*, 80.

130. Griffiths, "Secession," and Griffiths, *Age of Secession*.

131. Buchanan, *Secession*.

132. In 2022, there are a number of troubling signs that the Bosnian compromise is coming apart. As so often, the problems are both internal and external, unresolved ethnic conflicts and interference from foreign states.

133. Quoted in Getachew, *Worldmaking*, 102.

134. Siegelberg, *Statelessness*, is a new and insightful examination of this problem.

135. Collier, *Exodus*.

136. See, for example, Agnew and Crobridge, *Mastering Space*, 5. For a popular view on the power of globalization, Friedman, *World Is Flat*.

Conclusion

1. Stasavage, *Decline and Rise of Democracy*, chap. 11.

2. Kant, "Idea for a Universal History," in *Political Writings*, 44.

3. Alfred North Whitehead, *Symbolism*, 71. For a similar view of politics, see Rosanvallon, *Democracy*, 34.

4. Oakeshott, "Political Education," in Laslett, *Philosophy, Politics, and Society*, 21.

5. Quoted in Wolin, *Tocqueville*, 32. Thomas Kuhn says much the same thing about scientific revolutions; see Kuhn, *Structure of Scientific Revolutions*, 77.

BIBLIOGRAPHY

Abernethy, David B. *The Dynamics of Global Dominance: European Overseas Empires, 1415–1980.* New Haven, CT: Yale University Press, 2000.

Abrams, Philip. "Notes on the Difficulty of Studying a State." *Journal of Historical Sociology* 1, no. 1 (1988): 58–89.

Acton, Lord. *Essays on the Liberal Interpretation of History: Selected Papers.* Chicago: University of Chicago Press, 1967.

Agnew, John, and Stuart Crobridge. *Mastering Space: Hegemony, Territory and International Political Economy.* London: Routledge, 1995.

Albrecht-Carrié, René. *The Concert of Europe.* New York: Walker, 1968.

Alder, Ken. "Making Things the Same: Representation, Tolerance and the End of the Ancien Régime in France." *Social Studies of Science* 28, no. 4 (1998): 499–545.

Allen, Douglas W. *The Institutional Revolution: Measurement and the Economic Emergence of the Modern World.* Chicago: University of Chicago Press, 2011.

Alliès, Paul. *L'invention du territoire.* Grenoble: Presses universitaires de Grenoble, 1980.

Amos, Maurice. "The Code Napoléon and the Modern World." *Journal of Comparative Legislation and International Law* 10, no. 4 (1928): 222–36.

Anderson, Benedict. *Imagined Communities: Reflections on the Origins and Spread of Nationalism.* London: Verso, 1991.

Anderson, Margaret Lavinia. "The Kulturkampf and the Course of German History." *Central European History* 19, no. 1 (1986): 82–115.

———. *Practicing Democracy: Elections and Political Culture in Imperial Germany.* Princeton, NJ: Princeton University Press, 2000.

Anderson, M. S. *The Rise of Modern Diplomacy, 1450–1919.* London and New York: Longman, 1993.

Arendt, Hannah. *On Violence.* New York: Harcourt, Brace, 1969.

———. *The Origins of Totalitarianism.* New York: Harcourt, Brace, 1951.

Armitage, David. "The Contagion of Sovereignty: Declarations of Independence since 1776." *South African Historical Journal* 52 (2005): 1–18.

————. *The Declaration of Independence: A Global History*. Cambridge, MA: Harvard University Press, 2007.

Asemissen, Hermann Ulrich. *Jan Vermeer: Die Malkunst. Aspekte eines Berufsbildes*. Frankfurt: Fischer, 1988.

Axtmann, Roland. "The Formation of the Modern State: The Debate in the Social Sciences." In *National Histories and European History*, edited by Mary Fulbrook, 21–45. London: UCL Press, 1993.

Axton, Marie. *The Queen's Two Bodies: Drama and the Elizabethan Succession*. London: Royal Historical Society, 1977.

Aylmer, G. E. "The Peculiarities of the English State." *Journal of Historical Sociology* 3, no. 2 (1990): 91–108.

Badie, Bertrand. *The Imported State: The Westernization of the Political Order*. Stanford, CA: Stanford University Press, 2000.

Baecque, Antoine de. *The Body Politic: Corporeal Metaphor in Revolutionary France, 1770–1800*. Translated by Charlotte Mandell. Stanford, CA: Stanford University Press, 1997.

Bagehot, Walter. *The English Constitution*. London: Chapman and Hall, 1867.

————. *Physics and Politics: Or Thoughts on the Application of the Principles of "Natural Selection" and "Inheritance" in Political Society* (1867). Boston: Beacon, 1956.

Baker, Keith Michael. *Inventing the French Revolution: Essays on French Political Culture in the Eighteenth Century*. Cambridge: Cambridge University Press, 1990.

Baldwin, Peter. "Beyond Weak and Strong. Rethinking the State in Comparative Policy History." *Journal of Policy History* 17, no. 1 (2005): 12–33.

Ball, Terence, and J. G. A Pocock, eds. *Conceptual Change and the Constitution*. Lawrence: University Press of Kansas, 1988.

Barker, Ernest. *The Development of Public Services in Western Europe, 1660–1930*. New York: Oxford University Press, 1944.

————. *National Character and the Factors in Its Formation* (1927). London: Methuen, 1948.

————. *Principles of Social and Political Theory*. Oxford: Oxford University Press, 1951.

Bartov, Omer, and Eric D. Weitz, eds. *Shatterzone of Empires: Coexistence and Violence in the German, Habsburg, Russian, and Ottoman Borderlands*. Bloomington: Indiana University Press, 2013.

Bauer, Otto. *The Question of Nationalities and Social Democracy*. Minneapolis: University of Minnesota Press, 2000.

Becker, Peter, and William Clark, eds. *Little Tools of Knowledge: Historical Essays on Academic and Bureaucratic Practices*. Ann Arbor: Michigan University Press, 2001.

Bell, David A. *The First Total War: Napoleon's Europe and the Birth of Warfare as We Know It.* Boston: Houghton, Mifflin, 2007.

———. *Lawyers and Citizens: The Making of a Political Elite in Old Regime France.* New York: Oxford University Press, 1994.

Bellomo, Manlio. *The Common Legal Past of Europe, 1000–1800.* Washington, DC: Catholic University of America Press, 1995.

Bendix, Reinhard. *Kings or People: Power and the Mandate to Rule.* Berkeley: University of California Press, 1978.

Bentley, G. Carter. "Ethnicity and Practice." *Comparative Studies in Society and History* 29, no. 1 (1987): 24–55.

Benton, Lauren. *A Search for Sovereignty: Law and Geography in European Empires, 1400–1900.* Cambridge: Cambridge University Press, 2010.

Berlin, Isaiah. "Historical Inevitability." In *Liberty: Incorporating Four Essays on Liberty*, edited by Henry Hardy, 95–165. Oxford: Oxford University Press, 2002.

Bertelli, Sergio. *The King's Body: Sacred Rituals of Power in Medieval and Early Modern Europe.* Translated by R. Burr Litchfield. University Park: Pennsylvania State University Press, 2001.

Betts, Paul. *Ruin and Renewal: Civilizing Europe after World War II.* New York: Basic Books, 2020.

Bibó, István. *The Paralysis of International Institutions and Remedies: A Study of Self Determination, Concord among the Major Powers, and Political Arbitration.* Sussex: Harvester Press, 1976.

Biggs, Michael. "Putting the State on the Map: Cartography, Territory, and European State Formation." *Comparative Studies in Society and History* 41, no. 2 (1999): 374–405.

Billé, Franck, ed. *Voluminous States: Sovereignty, Materiality, and the Territorial Imagination.* Durham, NC: Duke University Press, 2020.

Binkley, Robert C. *Realism and Nationalism, 1852–1871.* New York: Harper and Brothers, 1935.

Blanning, T. C. W. *Frederick the Great: King of Prussia.* St. Ives: Allen Lane, 2015.

———. *The French Revolutionary Wars, 1787–1802.* London: Arnold, 1996.

Blum, Jerome. "The Internal Structure and Polity of the European Village Community from the Fifteenth to the Nineteenth Century." *Journal of Modern History* 43 (1971): 541–76.

Bobbio, Norberto. *Democracy and Dictatorship: The Nature and Limits of State Power.* Cambridge: Polity, 1989.

Bodin, Jean. *Six Books of the Commonwealth.* Abridged and translated by M. J. Tooley. Oxford: Oxford University Press, 1955.

Bödeker, Hans Erich. "On the Origins of the 'Statistical Gaze': Modes of Perception, Forms of Knowledge, and Ways of Writing in the Early Social

Sciences." In *Little Tools of Knowledge: Historical Essays on Academic and Bureaucratic Practices*, edited by Peter Becker and William Clark, 169–96. Ann Arbor: University of Michigan Press, 2001.

Boeckh, Katrin, and Sabine Rutar, eds. *The Balkan Wars from Contemporary Perception to Historic Memory*. Cham: Palgrave Macmillan, 2016.

Bonney, Richard, ed. *The Rise of the Fiscal State in Europe, c. 1200–1815*. Oxford: Oxford University Press, 1999.

Borst, Arno. *Der Turmbau von Babel: Geschichte der Meinungen über Ursprung und Vielfalt der Sprachen und Völker*. 4 vols in 6. Stuttgart: A. Hiersemann, 1957–1963.

Bossy, John. *Christianity in the West, 1400–1700*. Oxford: Oxford University Press, 1985.

Bourdieu, Pierre. *On the State: Lectures at the Collège de France, 1989–1992*. Cambridge: Polity, 2014.

Bowker, Geoffrey C., and Susan Leigh Star. *Sorting Things Out: Classification and Its Consequences*. Cambridge, MA: MIT Press, 1999.

Boyer, John W. "Silent War and Bitter Peace: The Revolution of 1918 in Austria." *Austrian History Yearbook* 34 (2003): 1–56.

Braddick, Michael J. *State Formation in Early Modern England, 1550–1700*. Cambridge: Cambridge University Press, 2000.

Branch, Jordan. *The Cartographic State: Maps, Territory, and the Origins of Sovereignty*. Cambridge: Cambridge University Press, 2014.

———. "Mapping the Sovereign State: Technology, Authority, and Systemic Change." *International Organization* 65 (2011): 1–31.

Braumoeller, Bear F. *Only the Dead: The Persistence of War in the Modern Age*. New York: Oxford University Press, 2019.

Bredekamp, Horst. *Leviathan: Body Politic as Visual Strategy in the Works of Thomas Hobbes*. Translated by Elizabeth Clegg. Berlin: DeGruyter, 2020.

Breuer, Stefan. *Der Staat: Entstehung, Typen, Organisationsstadien*. Reinbeck: Rowohlt, 1998.

Breuilly, John. *Nationalism and the State*. 2nd ed. Manchester: Manchester University Press, 1993.

Brix, Emil. *Die Umgangssprachen in Altösterreich zwischen Agitation und Assimilation: Die Sprachenstatistik in den zisleithanischen Volkszählungen, 1880 bis 1910*. Vienna: Böhlau, 1982.

Brodie, Bernard, and Frederick S. Dunn, et al., eds. *The Absolute Weapon: Atomic Power and World Order*. New York: Harcourt, Brace, 1946.

Brubaker, Rogers. *Ethnicity without Groups*. Cambridge: Cambridge University Press, 2004.

Brunner, Otto. *Land and Lordship: Structures of Governance in Medieval Austria*. Translated by Howard Kaminsky and James Van Horn Melton. Philadelphia: University of Pennsylvania Press, 1992.

Bryce, James. *Modern Democracies*. 2 vols. New York: MacMillan, 1921.

Buchanan, Allen. *Secession: The Morality of Political Divorce from Fort Sumter to Lithuania and Quebec*. Boulder: University of Colorado Press, 1991.

Buisseret, David. *Monarchs, Ministers, and Maps: The Emergence of Cartography as a Tool of Government in Early Modern Europe*. Chicago: University of Chicago Press, 1992.

Bukovansky, Mlada. *Legitimacy and Power Politics: The American and French Revolutions in International Political Culture*. Princeton, NJ: Princeton University Press, 2002.

Bull, Hedley. *The Anarchical Society: A Study of Order in World Politics*. New York: Columbia University Press, 1977.

Burbank, Jane, and Frederick Cooper. *Empires in World History: Power and the Politics of Difference*. Princeton, NJ: Princeton University Press, 2010.

Burgdorf, Wolfgang. "Proto-constitutionalism: The Imperial Constitution in the Electoral Capitulations and Basic Law Guarantees." *German History* 36, no. 3 (2018): 415–31.

Burke, Edmund. *Reflections on the Revolution in France and on the Proceedings in Certain Societies in London Relative to that Event*. Middlesex: Penguin, 1968.

———. *Revolutionary Writings*. Edited by Iain Hampsher-Monk. Cambridge: Cambridge University Press, 2014.

Burrow, John. *A History of Histories: Epics, Chronicles, and Inquiries from Herodotus and Thucydides to the Twentieth Century*. New York: Knopf, 2008.

Cairns, John. "Blackstone, an English Institutist: Legal Literature and the Rise of the Nation State." *Oxford Journal of Legal Studies* 4 (1984): 318–60.

Calhoun, Craig. *Nations Matter: Culture, History and the Cosmopolitan Dream*. New York: Routledge, 2007.

Calic, Marie-Janine. *The Great Cauldron: A History of Southeastern Europe*. Cambridge, MA: Harvard University Press, 2019.

Canovan, Margaret. *The People*. Cambridge: Polity, 2005.

Carrington, Dorothy. "The Corsican Constitution of Pasquale Paoli (1755–1769)." *English Historical Review* 88, no. 348 (1973): 481–503.

Carroll, Patrick. *Science, Culture, and Modern State Formation*. Berkeley: University of California Press, 2006.

Casper, Gerhard. "Changing Concepts of Constitutionalism: 18th to 20th Century." *Supreme Court Review* (1989): 311–32.

Cavell, Stanley. *The Claim of Reason*. Oxford: Oxford University Press, 1979.

Chapman, Brian. *The Profession of Government: The Public Service in Europe*. London: Macmillan, 1966.

Church, Clive H. *Revolution and Red Tape: The French Ministerial Bureaucracy, 1770–1850*. Oxford: Oxford University Press, 1981.

Clark, Christopher. "After 1848: The European Revolution in Government." *Transactions of the Royal Historical Society*, 6th ser., 22 (2012): 171–98.

———. *Iron Kingdom: The Rise and Downfall of Prussia, 1600–1947*. London: Allen Lane, 2006.

———. *Kaiser Wilhelm II: A Life in Power*. London: Penguin, 2009.

———. *The Sleepwalkers: How Europe Went to War in 1914*. New York: Harpers, 2012.

Clark, Christopher, and Wolfram Kaiser, eds. *Culture Wars: Secular–Catholic Conflict in Nineteenth-Century Europe*. Cambridge: Cambridge University Press, 2003.

Clark, George. *The Seventeenth Century*. New York: Oxford University Press, 1961.

Clark, Ian. *Legitimacy in International Society*. Oxford: Oxford University Press, 2005.

Claude, Inis L. "Collective Legitimization as a Political Function of the United Nations." *International Organization* 20, no. 3 (1966): 367–79.

Clausewitz, Carl von. *On War*. Princeton, NJ: Princeton University Press, 1976.

Cobban, Alfred. *The Nation State and National Self-Determination*. New York: Crowell, 1969.

Cohn, Bernard. *An Anthropologist among the Historians and Other Essays*. New York: Oxford University Press, 1987.

———. "The Census, Social Structure and Objectification in South Asia." In *An Anthropologist among the Historians and Other Essays*, 224–54.

Colley, Linda. *The Gun, the Ship, and the Pen: Warfare, Constitutions, and the Making of the Modern World*. New York: Liveright, 2021.

Collier, Paul. *Exodus: How Migration Is Changing Our World*. New York: Oxford University Press, 2013.

Collin, Peter, and Thomas Horstman, eds. *Das Wissen des Staates: Geschichte, Theorie und Praxis*. Baden-Baden: Nomos, 2004.

Collingwood, R. G. *An Autobiography*. London: Oxford University Press, 1939.

Connelly, John. *From Peoples into Nations: A History of Eastern Europe*. Princeton, NJ: Princeton University Press, 2020.

Connor, Walker. *The National Question in Marxist-Leninist Theory and Strategy*. Princeton, NJ: Princeton University Press, 1984.

Conrad, Christoph. "Was macht eigentlich der Wohlfahrsstaat?" *Geschichte und Gesellschaft* 41 (2013): 555–92.

Constant, Benjamin. *Political Writings*. Translated by Biancamaria Fontana. Cambridge: Cambridge University Press, 1988.

Crawford, Neta. *Argument and Change in World Politics: Ethics, Decolonization, and Humanitarian Intervention*. Cambridge: Cambridge University Press, 2002.

Croxton, Derek. *Westphalia: The Last Christian Peace*. New York: Palgrave Macmillan, 2013.

Cruttwell, C. R. M. F. *A History of Peaceful Change in the Modern World*. London: Oxford University Press, 1937.

Cubitt, Geoffrey, ed. *Imagining Nations*. Manchester: Manchester University Press, 1998.

Dandelet, Thomas. *The Renaissance of Empire in Early Modern Europe*. Cambridge: Cambridge University Press, 2014.

Daniel, Ute. *Postheroische Demokratiegeschichte*. Hamburg: Hamburger Edition, 2020.

Darwin, John. *After Tamerlane: The Global History of Empire since 1405*. New York: Bloomsbury, 2008.

————. *The Empire Project: The Rise and Fall of the British World-System, 1830–1970*. Cambridge: Cambridge University Press, 2009.

Davies, Norman. *Vanished Kingdoms: The Rise and Fall of States and Nations*. London: Allen Lane, 2011.

Deak, John. *Forging a Multinational State: State Making in Imperial Austria from the Enlightenment to the First World War*. Stanford, CA: Stanford University Press, 2015.

————. "The Great War and the Forgotten Realm: The Habsburg Monarchy and the First World War." *Journal of Modern History* 86, no. 2 (2014): 336–80.

De Callières, François. *The Art of Diplomacy* (1719). Edited by H. M. A. Keens-Soper and Karl Schweitzer. New York: Holmes and Meier, 1983.

De Dijn, Annelien. *Freedom: An Unruly History*. Cambridge, MA: Harvard University Press, 2020.

Diamond, Larry, and Marc Plattner, eds. *Nationalism, Ethnic Conflict, and Democracy*. Baltimore: Johns Hopkins University Press, 1994.

Dreitzel, Horst. *Monarchiebegriffe in der Fürstengesellschaft: Semantik und Theorie der Einherrschaft in Deutschland von der Reformation bis zum Vormärz*. 2 vols. Cologne: Böhlau, 1991.

Dudley, Leonard. *The Word and the Sword: How Techniques of Information and Violence Have Shaped Our World*. Cambridge: Blackwell, 1991.

Duffy, Eamon. *The Voices of Morebath: Reformation and Rebellion in an English Village*. New Haven, CT: Yale University Press, 2001.

Duindam, Jeroen. *Dynasties: A Global History of Power, 1300–1800*. Cambridge: Cambridge University Press, 2015.

————. *Myths of Power: Norbert Elias and the Early Modern European Court*. Amsterdam: Amsterdam University Press, 1995.

Dülffer, Jost, and Martin Kröger, et al., eds. *Vermiedene Kriege: Deeskalation von Konflikten der Großmächte zwischen Krimkrieg und Erstem Weltkrieg, 1865–1914*. Munich: Oldenbourg, 1997.

Dunlop, Catherine Tatiana. *Cartophilia: Maps and the Search for Identity in the French-German Borderland*. Chicago: University of Chicago Press, 2015.

Dunn, John. *Breaking Democracy's Spell*. New Haven, CT: Yale University Press, 2014.

Edney, Matthew. *Mapping an Empire. The Geographical Construction of British India, 1765–1843*. Chicago: University of Chicago Press, 1997.

Elden, Stuart. *The Birth of Territory*. Chicago: University of Chicago Press, 2013.

Elias, Norbert. *The Civilizing Process: Sociogenetic and Psychogenetic Investigations*. 2 vols. New York: Urizen Books, 1978–1982.

Elkins, Zachary, Tom Ginsburg, and James Melton. *The Endurance of National Constitutions*. Cambridge: Cambridge University Press, 2009.

Elliott, John. "A Europe of Composite Monarchies." *Past and Present* 137 (1992): 48–71.

Emsley, Clive. *Gendarmes and the State in Nineteenth-Century Europe*. Oxford: Oxford University Press, 1999.

———. *A Short History of Police and Policing*. Oxford: Oxford University Press, 2021.

Engberg-Pedersen, Anders. *Empire of Chance: The Napoleonic Wars and the Disorder of Things*. Cambridge: Cambridge University Press, 2015.

Engelstein, Laura. *Russia in Flames: War, Revolution, Civil War, 1914–1921*. New York: Oxford University Press, 2018.

Erasmus. *The Education of a Christian Prince* (1516). Edited by Lisa Jardine. Cambridge: Cambridge University Press, 1997.

Erbe, Michael. *Revolutionäre Erschütterung und Erneuertes Gleichgewicht. Internationale Beziehungen, 1785–1830*. Paderborn: Schöningh, 2004.

Ertman, Thomas. *Birth of the Leviathan: Building States and Regimes in Medieval and Early Modern Europe*. New York: Cambridge University Press, 1997.

Eulau, Heinz. "The Depersonalization of the Concept of Sovereignty." *Journal of Politics* 4, no. 1 (1942): 3–19.

Evans, Richard J. *Death in Hamburg: Society and Politics in the Cholera Years, 1830–1910*. Oxford: Oxford University Press, 1987.

Evans, R. J. W. "Language and State Building: The Case of the Habsburg Monarchy." *Austrian History Yearbook* 35 (2004): 1–23.

Fabry, Mikulas. *Recognizing States: International Society and the Establishment of New States since 1776*. Oxford: Oxford University Press, 2010.

Fahrmeir, Andreas. *Citizenship: The Rise and Fall of a Modern Concept*. New Haven, CT: Yale University Press, 2007.

———. "Nineteenth-Century German Citizenships: A Reconsideration." *Historical Journal* 40, no. 3 (1997): 721–52.

Faure, Fernand. "France." In Koren, ed., *History of Statistics*, 215–330.

Fazal, Tanisha. *State Death: The Politics and Geography of Conquest, Occupation, and Annexation*. Princeton, NJ: Princeton University Press, 2011.

Febvre, Lucien. *A Geographical Introduction to History*. New York: Knopf, 1950.

Feldman, Noah. *The Fall and Rise of the Islamic State*. Princeton, NJ: Princeton University Press, 2008.

Ferrero, Guglielmo. *The Principles of Power: The Great Political Crises of History*. New York: G. P. Putnam's Sons, 1942.

Fichtner, Paula. "Dynastic Marriage in Sixteenth-Century Habsburg Diplomacy and Statecraft: An Interdisciplinary Approach." *American Historical Review* 81, no. 2 (1976): 243–65.

Fieldhouse, D. K. *The Colonial Empires: A Comparative Survey from the Eighteenth Century*. New York: Delacourte, 1967.

Finer, Herman. *The Theory and Practice of Modern Government*. New York: H. Holt, 1949.

Finer, S. E. *The History of Government*. 3 vols. Oxford: Oxford University Press, 1997.

———. *A Primer of Public Administration*. London: F. Muller, 1950.

———. "State-Building, State Boundaries and Border Control." *Social Science Information* 13, no. 4/5 (1974): 79–126.

Fisch, Jörg, ed. *The Right of Self-Determination of Peoples: The Domestication of an Illusion*. Cambridge: Cambridge University Press, 2015.

———. *Die Verteilung der Welt: Selbstbestimmung und das Selbstbestimmungsrecht der Völker*. Munich: R. Oldenbourg, 2011.

Fisher, H. A. L. "The Codes." In *The Cambridge Modern History*, vol. 9, *Napoleon*, edited by A. W. Ward, Prothero Ward, et al., 148–79. New York: Cambridge University Press, 1934.

Fox, Edward W. *History in Geographic Perspective: The Other France*. New York: Norton, 1971.

Frank, Jason. *The Democratic Sublime. On Aesthetics and Popular Assembly*. New York: Oxford University Press, 2021.

Freedman, Lawrence. *The Evolution of Nuclear Strategy*. London: Macmillan, 1983.

Frevert, Ute. *A Nation in Barracks: Conscription, Military Service, and Civil Society in Modern Germany*. New York: Berg, 2004.

Friedman, Thomas. *The World Is Flat: A Brief History of the Twenty-First Century*. New York: Farrar, Straus and Giroux, 2005.

Fukuyama, Francis. *The Origins of Political Order: From Prehuman Times to the French Revolution*. New York: Farrar, Straus and Giroux, 2011.

Furet, François. *Interpreting the French Revolution*. Translated by Alborg Foster. Cambridge: Cambridge University Press, 1981.

———. *Revolutionary France, 1770–1880*. Oxford: Blackwell, 1992.

Gallagher, John. "Nationalisms and the Crisis of Empire, 1919–1922." *Modern Asian Studies* 15, no. 3 (1981): 355–68.

Gallie, W. B. "Essentially Contested Concepts." *Proceedings of the Aristotelian Society* 56 (1955–56): 167–98.

Gamberini, Andrea, and Isabella Lazzarini. *The Italian Renaissance State*. Cambridge: Cambridge University Press, 2012.

Gat, Azar. *Nations: The Long History and Deep Roots of Political Ethnicity and Nationalism*. Cambridge: Cambridge University Press, 2013.

Gauchet, Marcel. *The Disenchantment of the World: A Political History of Religion*. Princeton, NJ: Princeton University Press, 1997.

Geary, Patrick. *The Myth of Nations: The Medieval Origins of Europe*. Princeton, NJ: Princeton University Press, 2002.

Geertz, Clifford. "Ideology as a Cultural System." In *The Interpretation of Cultures*, 193–233.

———. "The Integrative Revolution: Primordial Sentiments and Civil Politics in the New States" (1963). In *The Interpretation of Cultures*, 255–310.

———. *The Interpretation of Cultures: Selected Essays*. New York: Basic Books, 1973.

———. "What Is a State If It Is Not a Sovereign? Reflections on Politics in Complicated Places." *Current Anthropology* 45, no. 5 (2004): 577–93.

———. "The World in Pieces: Culture and Politics at the End of the Century." In *Available Light: Anthropological Reflections on Philosophical Topics*, 218–63. Princeton, NJ: Princeton University Press, 2000.

Gellner, Ernest. *Conditions of Liberty: Civil Society and Its Rivals*. London: Hamish Hamilton, 1994.

———. *Contemporary Thought and Politics*. London: Routledge, 1974.

———. *Nations and Nationalism*. Ithaca, NY: Cornell University Press, 1983.

———. "Scale and Nation." In *Contemporary Thought and Politics*, 141–57.

Geppert, Dominik, William Mulligan, and Andreas Rose, eds. *The Wars before the Great War: Conflict and International Politics before the Outbreak of the First World War*. Cambridge: Cambridge University Press, 2015.

German Historical Institute. *German History in Documents and Images*. Vol. 4, *Forging an Empire*. https://germanhistorydocs.ghi-dc.org/Index.cfm?language=english.

Getachew, Adom. *Worldmaking after Empire: The Rise and Fall of Self-Determination*. Princeton, NJ: Princeton University Press, 2019.

Geuss, Raymond. *History and Illusion in Politics*. Cambridge: Cambridge University Press, 2001.

Ghervas, Stella. *Conquering Peace: From the Enlightenment to the European Union*. Cambridge, MA: Harvard University Press, 2021.

Gibbon, Edward. *The Decline and Fall of the Roman Empire*. 3 vols. New York: Modern Library, n.d.

Giddens, Anthony. *The Nation-State and Violence*. Berkeley: University of California Press, 1987.

Gierke, Otto. *Political Theories of the Middle Age*. Translated by F. W. Maitland. Cambridge: Cambridge University Press, 1900.

Glanville, Luke. "The Myth of 'Traditional' Sovereignty." *International Studies Quarterly* 57, no. 1 (2013): 79–90.

Glassman, Jonathon. *War of Words, War of Stones: Racial Thought and Violence in Colonial Zanzibar*. Bloomington: Indiana University Press, 2011.

Godlewska, Anne Marie Claire. *Geography Unbound: French Geographic Science from Cassini to Humboldt*. Chicago: University of Chicago Press, 1999.

Goettlich, Kerry. "The Rise of Linear Borders in World Politics." *European Journal of International Relations* 15, no. 1 (2019): 203–28.

Goody, Jack, and Ian Watt. "Consequences of Literacy." *Comparative Studies in Society and History* 5, no. 3 (1963): 304–45.

Gordon, Daniel. *Citizens without Sovereignty: Equality and Sociability in French Thought, 1670–1789*. Princeton, NJ: Princeton University Press, 1994.

Gosewinkel, Dieter. *Schutz und Freiheit? Staatsbürgerschaft in Europa im 20. und 21. Jahrhundert*. Berlin: Suhrkamp, 2016.

Gotthard, Axel. *In der Ferne: Die Wahrnehmung des Raums in der Vormoderne*. Frankfurt: Campus, 2007.

Gottmann, Jean. *A Geography of Europe*. 3rd ed. New York: Holt, Rhinehart, and Winston, 1962.

———. *The Significance of Territory*. Charlottesville: University Press of Virginia, 1973.

Gouldner, Alvin. "Metaphysical Pathos and the Theory of Bureaucracy." *American Political Science Review* 44, no. 2 (1955): 496–507.

Graeber, David, and Marshall Sahlins. *On Kings*. Chicago: Hau Books, 2017.

Greengrass, Mark. *Christendom Destroyed: Europe, 1517–1648*. New York: Viking Penguin, 2014.

———, ed. *Conquest and Coalescence: The Shaping of the State in Early Modern Europe*. London: E. Arnold, 1991.

Gregory, Brad. *Salvation at Stake: Christian Martyrdom in Early Modern Europe*. Cambridge, MA: Harvard University Press, 1999.

Griffiths, Ryan. *Age of Secession: The International and Domestic Determinants of State Birth*. Cambridge: Cambridge University Press, 2016.

———. "Secession and the Invisible Hand of the International System." *Review of International Studies* 40 (2014): 559–81.

Grimm, Dieter. *Recht und Staat der bürgerlichen Gesellschaft*. Frankfurt: Suhrkamp, 1987.

Grimmer-Solem, Erik. *Learning Empire: Globalization and the German Quest for World Status, 1875–1919*. Cambridge: Cambridge University Press, 2019.

Grosser, Pierre. *L'histoire du monde se fait en Asie: Une autre vision du XXe siècle*. Paris: Odile Jacob, 2017.

Guizot, François. *Historical Essays and Lectures*. Chicago: University of Chicago Press, 1972.

Habermas, Jürgen. *The Structural Transformation of the Public Sphere: An Inquiry into a Category of Bourgeois Society*. Cambridge, MA: MIT Press, 1989.

Hagen, William. *Ordinary Prussians: Brandenburg Junkers and Villagers, 1500–1840*. Cambridge: Cambridge University Press, 2002.

———. "The Partitions of Poland and the Crisis of the Old Regime in Prussia, 1772–1806." *Central European History* 9, no. 2 (1976): 115–28.

Hall, John, ed. *States in History*. Oxford: Blackwell, 1986.

Hampel, Karl. "The Dark(er) Side of 'State Failure': State Formation and Socio-Political Variation." *Third World Quarterly* 36, no. 9 (2015): 1629–48.

Harbutt, Fraser. *Yalta 1945: Europe and America at the Crossroads*. Cambridge: Cambridge University Press, 2010.

Harley, J. B. "Maps, Knowledge, and Power." In *The Iconography of Landscape: Essays on the Symbolic Representation, Design and Use of Past Environments*, edited by Denis Cosgrove and Stephen Daniels, 277–312. Cambridge: Cambridge University Press, 1988.

Hathaway, Oona, and Scott Shapiro. *The Internationalists: How a Radical Plan to Outlaw War Remade the World*. New York: Simon and Schuster, 2017.

Headrick, Daniel. *The Tools of Empire: Technology and European Imperialism in the Nineteenth Century*. New York: Oxford University Press, 1981.

———. *When Information Came of Age: Technologies of Knowledge in the Age of Reason and Revolution, 1700–1850*. New York: Oxford University Press, 2000.

Hegel, G. W. F. *Political Writings*. Edited by T. M. Knox. Oxford: Oxford University Press, 1964.

Held, David. *Political Theory and the Modern State*. Stanford, CA: Stanford University Press, 1989.

Hendrick, Burton Jesse. *The Life and Letters of Walter H. Page*. Vol 1. Garden City, NY: Doubleday, Page, 1922.

Hennock, E. P. *The Origin of the Welfare State in England and Germany, 1850–1914: Social Policies Compared*. Cambridge: Cambridge University Press, 2007.

Henshall, Nicholas. *The Myth of Absolutism: Change and Continuity in Early Modern European Monarchy*. London: Longman, 1992.

Herzfeld, Michael. *Cultural Intimacy: Social Poetics in the Nation-State*. New York: Routledge, 2005.

———. *The Social Production of Indifference: Exploring the Symbolic Roots of Western Bureaucracy*. New York: Berg, 1992.

Herzog, Tamar. *A Short History of European Law: The Last Two and a Half Millennia*. Cambridge, MA: Harvard University Press, 2018.

Hewitt, Rachel. *Map of a Nation: A Geography of the Ordnance Survey*. London: Granta, 2010.

Heyen, Erk Volkmar, ed. "Informations- und Kommunikationstechniken der öffentlichen Verwaltung." *Jahrbuch für europäische Verwaltungsgeschichte* 9. Baden-Baden: Nomos-Verl.-Ges., 1997.

Higgs, Edward. "The Rise of the Information State: The Development of Central State Surveillance of the Citizen in England, 1500–2000." *Journal of Historical Sociology* 14, no. 2 (2001): 175–97.

Hintze, Otto. "Staatsverfassung und Heeresverfassung" (1906). In *Staat und Verfassung*, 52–83.

———. *Staat und Verfassung: Gesammelte Abhandlungen zur Allgemeinen Verfassungsgeschichte*. 2nd ed. Göttingen: Vandenhoeck and Ruprecht, 1962.

———. "Wesen und Wandlung des modernen Staates" (1931). In *Staat und Verfassung*, 470–96.

Hirschman, Albert. *Exit, Voice, and Loyalty: Response to Decline in Firms, Organizations, and States*. Cambridge, MA: Harvard University Press, 1970.

Hobbes, Thomas. *Leviathan* (1651). Edited by Michael Oakeshott. Oxford: Blackwell, n. d.

———. *Leviathan*. Edited by Richard Flathman and David Johnston. New York: Norton, 1997.

Hobsbawm, E. J. *Nations and Nationalism since 1780: Programme, Myth, Reality*. Cambridge: Cambridge University Press, 1990.

Hocart, A. M. *Kings and Councillors: An Essay in the Comparative Anatomy of Human Society*. Chicago: University of Chicago Press, 1936.

———. *Kingship*. London: Oxford University Press, 1927.

Hochedlinger, Michael. "The Habsburg Monarchy: From 'Military-Fiscal State' to 'Militarization.'" In *The Fiscal-Military State in Eighteenth-Century Europe: Essays in Honour of P. G. M. Dickson*, edited by Christopher Storrs, 55–94. Farnham: Ashgate, 2009.

Hoffman, Philip T. *Why Did Europe Conquer the World?* Princeton, NJ: Princeton University Press, 2015.

Hoffmann, Stanley. "An Evaluation of the United Nations." *Ohio State Law Journal* 22, no. 3 (1961): 472–94.

Hont, Istvan. *Jealousy of Trade: International Competition and the Nation-State in Historical Perspective*. Cambridge, MA: Harvard University Press, 2005.

Hooson, David, ed. *Geography and National Identity*. Cambridge, MA: Blackwell, 1994.

Hopkins, A. G. *American Empire: A Global History*. Princeton, NJ: Princeton University Press, 2018.

Hopkins, Benjamin. *Ruling the Savage Periphery: Frontier Governance and the Making of the Modern State*. Cambridge, MA: Harvard University Press, 2020.

Horowitz, Donald. *Ethnic Groups in Conflict*. Berkeley: University of California Press, 1985.

Howard, Michael. *The Invention of Peace: Reflections on War and International Order*. New Haven, CT: Yale University Press, 2000.

———. *War in European History*. Oxford: Oxford University Press, 1976.

Howe, Richard Herbert. "Max Weber's Elective Affinities: Sociology within the Bounds of Pure Reason." *American Journal of Sociology* 84, no. 2 (1978): 366–85.

Hroch, Miroslav. *Social Preconditions of National Revival in Europe: A Comparative Analysis of the Social Composition of Patriotic Groups among the Smaller European Nations*. Cambridge: Cambridge University Press, 1985.

Huber, Ernst Rudolf. *Dokumente zur deutschen Verfassungsgeschichte*. Vol 1. Stuttgart: Kohlhammer, 1961.

Huntington, Samuel P. *Political Order in Changing Societies*. New Haven, CT: Yale University Press, 1968.

Immerwahr, Daniel. *How to Hide an Empire: A History of the Greater United States*. New York: Farrar, Straus and Giroux, 2019.

Isaacs, Harold. *Idols of the Tribe: Group Identity and Political Change*. New York: Harper and Row, 1975.

Jackson, Robert. *Quasi-States: Sovereignty, International Relations, and the Third World*. Cambridge: Cambridge University Press, 1990.

———. *Sovereignty: Evolution of an Idea*. Cambridge: Polity, 2007.

Jackson, Simon, and A. O'Malley, eds. *The Institution of International Order: From the League of Nations to the United Nations*. London: Routledge, Taylor, and Francis, 2018.

Jacob, Christian. *The Sovereign Map: Theoretical Approaches in Cartography throughout History*. Chicago: University of Chicago Press, 2006.

James, Alan. "The Equality of States: Contemporary Manifestations of an Ancient Doctrine." *Review of International Studies* 18 (1992): 377–92.

———. *Sovereign Statehood: The Basis of International Society*. London: Allen and Unwin, 1986.

James, Williams. "Great Men and Their Environment" (1880). In *Selected Papers on Philosophy*, 165–97. London: Dent, 1917.

Janowitz, Morris. "Military Institutions and Citizenship in Western Societies." In *The Military and the Problem of Legitimacy*, edited by G. Harries-Jenkins and J. Van Doorn, 77–92. Beverly Hills, CA: Sage, 1976.

Jarausch, Konrad. *The Enigmatic Chancellor: Bethmann Hollweg and the Hubris of Imperial Germany*. New Haven, CT: Yale University Press, 1973.

Jarrett, Mark. *The Congress of Vienna and Its Legacy: War and Great Power Diplomacy after Napoleon*. London: I. B. Tauris, 2013.

Jaszi, Oscar. *The Dissolution of the Habsburg Monarchy*. Chicago: University of Chicago Press, 1929.

Jaume, Lucien. "Citizens and State under the French Revolution." In *States and Citizens: History, Theory, Prospects*, edited by Quentin Skinner and Bo Stråth, 131–44. Cambridge: Cambridge University Press, 2003.

Jefferson, Mark. "The Civilizing Rails." *Economic Geography* 4, no. 3 (1928): 217–31.

Jellinek, Georg. *Allgemeine Staatslehre* (1900). 3rd ed. Berlin: O. Häring, 1922.

Jenks, Edward. "The European Codes." *Journal of the Society of Comparative Legislation* 4, no. 1 (1902): 71–72.

Jensen, A. "Denmark." In Koren, ed., *History of Statistics*, 199–214.

Joas, Hans. *The Power of the Sacred: An Alternative to the Narrative of Disenchantment.* New York: Oxford University Press, 2021.

Johannisson, Karin. "Society in Numbers: The Debate over Quantification in 18th-Century Political Economy." In *The Quantifying Spirit in the 18th Century*, edited by Tore Frängsmyr and J. L. Heilbron, et al., 343–61. Berkeley: University of California Press, 1990.

Joll, James. *1914: The Unspoken Assumptions.* London: University of London, 1968.

———. *The Second International, 1889–1914.* London: Weidenfeld and Nicolson, 1955.

Jones, Eric. *The European Miracle: Environments, Economies and Geopolitics in the History of Europe and Asia.* Cambridge: Cambridge University Press, 1981.

Jones, Gareth, ed. *The Sovereignty of the Law: Selections from Blackstone's Commentaries on the Laws of England.* Toronto: Toronto University Press, 1973.

Jones, Stephen B. "Boundary Concepts in the Setting of Place and Time." *Annals of the Association of American Geographers* 49, no. 3 (1959): 241–55.

Jordan, William. *Europe in the High Middle Ages.* London: Allen Lane, 2002.

Jouvenel, Bertrand de. *On Power: The Natural History of Its Growth.* New York: Viking, 1948.

Joyce, Patrick. *The State of Freedom: A Social History of the British State since 1800.* Cambridge: Cambridge University Press, 2013.

Judis, John. *The Nationalist Revival: Trade, Immigration, and the Revolt against Globalization.* New York: Columbia Global Reports, 2018.

Judson, Pieter. *The Habsburg Empire: A New History.* Cambridge, MA: Harvard University Press, 2016.

———. "Marking National Space on the Habsburg Austrian Borderlands, 1880–1918." In *Shatterzone of Empires: Coexistence and Violence in the German, Habsburg, Russian, and Ottoman Borderlands*, edited by Omer Bartov and Eric Weitz, 122–35. Bloomington: Indiana University Press, 2013.

Judson, Pieter, and Tara Zahra. "Introduction: Sites of Indifference to Nationhood." *Austrian History Yearbook* 43 (2012): 21–27.

Jusdanis, Gregory. *The Necessary Nation.* Princeton, NJ: Princeton University Press, 2001.

Jütte, Daniel, "Entering a City: On a Lost Early Modern Practice." *Urban History* 41, no. 2 (2014): 204–27.

———. *The Strait Gate: Threshold and Power in Western History*. New Haven, CT: Yale University Press, 2015.

Kafka, Ben. *The Demon of Writing: Powers and Failures of Paperwork*. New York: Zone, 2012.

Kafka, Franz. *The Office Writings*. Princeton, NJ: Princeton University Press, 2009.

Kant, Immanuel. *Political Writings*. Edited by Hans Reiss. Cambridge: Cambridge University Press, 1970.

Kantorowicz, Ernst. *The King's Two Bodies: A Study in Medieval Political Theology*. Princeton, NJ: Princeton University Press, 1957.

Keane, John. *The Life and Death of Democracy*. London: Simon and Schuster, 2009.

Kennan, George. *American Diplomacy*. Chicago: University of Chicago Press, 1984.

Kennedy, David. *Freedom from Fear: The American People in Depression and War, 1929–1945*. New York: Oxford University Press, 1999.

Kertzer, David, and Dominique Arel, eds. *Census and Identity: The Politics of Race, Ethnicity, and Language in National Censuses*. Cambridge: Cambridge University Press, 2002.

Kharkhordin, Oleg. "What Is the State? The Russian Concept of Gosudarstvo in the European Context." *History and Theory* 40, no. 2 (2001): 206–40.

Kiernan, V. G. "State and Nation in Western Europe." *Past and Present* 31, no. 1 (1965): 20–38.

King, Charles. *The Ghost of Freedom: A History of the Caucasus*. New York: Oxford University Press, 2008.

Kitromilides, Paschalis. "'Imagined Communities' and the Origins of the National Question in the Balkans." *European History Quarterly* 19, no. 2 (1989): 149–92.

Kivelson, Valerie. *Cartographies of Tsardom: The Land and Its Meanings in Seventeenth-Century Russia*. Ithaca, NY: Cornell University Press, 2006.

Klein, Robert. *Sovereign Equality among States: The History of an Idea*. Toronto: University of Toronto Press, 1974.

Klueting, Harm. *Die Lehre von der Macht der Staaten: Das aussenpolitische Machtproblem in der "politischen Wissenschaft" und in der praktischen Politik im 18. Jahrhundert*. Berlin: Duncker and Humblot, 1986.

Koenigsberger, H. G. *Monarchies, States Generals and Parliaments: The Netherlands in the Fifteenth and Sixteenth Centuries*. Cambridge: Cambridge University Press, 2001.

Kolla, Edward. *Sovereignty, International Law, and the French Revolution*. New York: Cambridge University Press, 2017.

Konvitz, Josef. *Cartography in France, 1600–1848: Science, Engineering, and Statecraft*. Chicago: University of Chicago Press, 1987.

Koren, John, ed. *History of Statistics: Their Development and Progress in Many Countries.* New York: Macmillan, 1918.

Korman, Sharon. *The Right of Conquest: The Acquisition of Territory by Force in International Law and Practice.* Oxford: Oxford University Press, 1996.

Körner, Axel. "Beyond Nation States: New Perspectives on the Habsburg Empire." *European History Quarterly* 48, no. 3 (2018): 516–33.

Koschorke, Albrecht, et al. *Der Fiktive Staat: Konstructionen des Politischen Körpers in der Geschichte Europas.* Frankfurt: Fischer, 2007.

Koselleck, Reinhart. *Preussen zwischen Reform und Revolution: Allgemeines Landrecht, Verwaltung, und soziale Bewegung von 1791 bis 1848.* Stuttgart: Klett, 1967.

Kostof, Spiro. *A History of Architecture: Settings and Rituals.* New York: Oxford University Press, 1985.

Kotkin, Stephen. *Stalin: Waiting for Hitler, 1929–1941.* New York: Penguin, 2017.

Kraehe, Enno. *Metternich's German Policy.* 2 vols. Princeton, NJ: Princeton University Press, 1963.

Krasner, Stephen D. *Sovereignty: Organized Hypocrisy.* Princeton, NJ: Princeton University Press, 1999.

Kuhn, Thomas. *The Structure of Scientific Revolutions.* 3rd ed. Chicago: University of Chicago Press, 1996.

Kula, Witold. *Measures and Men.* Princeton, NJ: Princeton University Press, 1986.

Kunisch, Johannes. *Staatsverfassung und Mächtepolitik: Zur Genese von Staatenkonflikten im Zeitalter des Absolutismus.* Berlin: Duncker and Humblot, 1979.

Ladd, Brian. *The Streets of Europe: The Sights, Sounds, and Smells That Shaped Its Great Cities.* Chicago: University of Chicago Press, 2020.

Laitin, David. *Nations, States, and Violence.* Oxford: Oxford University Press, 2007.

Lake, Peter. *How Shakespeare Put Politics on the Stage: Power and Succession in the History Plays.* New Haven, CT: Yale University Press, 2016.

Landwehr, Achim. "Diskurs—Macht—Wissen: Perspektiven einer Kulturgeschichte des Politischen." *Archiv für Kulturgeschichte* 85 (2003): 71–117.

———. *Die Erschaffung Venedigs.* Paderborn: Schöningh, 2007.

Langewiesche, Dieter. "Das Jahrhundert Europas: Eine Annäherung in globalhistorischer Perspektive." *Historische Zeitschrift* 296 (2013): 29–48.

———. *Die Monarchie im Jahrhundert Europas: Selbstbehauptung durch Wandel im 19. Jahrhundert.* Heidelberg: Winter, 2013.

Laslett, Peter. "The Face to Face Society." In Laslett, ed., *Philosophy, Politics and Society,* 157–84.

————, ed. *Philosophy, Politics, and Society*. Oxford: Oxford University Press, 1956.

Lazzarini, Isabella. *Communication and Conflict: Italian Diplomacy in the Early Renaissance, 1350–1520*. Oxford: Oxford University Press, 2015.

Le Bras, Hervé. "La Statistique Générale de la France." In *Les Lieux de Mémoire*, vol. 2, *La Nation*, edited by Pierre Nora, 317–53. Paris: Gallimard, 1986.

Lefort, Claude. *Democracy and Political Theory*. Minneapolis: University of Minnesota Press, 1985.

————. *The Political Forms of Modern Society: Bureaucracy, Democracy, Totalitarianism*. Cambridge, MA: Polity, 1986.

Leibnitz, Gottfried Wilhelm. *Politische Schriften: Sämtliche Schriften und Briefe*. 4th Series. Vol 3. Berlin: Akademie, 1986.

Lemay-Hérbert, Nicolas, Nicholas Onuf, Vojin Rakić, et al., eds. *Semantics of Statebuilding: Language, Meanings and Sovereignty*. London: Routledge, 2014.

Leonhard, Jörn. *Pandora's Box: A History of the First World War*. Cambridge, MA: Harvard University Press, 2018.

————. *Der überforderte Frieden: Versailles und die Welt, 1918–1923*. Munich: Beck, 2018.

Lesaffer, Randall, ed. *Peace Treaties and International Law in European History: From the Late Middle Ages to World War One*. Cambridge: Cambridge University Press, 2004.

Levitan, Kathrin. *A Cultural History of the British Census: Envisioning the Multitude in the Nineteenth Century*. New York: Palgrave Macmillan, 2011.

Lind, Gunner. "Great Friends and Small Friends: Clientelism and the Power Elite." In *Power Elites and State Building*, edited by Wolfgang Reinhard, 123–48. Oxford: Oxford University Press, 1996.

Lindley, M. F. *The Acquisition and Government of Backward Territory in International Law*. London: Longmans, Green, 1926.

Linklater, Andro. *Owning the Earth: The Transforming History of Land Ownership*. New York: Bloomsbury, 2013.

Longo, Matthew. *The Politics of Borders: Sovereignty, Security, and the Citizen after 9/11*. Cambridge: Cambridge University Press, 2018.

Lorenzini, Sara. *Global Development: A Cold War History*. Princeton, NJ: Princeton University Press, 2019.

Louis, William Roger, and Ronald Robinson. "The Imperialism of Decolonization." *Journal of Imperial and Commonwealth History* 102, no. 3 (1994): 462–511.

Lüthi, Lorenz. *Cold Wars: Asia, the Middle East, Europe*. Cambridge: Cambridge University Press, 2020.

Machiavelli, Niccolò. *The Prince*. Translated by Robert M. Adams. New York: Norton, 1972.

Machtan, Lothar. *Die Abdankung: Wie Deutschlands gekrönte Häupter aus der Geschichte fielen.* Berlin: Propyläen, 2008.

MacIver, R. M. *The Modern State.* Oxford: Oxford University Press, 1924.

Mackinder, Halford. "The Geographical Pivot of History." *The Geographical Journal* 23, no. 4 (1904): 421–44.

Mackridge, Peter. *Language and National Identity in Greece, 1766–1976.* New York: Oxford University Press, 2009.

MacLeod, Roy, ed. *Government and Expertise: Specialists, Administrators and Professionals, 1860–1919.* Cambridge: Cambridge University Press, 1988.

Maczak, Antoni. *Travel in Early Modern Europe.* Cambridge: Polity, 1995.

Mager, Wolfgang. *Zur Entstehung des modernen Staatsbegriffs.* Akademie der Wissenschaften und der Literatur, Mainz. Abhandlungen der geistes- und sozialwissenschaftlichen Klasse, Jahrgang 1968, no. 9. Wiesbaden, 1968.

Maier, Charles. *Leviathan 2.0: Inventing Modern Statehood.* Cambridge, MA: Harvard University Press, 2012.

———. "Leviathan 2.0: Inventing Modern Statehood." In *A World Connecting, 1870–1945,* edited by Emily Rosenberg, Akira Iriye, and Jürgen Osterhammel, 29–282. Cambridge, MA: Harvard University Press, 2012.

———. *Once within Borders: Territories of Power, Wealth, and Belonging since 1500.* Cambridge, MA: Harvard University Press, 2016.

Maistre, Joseph de. *Against Rousseau: "On the State of Nature" and "On the Sovereignty of the People."* Edited by Richard A. Lebrun. Montreal: McGill University Press, 1996.

Malia, Martin. *History's Locomotives: Revolutions and the Making of the Modern World.* New Haven, CT: Yale University Press, 2006.

———. *Russia under Western Eyes: From the Bronze Horseman to the Lenin Mausoleum.* Cambridge, MA: Harvard University Press, 1999.

Manela, Erez. *The Wilsonian Moment: Self-Determination and the International Origins of Anticolonial Nationalism.* New York: Oxford University Press, 2007.

Manent, Pierre. "Modern Democracy as a System of Separations." *Journal of Democracy* 14, no. 1 (2003): 114–25.

———. *A World beyond Politics? A Defense of the Nation-State.* Princeton, NJ: Princeton University Press, 2006.

Mann, Michael. "The Autonomous Power of the State: Its Origins, Mechanisms and Results." *European Journal of Sociology* 25, no. 2 (1984): 185–213.

———. *The Dark Side of Democracy: Explaining Ethnic Cleansing.* Cambridge: Cambridge University Press, 2005.

Mansfield, Harvey C., Jr. "On the Impersonality of the Modern State: A Comment on Machiavelli's Use of *Stato.*" *American Political Science Review* 77, no. 4 (1983): 849–57.

Marx, Karl, and Friedrich Engels. *The Communist Manifesto.* Edited by John Toews. Boston: Bedford/St. Martins, 1992.

Masaryk, T. G. *The Making of a State: Memories and Observations, 1914–1918*. New York: Allen Unwin, 1927.

Mattingly, Garrett. *Renaissance Diplomacy*. Boston: Houghton Mifflin, 1955.

Mayall, James. *Nationalism and International Society*. Cambridge: Cambridge University Press, 1990.

Mayer, Arno J. *Political Origins of the New Diplomacy, 1917–1918*. New Haven, CT: Yale University Press, 1959.

Mazower, Mark. *Governing the World: The History of an Idea, 1815 to the Present*. New York: Penguin, 2012.

———. *The Greek Revolution: 1821 and the Making of Modern Europe*. New York: Penguin, 2021.

McAdams, A. James. *Vanguard of the Revolution: The Global Idea of the Communist Party*. Princeton, NJ: Princeton University Press, 2017.

McNeill, William. *The Pursuit of Power: Technology, Armed Force, and Society since A.D. 1000*. Chicago: University of Chicago Press, 1982.

Mearsheimer, John J. *The Great Delusion: Liberal Dreams and International Realities*. New Haven, CT: Yale University Press, 2019.

Melton, James Van Horn. *The Rise of the Public in Enlightenment Europe*. Cambridge: Cambridge University Press, 2001.

Merriam, Charles. *Systematic Politics*. Chicago: University of Chicago Press, 1945.

Meyer, John. "The World Polity and the Authority of the Nation-State." In *Studies of the Modern World System*, edited by Albert Bergesen, 109–38. New York: Academic, 1980.

Middlekauff, Robert. *The Glorious Cause: The American Revolution, 1763–1789*. Rev. ed. Oxford: Oxford University Press, 2005.

Mill, John Stuart. "A Few Words on Non-Intervention" (1859). In *Essays on Politics and Culture*, edited by Gertrude Himmelfarb, 368–84. Garden City: Doubleday, 1963.

———. *Three Essays*. Oxford: Oxford University Press, 1975.

Miller, Alexei. "'National Indifference' as a Political Strategy?" *Kritika* 20, no. 1 (2019): 63–72.

Mintzker, Yair. *The Defortification of the German City, 1689–1866*. Cambridge: Cambridge University Press, 2012.

Møller, Jørgen. "The Ecclesiastical Roots of Representation and Consent." *Perspectives on Politics* 16, no. 4 (2018): 1075–84.

———. "The Medieval Roots of Democracy." *Journal of Democracy* 26, no. 3 (2015): 110–23.

Montesquieu, Charles-Louis de Secondat. *The Spirit of the Laws*. Edited by Anne M. Cohler, Basia Carolyn Miller, and Harold Samuel Stone. Cambridge: Cambridge University Press, 1989.

Morgan, Edmund. *Inventing the People: The Rise of Popular Sovereignty in England and America*. New York: Norton, 1988.

Morstein Marx, Fritz. *The Administrative State: An Introduction to Bureaucracy.* Chicago: University of Chicago Press, 1957.

Nexon, Daniel. *The Struggle for Power in Early Modern Europe: Religious Conflict, Dynastic Empires, and International Change.* Princeton, NJ: Princeton University Press, 2009.

Niebuhr, Reinhold. *Moral Man and Immoral Society: A Study in Ethics and Politics* (1932). New York: Continuum, 1960.

Nippel, Wilfred. *Ancient and Modern Democracy: Two Concepts of Liberty.* Cambridge: Cambridge University Press, 2916.

Nisbet, Robert. "Leadership and Social Crisis." In *Studies in Leadership: Leadership and Democratic Action*, edited by Alvin Ward Gouldner, 702–20. New York: Harper, 1950.

Nobles, Gregory. "Straight Lines and Stability: Mapping the Political Order of the Anglo-American Frontier." *Journal of American History* 80, no. 1 (1993): 9–35.

Nodia, Ghia. "Nationalism and Democracy." In *Nationalism, Ethnic Conflict, and Democracy*, edited by Larry Diamond and Marc Plattner, 3–22. Baltimore: Johns Hopkins University Press, 1994.

Noiriel, Gérard. *The French Melting Pot: Immigration, Citizenship, and National Identity.* Minneapolis: University of Minnesota Press, 1996.

Nolte, Paul. *Was ist Demokratie? Geschichte und Gegenwart.* Munich: C. H. Beck, 2012.

Nootens, Geneviève. "Liberal Nationalism and the Sovereign Territorial Ideal." *Nations and Nationalism* 12, no. 1 (2006): 35–50.

North, Douglass, John J. Wallis, and Barry R. Weingast. *Violence and Social Orders: A Conceptual Framework for Interpreting Recorded Human History.* Cambridge: Cambridge University Press, 2009.

Oakeshott, Michael. *On Human Conduct.* Oxford: Oxford University Press, 1975.

———. "Political Education." In Laslett, ed., *Philosophy, Politics and Society*, 1–21.

Oakley, Francis. *Kingship: The Politics of Enchantment.* Malden, MA: Blackwell, 2006.

Offen, Karen. *The Woman Question in France, 1400–1870.* New York: Cambridge University Press, 2017.

Ong, Walter. *Interfaces of the Word: Studies in the Evolution of Consciousness and Culture.* Ithaca, NY: Cornell University Press, 1977.

———. *Orality and Literacy: The Technologizing of the Word.* London: Routledge, 1995.

———. *The Presence of the Word: Some Prolegomena for Cultural and Religious History.* New Haven, CT: Yale University Press, 1967.

Onuf, Nicholas. "World-Making, State-Building." In *Semantics of Statebuilding: Language, Meanings and Sovereignty*, edited by Nicolas Lemay-Hérbert, Nicholas Onuf, Vojin Rakić, et al., 19–36. London: Routledge, 2014.

Osiander, Andreas. "Before Sovereignty: Society and Politics in Ancien Régime Europe." *Review of International Studies* 27, no. 5 (2001): 119–45.

———. *Before the State: Systemic Political Change in the West from the Greeks to the French Revolution*. Oxford: Oxford University Press, 2007.

———. *The States System of Europe, 1640–1990: Peacemaking and the Conditions of International Stability*. New York: Oxford University Press, 1994.

Osterhammel, Jürgen. *The Transformation of the World: A Global History of the Nineteenth Century*. Princeton, NJ: Princeton University Press, 2014.

Østerud, Øyvind. "The Narrow Gate: Entry into the Club of Sovereign States." *Review of International Studies* 13, no. 2 (1997): 167–84.

Overy, Richard. *Blood and Ruins: The Great Imperial War, 1931–1945*. Milton Keynes: Allen Lane, 2021.

Oxford Historical Treaties. Oxford, 2014. https://opil.ouplaw.com/home/OHT.

Parker, Geoffrey. *Geopolitics: Past, Present and Future*. London: Pinter, 1998.

Patel, Kiran Klaus. *Project Europe: A History*. Cambridge: Cambridge University Press, 2020.

Paulmann, Johannes. *Pomp und Politik: Monarchenbegegnungen in Europa zwischen Ancien Régime und Erstem Weltkrieg*. Paderborn: F. Schöningh, 2000.

Pedersen, Susan. *The Guardians: The League of Nations and the Crisis of Empire*. New York: Oxford University Press, 2015.

Pelletier, Monique. *Les Cartes des Cassini: La Science au service de l'État et des régions*. Paris: Editions du CTHS, 2002.

Petersen, E. Ladewig. "From Domain State to Tax State: Synthesis and Interpretation." *Scandinavian Economic History Review* 23, no. 2 (1975): 116–48.

Pflanze, Otto. *Bismarck and the Development of Germany: The Period of Unification, 1815–1871*. Princeton, NJ: Princeton University Press, 1963.

Pinker, Steven. *The Better Angels of Our Nature: Why Violence Has Declined*. New York: Viking, 2011.

Pitkin, Hanna. "Idea of a Constitution." *Journal of Legal Education* 37, no. 2 (1987): 167–69.

Pitts, Jennifer. *Boundaries of the International: Law and Empire*. Cambridge, MA: Harvard University Press, 2018.

Plamenatz, J. P. *Consent, Freedom and Political Obligation*. Oxford: Oxford University Press, 1938.

Plato. *The Collected Dialogues*. Princeton, NJ: Princeton University Press, 1961.

Poggi, Gianfranco. *The State: Its Nature, Development, and Prospects*. Stanford, CA: Stanford University Press, 1990.

Pointon, Marcia. "Money and Nationalism." In *Imagining Nations*, edited by Geoffrey Cubitt, 229–54. Manchester: Manchester University Press, 1998.

Pölitz, Karl Heinrich. *Die europäischen Verfassungen seit dem Jahre 1789 bis auf die neueste Zeit*. 4 vols. Leipzig: Brockhaus, 1817–1825.

Popkin, Jeremy. *A New World Begins: The History of the French Revolution*. New York: Oxford University Press, 2019.

Porter, Dorothy. *Health, Civilization and the State: A History of Public Health from Ancient to Modern Times*. London: Routledge, 1999.

Porter, Theodore. *The Rise of Statistical Thinking, 1820–1900*. Princeton, NJ: Princeton University Press, 1986.

Potter, David. "The Historian's Use of Nationalism and Vice Versa." *American Historical Review* 67, no. 4 (1962): 924–50.

Pounds, N. J. G. *A Historical Geography of Europe, 1800–1914*. Cambridge: Cambridge University Press, 1990.

Press, Steven. *Rogue Empires: Contracts and Conmen in Europe's Scramble for Africa*. Cambridge: Cambridge University Press, 2017.

Price, J. L. *The Dutch Republic in the Seventeenth Century*. New York: St. Martin's, 1998.

Prott, Volker. *The Politics of Self-Determination: Remaking Territories and National Identities in Europe, 1917–1923*. Oxford: Oxford University Press, 2016.

Prussia. *Allgemeines Landrecht für die Preußischen Staaten von 1794*. 2 vols. Frankfurt: Metzner, 1970–73.

Prutsch, Markus. *Making Sense of Constitutional Monarchism in Post-Napoleonic France and Germany*. Basingstoke: Palgrave Macmillan, 2013.

Rady, Martyn. *The Habsburgs: To Rule the World*. New York: Basic Books, 2020.

Raeff, Marc. *The Well-Ordered Police State: Social and Institutional Change through Law in the Germanies and Russia, 1600–1800*. New Haven, CT: Yale University Press, 1983.

Rakove, Jack N., ed. *The Annotated U.S. Constitution and Declaration of Independence*. Cambridge, MA: Harvard University Press, 2009.

Randeraad, Nico. *States and Statistics in the Nineteenth Century: Europe by Numbers*. Manchester: Manchester University Press, 2010.

Raphael, Lutz. *Recht und Ordnung: Herrschaft durch Verwaltung im 19. Jahrhundert*. Frankfurt: Fischer, 2000.

Reed, Isaac Arial. *Power in Modernity: Agency Relations and the Creative Destruction of the King's Two Bodies*. Chicago: University of Chicago Press, 2020.

Reinhard, Wolfgang. *Geschichte der Staatsgewalt: Eine vergleichende Verfassungsgeschichte Europas von den Anfängen bis zur Gegenwart*. Munich, 1999.

———, ed. *Power Elites and State Building*. Oxford: Oxford University Press, 1996.

————, ed. *Verstaatlichung der Welt? Europäische Staatsmodelle und aussereuropäische Machtprozesse*. Munich: R. Oldenbourg, 1998.

Reiter, Dan, Allan C. Stam, and Michael C. Horowitz. "A Revised Look at Interstate Wars, 1816–2007." *Journal of Conflict Resolution* 60, no. 5 (2016): 956–76.

Renan, Ernest. *What Is a Nation? And Other Political Writings*. Edited by M. F. N. Giglioli. New York: Columbia University Press, 2018.

Revel, Jean François. *The Totalitarian Temptation*. Translated by David Hapgood. New York: Doubleday, 1977.

Reynolds, Michael. *Shattering Empires: The Clash and Collapse of the Ottoman and Russian Empires, 1908–1918*. Cambridge: Cambridge University Press, 2011.

Richter, Hedwig. *Moderne Wahlen: Eine Geschichte der Demokratie in Preußen und den USA im 19. Jahrhundert*. Hamburg, 2017.

Rieff, Philip. "Aesthetic Functions in Modern Politics." *World Politics* 5, no. 4 (1953): 478–502.

Ritter, Gerhard A. *Der Sozialstaat: Entstehung und Entwicklung im internationalen Vergleich*. 3rd ed. Munich: R. Oldenbourg, 2010.

Ritvo, Harriet. *The Platypus and the Mermaid: And Other Figments of the Classifying Imagination*. Cambridge: Cambridge University Press, 1997.

Robertson, John. "Empire and Union: Two Concepts of the Early Modern European Political Order." In *A Union for Empire: Political Thought and the Union of 1707*, edited by John Robertson, 3–36. Cambridge: Cambridge University Press, 1995.

Rosanvallon, Pierre. *The Demands of Liberty: Civil Society in France since the Revolution*. Translated by Arthur Goldhammer. Cambridge, 2007.

————. *Democracy: Past and Future*. Edited by Samuel Moyn. New York: Columbia University Press, 2006.

————. *The Society of Equals*. Translated by Arthur Goldhammer. Cambridge, MA: Harvard University Press, 2013.

Rose, Richard, ed. *Public Employment in Western Nations*. Cambridge: Cambridge University Press, 1985.

Rosenberg, Emily, Akira Iriye, and Jürgen Osterhammel, eds. *A World Connecting, 1870–1945*. Cambridge, MA: Harvard University Press, 2012.

Roshwald, Ariel. *Ethnic Nationalism and the Fall of Empires: Central Europe, Russia, and the Middle East, 1914–1923*. London: Routledge, 2001.

Ross, Anna. *Beyond the Barricades: Government and State-Building in Post-Revolutionary Prussia, 1848–1858*. Oxford: Oxford University Press, 2019.

Rousseau, Jean-Jacques. *The Social Contract and Discourses*. London: J. M. Dent, 1993.

Rowe, Michael. *From Reich to State: The Rhineland in the Revolutionary Age, 1780–1830*. Cambridge: Cambridge University Press, 2003.

Rowen, Herbert. *The King's State: Proprietary Dynasticism in Early Modern France*. New Brunswick, NJ: Rutgers University Press, 1980.

Runciman, David. "The Concept of the State: The Sovereignty of a Fiction." In *States and Citizens: History, Theory, Prospects*, edited by Quentin Skinner and Bo Stråth, 28–38. Cambridge: Cambridge University Press, 2003.

———. *The Confidence Trap: A History of Democracy in Crisis from World War I to the Present*. Princeton, NJ: Princeton University Press, 2015.

Rusnock, Andrea. "Quantification, Precision, and Accuracy: Determinations of Population in the Ancien Régime." In *The Values of Precision*, edited by M. Norton Wise, 17–38. Princeton, NJ: Princeton University Press, 1995.

Rustow, Dankwart. "Transitions to Democracy: Toward a Dynamic Model." *Comparative Politics* 2, no. 3 (1970): 337–63.

Ryan, Alan. *On Politics: A History of Political Thought from Herodotus to the Present*. 2 vols. New York: Liveright, 2012.

Sabean, David. *Property, Production, and Family in Neckarhausen, 1700–1870*. Cambridge: Cambridge University Press, 1990.

Sack, Robert. *Human Territoriality: Its Theory and History*. Cambridge: Cambridge University Press, 1986.

Sahlins, Peter. *Boundaries: The Making of France and Spain in the Pyrenees*. Berkeley: University of California Press, 1989.

———. "Natural Frontiers Revisited: France's Boundaries since the Seventeenth Century." *American Historical Review* 95, no. 5 (1990): 1423–51.

———. *Unnaturally French: Foreign Citizens in the Old Regime and After*. Ithaca, NY: Cornell University Press, 2004.

Santner, Erik. *The Royal Remains: The People's Two Bodies and the Endgames of Sovereignty*. Chicago: University of Chicago Press, 2011.

Sassen, Sakia. *Territory, Authority, Rights: From Medieval to Global Assemblages*. Princeton, NJ: Princeton University Press, 2006.

Scheidel, Walter. *Escape from Rome: The Failure of Empire and the Road to Prosperity*. Princeton, NJ: Princeton University Press, 2019.

Schieder, Theodor. "Shakespeare und Machiavelli." In *Begegnungen mit der Geschichte*, 9–55. Göttingen: Vandenhoeck and Ruprecht, 1962.

Schilling, Heinz. *Konfessionalisierung und Staatsinteressen: Internationale Beziehungen, 1559–1660*. Paderborn: Fink, 2007.

Schlögel, Karl. *Im Raume lesen wir die Zeit: Über Zivilisationsgeschichte und Geopolitik*. Munich: Carl Hanser, 2003.

Schmidt, Daniel. *Statistik und Staatlichkeit*. Wiesbaden: VS Verlag, 2005.

Schnapper, Dominique. *Community of Citizens: On the Modern Idea of Nationality*. New Brunswick, NJ: Transaction Publishers, 1998.

Schoch, Rainer. *Das Herrscherbild in der Malerei des 19. Jahrhunderts*. Munich: Prestel, 1975.

Scholz, Luca. *Borders and Freedom of Movement in the Holy Roman Empire.* Oxford: Oxford University Press, 2020.

Schöpflin, George. *Nations, Identity, Power.* New York: New York University Press, 2000.

Schremmer, Eckart. *Steuern und Staatsfinanzen während der Industrialisierung Europas: England, Frankreich, Preußen und das Deutsche Reich, 1800 bis 1914.* Berlin: Springer, 1994.

Schroeder, Paul. *Systems, Stability, and Statecraft: Essays on the International History of Modern Europe.* New York: Oxford University Press, 2004.

———. *The Transformation of European Politics, 1763–1848.* Oxford: Oxford University Press, 1994.

Scott, Hamish. *The Birth of a Great Power System, 1740–1815.* Harlowe: Pearson/Longman, 2006.

Scott, James C. *Seeing Like a State: How Certain Schemes to Improve the Human Condition Have Failed.* New Haven, CT: Yale University Press, 1998.

Scott, Jonathan. *How the Old World Ended: The Anglo-Dutch-American Revolution, 1500–1800.* New Haven, CT: Yale University Press, 2019.

Scott, Tom. *The City-State in Europe, 1000–1600: Hinterland, Territory, Region.* Oxford: Oxford University Press, 2012.

Scribner, Robert. "Symbolizing Boundaries: Defining Social Space in the Daily Life of Early Modern Germany." In *Symbole des Alltags, Alltag der Symbole: Festschrift für Harry Kühnel zum 65. Geburtstag,* edited by Gertrud Blaschitz et al., 821–41. Graz: Akademische Druch- und Verlagsanstalt, 1992.

Seegel, Steven. *Mapping Europe's Borderlands: Russian Cartography in the Age of Empire.* Chicago: University of Chicago Press, 2012.

Seligman, Adam. *Modernity's Wager: Authority, the Self, and Transcendence.* Princeton, NJ: Princeton University Press, 2000.

Sellin, Volker. *Gewalt und Legitimität: Die europäische Monarchie im Zeitalter der Revolutionen.* Munich: R. Oldenbourg, 2011.

Seton-Watson, Hugh. *Eastern Europe between the Wars, 1918–1941.* 3rd ed. New York: Harper and Row, 1967.

Sewell, William. *Capitalism and the Emergence of Civil Equality in Eighteenth-century France.* Chicago: University of Chicago Press, 2021.

———. "The French Revolution and the Emergence of the Nation Form." In *Revolutionary Currents: Nation Building in the Transatlantic World,* edited by Michael Morrison and Melinda Zook, 91–126. Lanham, MD: Rowman and Littlefield, 2004.

———. *A Rhetoric of Bourgeois Revolution: The Abbé Sieyès and "What Is the Third Estate?"* Durham, NC: Duke University Press, 1994.

Sharma, Aradhana, and Akhil Gupta, eds. *The Anthropology of the State: A Reader.* Oxford: Blackwell, 2006.

Sheehan, James J. "The Future of Conscription: Some Comparative Reflections." In *The Modern American Military*, edited by David Kennedy, 177–91. New York: Oxford University Press, 2013.

———. *German History, 1770–1866*. Oxford: Oxford University Press, 1989.

———. *Where Have All the Soldiers Gone? The Transformation of Modern Europe*. Boston: Houghton Mifflin, 2008.

Shils, Edward. *The Constitution of Society*. Chicago: University of Chicago Press, 1982.

Siegelberg, Mira. *Statelessness: A Modern History*. Cambridge, MA: Harvard University Press, 2020.

Siemann, Wolfram. *Metternich: Strategist and Visionary*. Cambridge, MA: Harvard University Press, 2019.

Sieyès, Emmanuel Joseph. *Political Writings*. Edited by Michael Sonenscher. Indianapolis: Hackett, 2003.

Simms, Brendan. *Europe: The Struggle of Supremacy, from 1453 to the Present*. New York: Basic Books, 2013.

Simpson, Gerry. *Great Powers and Outlaw States: Unequal Sovereigns in the International Legal Order*. Cambridge: Cambridge University Press, 2004.

Skinner, Quentin. "From the State of Princes to the Person of the State." In *Visions of Politics*, 2:368–413. Cambridge: Cambridge University Press, 2002.

Smith, Anthony. *The Antiquity of Nations*. Cambridge: Cambridge University Press, 2004.

Smith, Rupert. *The Utility of Force: The Art of War in the Modern World*. New York: Allen Lane, 2007.

Smith, William Robertson. *Lectures on the Religion of the Semites. First Series: The Fundamental Institutions*. New York: Oxford University Press, 1989.

Somaini, Francesco. "The Collapse of City-States and the Role of Urban Centers in the New Political Geography of Renaissance Italy." In *The Italian Renaissance State*, edited by Andrea Gamberini and Isabella Lazzarini, 239–60. Cambridge: Cambridge University Press, 2012.

Sorel, Albert. *Europe under the Old Regime: Power, Politics, and Diplomacy in the Eighteenth Century*. Los Angeles: Ward Richie Press, 1947.

Soutou, Georges-Henri. *La Guerre de Cinquante Ans: Les relations Est–Ouest, 1943–1990*. Paris: Fayard, 2001.

———. "L'ordre européen de Versailles à Locarno." In *1918–1925: Comment faire la paix?*, edited by Claude Carlier and Georges-Henri Soutou, 301–31. Paris: Economica, 2001.

———. "Was There a European Order in the Twentieth Century? From the Concert of Europe to the End of the Cold War." *Contemporary European History* 9, no. 3 (2000): 329–53.

Spawforth, Tony. *Versailles: A Biography of a Palace*. New York: St. Martin's, 2008.

Sperber, Jonathan. *The European Revolutions, 1848–1851.* New York: Cambridge University Press, 2005.

Spruyt, Hendrik. *The Sovereign State and Its Competitors: An Analysis of Systems Change.* Princeton, NJ: Princeton University Press, 1994.

Stansky, Peter, ed. *The Victorian Revolution: Government and Society in Victoria's Britain.* New York: New Viewpoints, 1973.

Stargardt, Nicholas. "Beyond the Liberal Idea of the Nation." In *Imagining Nations*, edited by Geoffrey Cubitt, 22–34. Manchester: Manchester University Press, 1998.

Stasavage, David. *The Decline and Rise of Democracy: A Global History from Antiquity to Today.* Princeton, NJ: Princeton University Press, 2020.

———. "Representation and Consent: Why They Arose in Europe and Not Elsewhere." *Annual Review of Political Science* 19 (2016): 145–62.

Stead, W. T., ed. *The Last Will and Testament of Cecil John Rhodes with Elucidatory Notes.* London: Review of Books Office, 1902.

Steiner, Zara. *The Light That Failed: European International History, 1919–1933.* Oxford: Oxford University Press, 2005.

———. *The Triumph of the Dark: European International History, 1933–1939.* Oxford: Oxford University Press, 2011.

Stevenson, David. *The First World War and International Politics.* New York: Oxford University Press, 1988.

Stewart, John Hall. *A Documentary Survey of the French Revolution.* New York: Macmillan, 1951.

Stokes, Gale. *Three Eras of Political Change in Eastern Europe.* Oxford: Oxford University Press, 1997.

Stollberg-Rilinger, Barbara. *The Emperor's Old Clothes: Constitutional History and the Symbolic Language of the Holy Roman Empire.* New York: Berghahn Books, 2015.

Stolleis, Michael. "Die Entstehung des Interventionsstaates und das öffentliche Recht." *Zeitschrift für neuere Rechtsgeschichte* 11 (1989): 129–46.

———. *Konstitution und Intervention: Studien zur Geschichte des öffentlichen Rechts im 19. Jahrhunderts.* Frankfurt: Suhrkamp, 2001.

———. "Verfassungsideale der Bürgerlichen Revolution." In *Konstitution und Intervention*, 17–32.

Storm, Eric. "A New Dawn in Nationalism Studies? Some French Incentives to Overcome Historiographical Nationalism." *European History Quarterly* 48, no. 1 (2018): 113–29.

Storrs, Christopher, ed. *The Fiscal-Military State in Eighteenth-Century Europe.* Farnham, Surrey: Ashgate, 2009.

Stourzh, Gerald. "*Constitution*: Changing Meanings of the Term from the Early Seventeenth to the Late Eighteenth Century." In *Conceptual Change and the Constitution*, edited by Terence Ball and J. G. A. Pocock, 35–54. Lawrence: University Press of Kansas, 1988.

Strakosch, Henry. *State Absolutism and the Rule of Law: The Struggle for the Codification of Civil Law in Austria, 1753–1811.* Sydney: Sydney University Press, 1967.

Symonds, Craig. *World War II at Sea: A Global History.* New York: Oxford University Press, 2008.

Szücs, Jenő. "The Three Historic Regions of Europe: An Outline." *Acta Historica Academiae Scientiarum Hungaricae* 29, no. 2/4 (1983): 131–84.

Tantner, Anton. "Addressing the Houses: The Introduction of House Numbering in Europe." *Histoire et Mesure* 14, no. 2 (2009): 7–30.

Tarello, Giovanni. *Storia della cultura giuridica moderna.* Vol 1, *Assolutismo e codificazione del diritto.* Bologna: Il Molino, 1976.

Taylor, Brian, and Roxana Botea. "Tilly Tally: War-Making and State-Making in the Contemporary Third World." *International Studies Review* 10, no. 1 (2008): 27–56.

Taylor, Charles. *Modern Social Imaginaries.* Durham, NC: Duke University Press, 2004.

Teschke, Benno. *The Myth of 1648: Class, Geopolitics, and the Making of Modern International Relations.* London: Verso, 2003.

Thompson, E. P. *The Making of the English Working Class.* Harmondsworth: Penguin, 1968.

Thompson, John. *A Sense of Power: The Roots of America's Global Role.* Ithaca, NY: Cornell University Press, 2015.

Thomson, Janice. *Mercenaries, Pirates, and Sovereigns: State-Building and Extraterritorial Violence in Early Modern Europe.* Princeton, NJ: Princeton University Press, 1994.

Tilly, Charles. *Coercion, Capital, and European States, AD 990–1990.* Cambridge, MA: Blackwell, 1990.

———, ed. *The Formation of National States in Western Europe.* Princeton: Princeton University Press, 1975.

Tischer, Anuschka. *Offizielle Kriegsbegründungen in der Frühen Neuzeit: Herrscherkommunikation in Europa zwischen Souveränität und Korporativem Selbstverständnis.* Berlin: Lit, 2012.

Tocqueville, Alexis de. *Democracy in America.* Chicago: University of Chicago Press, 2000.

———. *Recollections: The French Revolution of 1848 and Its Aftermath.* Charlottesville: University of Virginia Press, 2016.

Toft, Monica Duffy. *The Geography of Ethnic Violence: Identity, Interests, and the Indivisibility of Territory.* Princeton, NJ: Princeton University Press, 2003.

Tooze, Adam. *The Deluge: The Great War, America and the Remaking of the Global Order, 1916–1931.* New York: Viking, 2014.

———. *Statistics and the German State, 1900–1945: The Making of Modern Economic Knowledge.* Cambridge: Cambridge University Press, 2001.

Tooze, Adam, and Ted Fertik. "The World Economy and the Great War." *Geschichte und Gesellschaft* 40 (2014): 214–38.

Toulmin, Stephen. *Cosmopolis: The Hidden Agenda of Modernity*. Chicago: University of Chicago Press, 1990.

Toynbee, Arnold. *The Western Question in Greece and Turkey: A Study in the Contact of Civilizations*. 2nd ed. London: Constable, 1923.

Tuck, Richard. *The Sleeping Sovereign: The Invention of Modern Democracy*. Cambridge: Cambridge University Press, 2015.

Ullmann, Hans-Peter. *Der deutsche Steuerstaat: Geschichte der öffentlichen Finanzen*. Munich: Beck Verlag, 2005.

Valéry, Paul. "Letters from France." *The Athenaeum*, April 11 and May 2, 1919, 182–84, 279–84. London.

Vance, James. *Capturing the Horizon: The Historical Geography of Transportation since the Transportation Revolution of the Sixteenth Century*. New York: Harper and Row, 1986.

Van Creveld, Martin. *The Rise and Decline of the State*. Cambridge: Cambridge University Press, 1999.

Van Middelaar, Luuk. *The Passage to Europe: How a Continent Became a Union*. New ed. New Haven, CT: Yale University Press, 2020.

Vann, James. "Mapping under the Austrian Habsburgs." In *Monarchs, Ministers and Maps: The Emergence of Cartography as a Tool of Government in Early Modern Europe*, edited by David Buisseret, 153–67. Chicago: University of Chicago Press, 1992.

Van Panhuys, H. F. *The Role of Nationality in International Law: An Outline*. Leyden: A. W. Sythoff, 1959.

Van Zanden, Jan Luiten, Eltjo Buringh, and Maarten Bosker. "The Rise and Decline of European Parliaments, 1188–1789." *Economic History Review* 65, no. 3 (2012): 835–61.

Vargas Llosa, Mario. "A Novel for the Twenty-First Century." Translated by Johanna Damgaard Liander. *Harvard Review*, no. 28 (2005): 125–36.

Vec, Miloš. *Recht und Normierung in der industriellen Revolution: Neue Strukturen der Normsetzung in Völkerrecht, staatlicher Gesetzgebung und gesellschaftlicher Selbstnormierung*. Frankfurt: Klostermann, 2006.

Vernon, James. *Distant Strangers: How Britain Became Modern*. Berkeley: University of California Press, 2014.

Vick, Brian. *The Congress of Vienna: Power and Politics after Napoleon*. Cambridge: Cambridge University Press, 2014.

Vital, David. *A People Apart: The Jews in Europe, 1789–1939*. Oxford: Oxford University Press, 1999.

Vries, Peer. "States: A Subject in Global History." In *Explorations in History and Globalization*, edited by Cátia Antunes and Karwan Fatah-Black, 155–77. London: Routledge, 2016.

Wagner, Adolf. *Die Ordnung des österreichischen Staatshaushaltes*. Vienna: Christian Brandstätter, 1863.

Walker, Mack. *German Home Towns: Community, State, and General Estate, 1468–1871*. Ithaca, NY: Cornell University Press, 1971.

Walzer, Michael. "On the Role of Symbolism in Political Thought." *Political Science Quarterly* 82, no. 2 (1967): 191–204.

Wambaugh, Sarah. *A Monograph on Plebiscites with a Collection of Official Documents*. New York: Carnegie Endowment, 1920.

Warnock, Mary. *Imagination*. Berkeley: University of California Press, 1978.

Weber, Eugen. *Peasants into Frenchmen: The Modernization of Rural France, 1870–1914*. Stanford, CA: Stanford University Press, 1976.

Weber, Max. *Economy and Society*. 2 vols. Berkeley: University of California Press, 1978.

———. *The Protestant Ethic and the Spirit of Capitalism*. New York: Penguin, 2002.

Weber, Thomas. *Becoming Hitler: The Making of a Nazi*. New York: Basic Books, 2017.

Weinberg, Gerhard. *A World at Arms: A Global History of World War II*. 2nd ed. New York: Oxford University Press, 2005.

Weitz, Eric. "Self-Determination: How a German Enlightenment Idea Became the Slogan of a National Liberation and a Human Right." *American Historical Review* 120, no. 2 (2015): 462–96.

———. *A World Divided: The Global Struggle for Human Rights in the Age of Nation-States*. Princeton, NJ: Princeton University Press, 2019.

Welu, James. "The Map in Vermeer's *Art of Painting*." *Imago Mundi* 30, no. 1 (1978): 9–30.

Wendt, Alexander. "Anarchy Is What States Make of It: The Social Construction of Power Politics." *International Organization* 46, no. 2 (1992): 391–425.

Westad, Odd Arne. *The Cold War: A World History*. London: Allen Lane, 2017.

———. *The Global Cold War: Third World Interventions and the Making of Our Times*. New York: Cambridge University Press, 2005.

Wheare, K. C. *Modern Constitutions*. Oxford: Oxford University Press, 1951.

White, Leonard, et al., eds. *Civil Service Abroad: Great Britain, Canada, France, Germany*. New York,: McGraw-Hill, 1935.

Whitehead, Alfred North. *Symbolism: Its Meaning and Effect*. New York: Macmillan, 1927.

Whitman, James Q. *The Verdict of Battle: The Law of Victory and the Making of Modern War*. Cambridge, MA: Harvard University Press, 2012.

Wiebe, Robert. *Who We Are: A History of Popular Nationalism*. Princeton, NJ: Princeton University Press, 2002.

Wight, Martin. "International Legitimacy." *International Relations* 4 (1972): 1–28.

———. *Power Politics*. Edited by Hedley Bull and Carsten Holbraad. Leicester: Leicester University Press, 1978.

———. *Systems of States*. Edited by Hedley Bull. Leicester: Leicester University Press, 1977.

Wimmer, Andreas. "The Rise of the Nation-State across the World, 1816–2001." *American Sociological Review* 75, no. 5 (2010): 764–90.

———. *Waves of War: Nationalism, State Formation, and Ethnic Exclusion in the Modern World*. Cambridge: Cambridge University Press, 2013.

Winter, Jay, ed. *The Cambridge History of the First World War*. 3 vols. Cambridge: Cambridge University Press, 2014.

Winter, Jay, and Antoine Prost. *The Great War in History: Debates and Controversies, 1914 to the Present*. New York: Cambridge University Press, 2020.

Wirsching, Andreas. *Der Preis der Freiheit: Geschichte Europas in unserer Zeit*. Munich: Beck Verlag, 2012.

Wittgenstein, Ludwig. *Philosophical Investigations*. Oxford: Blackwell, 1972.

Wolff, Larry. *Woodrow Wilson and the Reimagining of Eastern Europe*. Stanford, NJ: Stanford University Press, 2020.

Wolin, Sheldon. *Fugitive Democracy and Other Essays*. Princeton, NJ: Princeton University Press, 2016.

———. *Tocqueville between Two Worlds: The Making of a Political and Theoretical Life*. Princeton, NJ: Princeton University Press, 2001.

Woloch, Isser. *The New Regime: Transformations of the French Civic Order, 1789–1820s*. New York: W. W. Norton, 1994.

Woolf, Stuart. "Statistics and the Modern State." *Comparative Studies in Society and History* 31, no. 3 (1989): 588–604.

Wright, Quincy. *Mandates under the League of Nations*. Chicago: University of Chicago Press, 1930.

Wright, Richard. *The Color Curtain: A Report on the Bandung Conference*. Cleveland: World Publishing, 1956.

Yack, Bernard. *Nationalism and the Moral Psychology of Community*. Chicago: University of Chicago Press, 2012.

———. "Popular Sovereignty and Nationalism." *Political Theory* 29, no. 4 (2001): 517–36.

Yates, JoAnne. *Control through Communication: The Rise of System in American Management*. Baltimore: Johns Hopkins University Press, 1989.

INDEX

accident insurance, 50, 71
Acton, John Emerich Edward
    Dalberg- (Lord Acton), 105, 117
Adams, John, 64
administration
    critique of, 67
    growth, 65–66
    law, 66
Allgemeines Landrecht (Prussia), 10,
    56–57
Ancien régime, 5, 7
Anderson, Benedict, 26, 80, 102
Appadurai, Arjun, 46
Arendt, Hannah, 159, 161
Armenian genocide, 132
Armitage, David, 150
Aron, Raymond, 81
Atlantic Charter, 143–44, 154
Augsburg, Treaty of, 39–40

Bacon, Francis, 20, 166
Bagehot, Walter, 79–80
Balkan Wars, 129
Barker, Ernest, 54, 106, 110
Bauer, Otto, 99, 100–101, 111
Beaton, Cecil, 20
Belgium, creation of, 124
Bentham, Jeremy, 32
Benton, Lauren, 11

Berlin, Isaiah, 115–16
Bethmann Hollweg, Theobald von,
    133
Bismarck, Otto von, 106–7
Blackstone, William, 57, 82
Bloch, Marc, 28
Bluntschli, J. C., 110
Bodin, Jean, 14–15, 18, 35–36, 39
Bologna, 32
Boswell, James, 59
Botero, Giovanni, 13
Bourdieu, Pierre, 19, 77
Braunschweig-Wolfenbüttel, 11
Breuilly, John, 110
Bryce, James, 137
budgets, and state making, 69
Buffon, Georges-Louis, 53
Bull, Hedley, 121, 157
Burgdorf, Wolff, 58
Burke, Edmund, 51, 91, 118
Byron, George Gordon (Lord
    Byron), 123

Cahiers de doléances, 87
Calhoun, Craig, 92
Callières, François, 36
Cassini family, 44–45, 161
Castlereagh, Robert Stewart
    Viscount, 120

225

JAMES J. SHEEHAN

is the Dickason Professor in the Humanities, Emeritus, at Stanford University. He was president of the American Historical Association in 2005 and is the author and editor of numerous books, including *Where Have All the Soldiers Gone?*

CPSIA information can be obtained
at www.ICGtesting.com
Printed in the USA
LVHW021257060423
743668LV00002B/205